The NATURAL

IRONBARK PRESS

The NATURAL

Brett Kenny's life in league

with
NEIL CADIGAN

Foreword by PETER STERLING

IRONBARK
PRESS

DEDICATION

To Julie, Joshua, Nikolah and Mitchell, for all the hours I haven't been there.

Neil Cadigan has had a varied career in journalism and rugby league. In 1985 he won the prestigious Australian Sportswriters' Association award for his profile of Paul Hayward, the former rugby league star jailed for drug offences in Bangkok.

After seven years with *Rugby League Week* magazine, during which time he covered all of Brett Kenny's grand final appearances and represented RLW on several overseas campaigns, he was appointed editor of the *Central Coast Express* newspaper. During his time at the helm, the paper won the Australian Suburban Newspaper-of-the-Year award. After a brief stint as general manager of English first division club Wakefield Trinity, he returned to Australia, rejoining *Rugby League Week* as associate editor.

Neil has written two previous books: *Quest for Glory*, the story of Parramatta club's rise to rugby league glory and *Perpetual Motion*, the biography of champion lock forward Ray Price.

Photographs: Thanks to the managing editor of *Rugby League Week,* Norm Tasker, for access to the magazine's photo files. Thanks also to the Kenny family, David Middleton and Andrew Varley for their assistance.

Published in 1993 by Ironbark Press Level 1,
175 Alison Road, Randwick NSW 2031

National Library of Australia
Cataloguing-in-Publication

Kenny, Brett. The Natural

ISBN 1 875471 32 4.

1. Kenny, Brett. 2. Rugby League football players — New South Wales — Biography. I. Title.

796.338

Editor: Ian Heads
Production: Geoff Armstrong
Design and Finished Art: Kylie Prats
Cover Design: Jayem Productions
Cover photography: Rugby League Week
Printed by McPhersons Print Group, Mulgrave, Victoria.

Contents

Foreword by Peter Sterling

It should come as no great surprise that I was asked to write the foreword to Brett Kenny's book. After all, I spent more than 10 years making him look good; why shouldn't I now make him sound good!

Unfortunately, if you believe that, you probably believe that halfbacks put the ball in the middle of the scrum, or that blokes who play in the front-row are really highly intelligent people, but misunderstood.

The real truth is that during one of the truly outstanding careers of rugby league, on whatever ground he graced, it was Brett Kenny who made all his team-mates look great.

In all sports, we hear the words "gifted", "champion", "a natural". In most cases the words are overused and in many cases they're misdirected. When it comes to "Bert" Kenny however, such words don't provide adequate descriptions of just what the guy possesses, and the unbelievable talent that he really is.

I was fortunate enough to play inside Brett for 13 seasons, and in that period of time saw him do things in the game that only the true greats could come close to. It was a joy to stand back and watch a form of poetry in motion.

His command over the basic skills seemed intrinsic, the fluency of movement would have been comfortably at home at the ballet. And along with all the exceptional competitors on the world sporting stage, he had time. What Brett Kenny did on the football field was make it all look oh-so-easy.

To best understand how this was achieved, we need to look at the man himself.

From his early days in age divisions at McCredie Park in Guildford, through to Test football on the famous Old Trafford ground in Manchester, Brett has always taken things in his stride.

He is unfazed by occasion, laconic in his approach to pressure. We've all seen him walk onto grounds, invariably the last in line. He could be out for a Sunday afternoon stroll.

In 1985, many in the crowd of 97,000 English supporters at Wembley Stadium for the Challenge Cup final between Wigan and Hull, judged this approach as insulting and arrogant. But to the fans who had seen the Kenny walk before, it was neither. As an opponent that day, all it did was make me less confident — because I knew it meant that Brett Kenny was ready to roll.

What was arrogant was the manner in which he took England's premier game by the scruff of the neck, and made it his in a totally dominant performance. With a brilliant display he rightly took out the Lance Todd Trophy, becoming the first Aussie to be afforded that honour.

Some people have labelled him a "dressing-room comedian", which again is a misnomer. One thing never abided at the Parramatta club over the years has been the "joker" in the sheds when it was time to go to work.

The way players ready themselves for football matches is a very personal thing; Brett's preparation always seemed more relaxed than anyone else's. Steven Sharp sang Elvis songs, Geoff Bugden was physically ill, Brett Kenny was quiet and confident. I must reveal that before some games, listening to Sharpy's vocal ability had a few of us adopting the preparation of "Big Bugs"!

Off the paddock, I'm not Brett's best mate ... but we're good mates. He is popular with his peers, a bloke who has always just heard the latest joke or knows the newest gossip. On most occasions, the delivery is more entertaining than the information.

Like most of us, he is a mixture of things in character and personality. He can be very serious, a deep-thinker about the things he sees as important in life. At social gatherings he is comfortable being the life of the party. After a few drinks (and I mean a few), John Travolta is liable to make an appearance. Brett, in fact, knows the words to every song in the world, and if he doesn't, he'll make them up anyway.

I realise that this foreword isn't supposed to be a roast, but looking back over many years spent in Brett's company, all I know of him are good times.

Over the passing seasons I have witnessed the transformation of a scrawny, gangly teenager, who was terrified of being in the same room as a microphone, into a well-known, respected and articulate adult, married to a loving wife and the father of three gorgeous children.

Brett's has been a heady rise, but one that has never gone to his head. In a day and age where it seems every sporting personality ends up with a book on his life this is one story that truly should be told. It's the story of a champion.

So, sit back and enjoy the life and times of Brett Kenny, a man who if he had not become a rugby league legend, would be playing major league baseball in the US, or cracking a boundary at Lord's.

Fortunately for us, it was in our great game that he chose to weave his magic.

1 Tiger Bait

It was in the plush foyer of the Parkroyal Parramatta, as I shook hands with Balmain coach and Sydney radio personality Alan Jones, that it first really hit me. I had just had an incredible conversation with Jones in a suite upstairs. Alan had impressed me as an intelligent and convincing bloke and I had left the meeting with plenty of respect and admiration for him. It was a decade since I had become a rugby league international, and yet in less than half an hour he had driven it home to me that I should have and could have made a lot more of my life in football. Oh, yeah, and by the way, he also wanted me to play with the Tigers. And *that* was the reason we had got together. Now, the meeting over, it was sinking in. After all my Parramatta years, good and bad, I saw myself seriously looking at the prospect of playing for another club.

Only once before in 13 seasons of first grade football had I had a genuine discussion with another club. That was back in 1984 when Manly wined and dined me. On that occasion my pending agreement with Wigan to play a season with them ended any real chance that I'd leave the Eels. Not that I wanted to. I was surprised it took until I was almost 32, and near the end, before someone else came knocking on my door.

I drove home from that October 1992 meeting with Jones, my head spinning with his words. Footballwise things hadn't been particularly marvellous. It had been another very ordinary season with Parramatta. I realised I faced a pretty big decision — whether to play my 14th and final season with Parramatta, or to have a last throw of the dice somewhere else. The choice was to remain a one-club man or to "cash in" elsewhere.

My wife Julie was keen for me to leave Parramatta. She was really disappointed, as I was, with certain things that had happened between me and the Parramatta management, and she thought I'd be better off enjoying a final season somewhere else. But I explained to her as we talked that day that deep down I wanted to stay — not because of the club and the management, but for the players and the coaching staff. These were people I'd really enjoyed having as part of my life, for a long time. Even though we'd had some pretty lean years since our last premiership win in 1986, and things hadn't been as enjoyable as anybody would have wanted, playing at Parramatta was a big, big habit to break.

I'll admit there were times when getting beaten each week really got to me. I seriously thought of tossing it in, of making a pretty ordinary 1992 my last year. People had been asking me for months whether I'd back up again and I kept saying, "I don't know, I want to think about it."

Of those terrible last couple of months of the '92 premiership season I remember especially the game against North Sydney — the second-last match of the year. For Parramatta it was a shocker and they gave us a real hiding, 28-8. I was really down after that one, and I was getting used to the feeling. We'd only won one match in the past six games — 26-16 over Wests at Campbelltown. But there was something about the day of the Norths game that really got to me.

I remember talking to the *Telegraph Mirror's* Peter Frilingos and a few other media blokes in the dressing room after the game. They all asked how I felt, and had I decided if I would play again. I told them that my feeling right then was to give it all up, and retire. The next day's papers carried the headlines that I was going to call it quits.

On the way out of the dressing room I talked with our coach Mick Cronin. Maybe someone had told him of my conversation with the press guys earlier, and he made a point of asking me how I was feeling. I said obviously I wasn't real happy; it had been such a poor game for us again and anyone would get sick of floggings like the one that day. Mick asked me not to make up my mind straight away, but to go away and think about it. I told "Crow" I was never going to make up my mind until after the last match, and that I wanted to get away from the game, have a break at home with the family — just to sit down and work out what I wanted to do.

Julie and I had some talking to do — about what she wanted in life and what I wanted, and what we wanted to achieve together — and whether we could do those things without one more season of footy. Also I had to work out deep within myself whether I had the desire to put everything into one more season as a football player and so not let myself or my club down.

Julie and I never actually got around to having that talk. I got a phone call from Ken Shine, who used to coach Parramatta's under-23s and who had become Alan Jones' right-hand man at Balmain. He asked me what I was doing, and told me Jonesy was interested in me playing at Leichhardt if I decided to go around again.

It wasn't *just* the fact that Balmain rang and showed interest in me, but it certainly helped. I told Julie my mind was suddenly made up, that I wanted to keep playing. If another club felt I had something to offer them, I thought, I must still be playing well enough to justify going on.

Way down deep my underlying feeling was that I wanted to play one more year at Parramatta and help my club back towards the top of the competition — or at the very least to struggle out of the basement. We'd finished second-last the previous two years and if it hadn't been for Gold Coast being stripped of two points for a technical breach, we would have had the wooden spoon in 1992. That wasn't the note on which to end a career.

Balmain made contact again and I told them that I had decided I'd like to play one more season and would be interested in talking with them. I went through the right channels and put them in touch with my manager David Collins. In the interests of doing it "right" I asked David to talk to Parramatta chief executive Denis Fitzgerald to let him know I wanted to keep playing. I rang Mick Cronin myself. I wanted Crow to know before anyone else that I wanted to have another year — and also that I had been approached by Balmain.

The disappointing thing was how much more quickly and purposefully Balmain worked towards getting my signature than did Parramatta. I had the sense that Parra were just taking me for granted. Maybe they saw me as part of the furniture; perhaps they considered I'd never leave and there was no rush to sit me down. In contrast, Balmain were all "go".

I spoke with Alan Jones a few times and finally it got to the point where he said he'd like to sit down with me and have a serious discussion about my future plans. So it was that we met that day at the Parramatta Parkroyal. We met in the foyer and Alan said he didn't want to talk in the bar or anywhere public where we'd be spotted. He'd organised a room and it was there that we talked for 45 minutes or so about the past and future football life of B. Kenny. In retrospect it was an important event in my life at that time, a real eye-opener for me. Alan is a persuasive and articulate bloke, and he had me realising I should have been doing a lot more than I had in my 13 seasons. He explained there were avenues through which I could cash in on what I had achieved. That day Alan Jones put a very good proposal to me which included radio work with 2UE.

I'd felt at ease with him and got the strong impression that Balmain genuinely wanted to look after me — far more than Parramatta did. The Balmain approach was about a lot more than football. I felt Parramatta weren't too interested or worried about what you did outside football. On that score maybe I hadn't been worried enough about myself, although the Eels' marketing manager Steve Edge, more as a friend, had helped me find a few jobs over the years.

Alan Jones mentioned the possibility of media work to me, although he reckoned it was something I would have to work on because I wasn't naturally a very open sort of person. As a footballer, confidence had never been a problem for me — but Jones that day touched on possibilities that could exist for me *outside* football. He talked about a potential that I had perhaps never tapped. The meeting with him was an enlightening experience for me.

I thanked Jones, expressed my appreciation and told him I was obliged, of course, to go back to Parramatta to give them the last option. I'd been at the club all my life, and I owed them that. It would have been the same if I'd spent all my career at Balmain. He was willing to accept that — but he needed an answer within a week.

In the days that followed, as I waited to see what counter-offer Parramatta would come up with, I visualised myself running out on Leichhardt Oval in the black and gold and contemplated what a challenge it would be. At other times I thought "nah, not really" — that I'd like to have my last year at Parramatta.

David Collins spoke with Denis Fitzgerald during those days and we awaited Parramatta's response. But the first conversation I subsequently had with Fitzgerald was virtually by accident — and yet another example, I thought, of the lack of professionalism at the club — Parramatta's deficiencies in communication skills in dealing with players. I just happened to be in the football office and Fitzy walked downstairs and noticed me. "Got five minutes, Bert?" he asked. I said yes and we tramped upstairs to his office. There he made an offer to me —

a very disappointing offer. It was considerably less than what I'd received the previous year and way below what Balmain had put to me. I was absolutely stunned. There had been no phone call to arrange a meeting, no appointment set up for me to come in and discuss things. Yet I was the club's longest serving player. Our meeting happened by chance. I just happened to be passing by, got asked if I had a minute and then informed that I was suddenly worth a whole lot less than a few months ago.

There was more to it than that, though. There were the reasons given to me at that impromptu meeting — that I was not getting any younger, that there was no improvement left in me. I was being pensioned off! Yet, strangely, by the end of the conversation I was being told how the side would be in trouble if I didn't sign and that they needed my experience. What a contradiction!

I was shocked. In the days that followed, as news of my situation became more public, people were stopping me in the street and declaring that if Parramatta don't sign me, Fitzy — who was already under enormous pressure from the fans — would be in a tonne of trouble. I interpreted Fitzgerald's message that day as being that after 13 years I wasn't wanted; Parramatta didn't have room for me.

When I walked out of his office my prime thought was: "Well, why should I stay?" I had to look way past my disappointment with Fitzy to find the answers. In fact, there were plenty of reasons. Management wasn't one of them.

I honestly believed that my standing in the side justified me being worth at least the same money, if not more, than I had earned the previous year. My form had been okay, and I was at a club where there were a lot of kids who needed some experienced hands around them. If I had gone to the Brisbane Broncos, for example, I realised I wouldn't be worth anywhere near as much. They had internationals right through their team. But at Parramatta, it was different. I felt I still had something to offer.

I asked David Collins to let Denis Fitzgerald know that, unless he made me an offer a lot better than the original, then I wouldn't be staying. I couldn't let things go on too long. It was only fair that I give Balmain a quick answer. I had to go to the country to fulfil a work obligation but I knew that when I got back, I had to make a decision one way or the other.

I enjoyed the few days away from the dilemma, and had time while on the road to think about it. I called David Collins a few times and he reported that Fitzy's revised offer was getting closer to the mark everytime they spoke. On the Friday night I returned, David called and told me the final Parramatta deal. Let's just say that it was a *helluva* lot better than the original. In straight money terms it was worth more than Balmain's deal, but Balmain's offer had more advantages off-field.

I kept thinking of what Alan Jones had said — that I was only going to play for one more year, and to focus on what I was going to do past that.

There were other considerations as I weighed up the two offers. Jobwise, I was happy at Berrivale Orchards and thought I had a good enough future there. Maybe some media work might come along anyway. And Mick Cronin was a major factor. He'd been like a big brother to me way back when it all began in 1980, my partner in the centres. Now he was my coach. I expected it was going to be his last year as coach and the thought of finishing my career with The Crow – – just as I had started it — meant something to me.

So I made my decision. I was going to stay at Parramatta, finish at Parramatta. It felt as if a great weight had been lifted from my shoulders. I rang Alan Jones to tell him the news — that I had decided I couldn't leave Parramatta despite the appeal of the Balmain offer. He was terrific. He told me he was disappointed but that if my heart was still at Parramatta then I had done the right thing. He wished me well, and I hung up the phone, mightily impressed with the way he had handled the whole thing.

I went into the football office soon afterwards to sign my last contract. Fitzy wasn't there — he'd left the contracts with his secretary. So it was that I had the rather impersonal experience of signing the last contract of my long career with Parramatta in the secretary's office — with the club general manager nowhere in sight. I didn't want TV cameras there or any of that fuss, but I thought what with it being my last year and in view of the long stay I had had at Parramatta, and the fact there had been another club trying to get me, that *at least* the GM might have made a point of organising five minutes of his time to sign me. It would have been nice to shake on it and wish each other well. There was none of that. It was a "cold" signing and a disappointing one.

It got me thinking. I thought, gee, if this is how I am treated after 13 years, how do they treat young up-and-comers, or players from other clubs who they are trying to attract? Better than they treated me, I hoped.

Please don't get me wrong. I will always be proud and pleased to have played all my career at Parramatta. There were some wonderful times — the very best memories of my life, all of them irreplaceable. And Parramatta and football have provided things for me and my family I could not have hoped for without my career in league. Despite the disappointment I felt at the way I was signed, deep down I was over the moon. Now I would be able to say I was a one-club man; now I could finish my career at Parramatta Stadium — ironically (if we didn't make the '93 finals) against Balmain.

People have asked me since if Ray Price's club record of 258 first grade games was a motivation for me to keep going. At the start of season 1993 I only needed eight to equal him. I really wasn't aware I was that close and, no, it wasn't a big factor. The bigger influence was that I wanted to finish with Parramatta on the rise — not as cellar-dwellers of the competition. I wanted to look back on those last few tougher years and think, well, I achieved something worthwhile for the club.

As it turned out I hadn't even made it to Parramatta Stadium for the first match of my last season when I realised, painfully, that things were not necessarily going to go according to plan.

2 A Shoulder to Cry On

As I shaped up for my last year as a football player, people asked me how would I be able to get myself geed up again after so many poor Parramatta seasons. I was 32 then, with 250 first grade games on the board; a genuine veteran. With our half and captain Peter Sterling having succumbed to his chronic shoulder problem in 1992 and lock Mark "Pebbles" Laurie retiring (although he went to Salford in England for a brief spell), I was the last survivor of the golden era of the 1980s. People would say: "You've done everything there was to do in the game, you've got nothing to prove, why be a glutton for punishment again?" Well, there were the financial considerations to start with; you don't just replace your foootball earnings the day you hang up your boots. More than that, I realised that I still enjoyed playing. I believed that I still had something to offer the club. And I had things to achieve. As much as anything, I wanted to help lift Parramatta back to premiership respectability.

One thing still gnawed away at the back of my mind. Despite having played against every league country in the world, winning the Golden Boot (as the world's best player), being on two undefeated Kangaroo tours, and winning and losing State of Origin series, I'd never won a Dally M five-eighth of the year award. In fact the only Dally M award — the only award I ever won in the Winfield Cup — was as representative player of the year in 1986. I knew '93 was going to be my last year and I wanted to go out with a good season *individually*. A good season for me hopefully would help Parramatta to a good season. That Dally M had become a real aim, a goal.

Even in the years when I was chosen as the best five-eighth in NSW in the Origin side, I was never regarded the best by the Dally M judges. Terry Lamb or Cliff Lyons invariably beat me. As it turned out, Mick Cronin had decided to play me lock anyway in '93 — but with Canberra's Bradley Clyde starting the season late because of injury suffered in the World Cup final, maybe I could snare the lock's prize instead.

Once I made my decision to play and to play for Parramatta, I couldn't wait for the get-together when all the training details were announced. It's not really like me to look forward to training, but I was just so keen this time. Mind you, it didn't take long for a few sessions to knock that out of me! I felt good about the season and confident that the side would improve. We'd bought some experienced players in Paul Dunn, Michael Speechley and Peter McPhail, plus a couple of keen young blokes from Queensland in Darren Winmill and Marty McKenzie. Another thing which helped my attitude was that I was given special dispensation to miss some training sessions during the summer if I felt a bit stale or had other commitments. In the previous 13 seasons I wasn't offered this luxury but obviously the coaching staff felt, with the club stepping up intensity of pre-season training to five times a week, that at that stage of my football life I didn't necessarily need all of that. They knew I'd do the training I felt was needed to get me in good enough shape for the season. I felt good. We were training five times a week. I was doing one or two weight sessions instead of three and occasionally missed another session. I didn't take any unfair advantage of the concession I had been offered, but having that little bit of breathing space really worked for me.

By December I was counting the weeks to the first game, the annual match up at Nelson Bay on the NSW mid-north coast. We'd go up on a Saturday, play Saturday night and come back late Sunday after a few beers and a morning run. It was always a relaxing time and great for morale. The last training session of the year was always a few days before Christmas, and always a 10km time trial. After it we'd have a barbecue and a game of cricket, and the coaches would say: "Have a nice Christmas and enjoy the break" — which was all very well when you were almost sick from exhaustion after running 10km flat out! Once the Christmas break was over, you knew you were on a downhill run towards the season. Training got quicker, more intense. You started on ballwork, and you started looking ahead keenly to that first trial.

Every Paramatta year we went to Nelson Bay. I used to joke that I'd only play for 25 minutes and be dressed, having a cold beer on the sideline when the rest of the blokes came off. This time we had the prospect of the World Sevens the following weekend — an event I wasn't particularly keen on playing in. I reckoned I was getting too old for that frantic stuff. We were told anyone who was going to be in the Sevens squad would only play 20 or 30 minutes at Nelson Bay. I had a quick change of heart and my arm went straight up to volunteer!

When we got to Nelson Bay everything was fine. It was overcast, not too hot and I was looking forward to a bit of a jog for 25 minutes then off and into a few cold ones. Well, I was off and into the cold cans nice and early — but for the wrong reason. It became a day I'd never forget, that last visit to Nelson Bay.

I can recall the moment vividly. About 15 minutes into the game and I was tackled front-on. I had the ball in my left hand, swivelling to try and offload, but there was no-one there. A player was coming from deeper behind the line, so I delayed the pass, and got the ball away. As I did I was driven into the ground while my arm was still horizontal. I landed with my left arm outstretched and it came up on impact and actually hit my head. I was in a little bit of pain, so our trainer Peter Cohen came out. I started to move the arm around and I told him I'd be OK. We scored shortly afterwards and when we went back to halfway I had fair movement in the arm, but it was still a bit sore. I played on till the break (we played the match in "thirds" that night), then went to our physio and told him I was crook; he put ice on my shoulder. Crow (Mick Cronin) said he didn't want me going back on if I wasn't right. I said I'd be OK for another 10 minutes but the coach over-ruled me.

I thought I'd just strained the ligaments — until the next day. In a training session in the sparkling waters of Port Stephens we donned these special vests. The idea was to go out beyond where we could touch bottom, and run in the water with the vests keeping us afloat. I got out there and I couldn't move my arm, I couldn't swim. I had to dog paddle back in well behind the other blokes.

I saw the doctor on the Monday and I was ordered to have physio on the following days. But our team co-ordinator Ron Massey called on Monday to ask how I'd be for the Sevens as they had to nominate their side that day, and weren't allowed to make any changes. I told him I didn't know how I'd be; in hindsight I suppose I should have made myself unavailable. Anyhow, they picked me in the side, with the plan being to monitor my progress over the week.

I couldn't get to the physio on the Friday of our first match, so I arranged to meet him at the Sydney Football Stadium. He said the shoulder was "stable" although it was still sore, so there shouldn't be any problems. It took about two minutes of play to find there sure were some problems.

Beforehand I was joking how I mightn't be out there too long — if things got too fast or my shoulder took a bang. I told them I'd be off and in the stand before the young blokes could blink. I strapped the shoulder, and it felt pretty good. This day I put on pads, which I wouldn't normally do in Sevens football — and led the side out at Sydney Football Stadium against St George.

Saints kicked off and in about the third tackle of the match I fell back on my elbow in a Brad Mackay tackle; I'd been studded in the ankle at the same time. I was struggling but our new prop Paul Dunn wasn't interested, he was at dummy-half swearing at me to play the ball. I got up gingerly and played it. In the ensuing move we kicked downfield and Michael Speechley was knocked down after he kicked. Trainer Peter Cohen came on to see him, raced passed me on the way and, in the immortal words of Fatty Vautin, told me he'd get back to me shortly. I think we scored a try from the kick, so by the time Peter got back to me I was moving my arm around and I thought I'd be OK. He went back and reported to the coaches and they instructed him to get me off straight away. In the dressing room, club doctor Peter Manollaras discovered the shoulder was "clicking". It was one of two things, he told me — either cartilage damage, which meant a minor operation and a couple of weeks out, or ligament damage which meant, well, six months on the sidelines. I looked him in the eye and said there was no way I could spend that long out. This was my last season. What about all the agonising over the decision to play again? And all the summer training? The plans for a fairytale farewell? I couldn't let a mishap at Nelson Bay or in a Sevens tournament wreck it all.

I wasn't going to retire like that. Surely I could get a painkiller every week and get through? Put the shoulder in a special sling?... anything but that, anything but the end before the end was right.

People have asked me, if I hadn't played the Sevens, what would have happened with the extra few weeks' rest? Doctors told me it wouldn't have mattered — it was an injury waiting to happen. The initial damage was done at Nelson

Bay; a subsequent knock any time, even at training, would have had the same effect. It was just extra-disappointing that it all came to a head before we got anywhere near running onto Parramatta Stadium for a premiership match.

I was supposed to have an arthroscope on the Saturday but we were looking after my sister's girl, so I said I'd wait; otherwise Julie would be home with four kids all weekend. The following Tuesday I was starting this book. I'll go in and have it done on Wednesday, I thought, when I had everything out of the road.

Julie convinced me I shouldn't delay. So I rang Michael Johnson, our orthopaedic specialist, and he booked me in for Sunday morning. About 8 o'clock that night I went back to the hospital and Doc Johnson asked me just one question: was this definitely my last season? He'd already rung Julie and told her it was ligament damage. I knew what that meant.

I told him yes, it was my last season, and that all I wanted in life was the chance to to run out at Parramatta Stadium for the last match against Balmain, to wave goodbye to the fans and shake hands with all my mates.

He said if that was the case, I wouldn't have to rush to have the operation. My shoulder wouldn't deteriorate further if I waited until after the season. But could I play? The doc wouldn't give me any guarantees.

I was to leave the arm in a sling for four weeks, have extensive physiotherapy, build the strength up in the shoulder and then ... it was a case of luck. I could play my first game, fall heavily and it would pop again; or I might go three or four weeks before it happened. I might even last the season. When he said that, when he gave me even that slight chance, I had to take it.

The worst thing that could happen, I thought, was that the shoulder would keep popping. It might just become a case of how well I could handle the pain. The thought of that last premiership game of the season at Parramatta Stadium was set in my mind. Maybe if I came back and the shoulder wasn't standing up week after week, I'd ask Mick Cronin if I could work on my shoulder, get it right just for that one last game. I was desperate to do that — to finish where I had started ... even though the rubble of Cumberland Oval was buried somewhere deep beneath the new stadium.

When I went to bed that Sunday night I hardly slept. I should have been thankful that at least I had the chance, no matter how slim, to play again. I knew I'd run out in the blue and gold at least once more ... maybe a dozen times more if I was lucky. But it's hard to explain how desperate I felt, how utterly frustrated and dejected. It wasn't fair. My future was in the lap of the gods, resting on a dicky ligament. This wasn't the way it was supposed to happen. Damn it!!!

3 Brett the Baseballer

I have always been flattered when people have referred to me as "naturally gifted". The presumption is inherent in such an assessment that I was born to be a good footballer. It is far from the truth. Firstly, if I was born to be anything, it was a baseballer! And secondly, there was a time when I couldn't even make my school football side (although I thought that wasn't very fair at the time) and I didn't play any representative rugby league until I was 18 — and I almost missed the boat then because of an oversight.

I grew up at Greystanes in Sydney's western suburbs (my parents still live in the house where I spent my early years) and I was a baseball spectator before I could speak. My mum Marj took me to one of dad's matches when I was a couple of weeks old and it was a logical progression that I took up the game when I was older. My Dad, Alan Kenny, played for NSW and was chosen in the Australian merit side plenty of times. Many people have told me his brother Archie Kenny was the "Bradman" of Australian baseball. They both played for the Petersham club near where they grew up, and I used to love watching them when I was young. Dad told me of the time he played against Ian Chappell in the Caxton Shield interstate series. Chappell, although better known as a cricketer, was a first-class baseballer as well. Once when I was at the Channel 9 studios for the Wide World of Sports show, Ian mentioned how he played against my dad and what a good baseballer he was. It was nice to hear praise from someone like Ian Chappell and I thought: gee, here's a bloke famous throughout the sporting world, and my father played against him.

I actually got to play with Dad in first grade at Blacktown, after that club had amalgamated with Petersham after Petersham hit some financial problems. Rugby league was always my number one, though; it was league in winter and baseball in summer. Cricket? No way; I could never get into standing around in the field for four hours at a time.

By the time I was 15 I was in the Cumberland baseball side in the representative games, and probably wasn't that far away from making the NSW team. When I was 17 I was picked in the Blacktown Workers firsts, alongside my father. I was the youngest in the team. It was second division, not the major league in NSW, so I can't brag too much about how I sacrificed potential stardom as a baseballer! When I made the decision to give the game away I was an occasional first-grader with Petersham in the major league. I probably only got a start then because my uncle was the coach.

There was never any real doubt about which direction my sporting career would take after I joined Parramatta, and the two sports clashed for the first time. My parents and I could see straight away that rugby league offered a good income if I was successful enough at it. That was not a possibility in baseball. By the time I was 19, I had played my last game of baseball. If Dad was disappointed I didn't follow his footsteps, he never showed it. He was always right behind my rugby league career and I remember him telling me one day: "This is the way to go; you're going to make a good career out of this." I was the only one in the family who was really into rugby league.

I am the oldest of the three Kenny children. My brother Troy is 18 months younger and there is another 18 months between Troy and Debbie. I was only a toddler when I was responsible for the biggest family drama of the growing-up years — an accident which could have been far more serious than it turned out. I was taken to hospital with burns to most of my body after my grandfather Mick accidentally knocked a pot of tea off a kitchen bench onto me while we were visiting his place. I only vaguely remember it, but my parents told me that I was covered with bandages from head to toe with only one eye visible.

I still carry scars from the burns, on the right side of my neck and shoulder, but they have never worried me much. In fact, I have had some fun because of the marks. Whenever someone asks me what happened to me, I tell them I was attacked by a shark when I was surfing one day. I change the story from time to time, but usually it goes that I was surfing when the shark came at me and knocked me off my board. I'll tell graphically how I remembered the shark programmes on TV, where they let you know that the best chance you have is to poke the shark in the eye or punch it on the nose. My story is that I tried to punch it but as I threw my arm at it, it lunged at my arm around the top of the shoulder. But by this time the other surfers had paddled over and started making a racket in the water and charged at the shark and scared it away. Luckily skin grafts and stitches were able to save the arm. It gets people in for a while, though I'm not sure anyone has ever really believed me.

The sad thing about the accident is that my grandfather has never quite forgiven himself, and I have been his favourite ever since. Even when his wife died and he decided to sell his house, he split all the money up between his children, but also wanted to give me a share as a sort of repayment. God bless him. He's a great old bloke and the accident has never done me any harm in life. It was just one of those things that can happen.

Our home backed on to an old brickyard and there was a vast paddock right over the back fence which ran down to a canal. The people a few houses down had a horse which they kept in the paddock, tied to the back fence. Troy was always jumping the fence and patting the horse, so eventually Mum and Dad bought him one and we put a stable in the backyard. There were a few horses in the paddock and the kids used to congregate around them after school. The residents ended up getting the council to fence off the canal, and it was a great spot for kids and horses.

Troy and Debbie really got involved, and showed horses for years — but I was too busy playing football. I could ride a horse OK, but I was no Roy Rogers. Troy left for Yass for a while where he broke in thoroughbreds for a job and rode buckjumpers at the rodeos. He could have that on his own.

While we were growing up, the family juggled weekends between baseball, football and gymkhanas — but mum and dad always supported all of us and were happy to drive halfway around Sydney some weekends so they could see all of us follow our chosen pastimes. I remember well the many times I went with Mum, Debbie and Troy to Bossley Park for the gymkhana to help get things set up, while Dad went to baseball early to mark the field at Laybutt Reserve. Mum would arrange to get a lift home from Bossley Park and I'd take her car to Blacktown to play baseball. We all took an interest in each other's activities and tried to fit everything in each weekend.

The days at the gymkhanas remain as great memories. They'd most often be held at Bossley Park and there'd be kids everywhere. I recall the barrel races and the flag races. It was a big family thing and we'd all help out with the horses. Troy started riding poddy calves and then horses, bareback. Finally he was onto the buckjumpers. He never rode the bulls, though.

I was eight when a kid who lived in the same street came and asked if I wanted to play football with him, at Guildford. So I went down and instantly loved it. I finished up being captain. By the next year I was so hooked I lived for the weekends, and football. I remember once I had the chicken-pox and I wasn't allowed to play. I wasn't happy at all and asked my parents whether, even though I couldn't play, could I at least go to the game? It was pouring rain and we were playing away, but I still put all my gear on even though I was told I couldn't get out of the car. I was thinking if the team was short they might have to let me play, but unfortunately it didn't turn out anything like that. I reckon Mum would have handcuffed me to the steering wheel rather than let me out in the rain.

My Guildford side wasn't too successful. We never got near a grand final and I think we only made the semi-finals once. I played five-eighth right through until I was about 15 or 16 and then was switched to the centres, and that's where I finished my junior football.

I was always fairly tall and thin — "gangly" I suppose was a good way of describing me. I had collar-length hair and could be seen around most of the time wearing a shirt or footy jumper and a pair of tracksuit pants and joggers. I wouldn't say I was lazy, but training hard wasn't my definition of fun.

When I made it to grade level with Parramatta, there had only been two Guildford players I knew of who had made anything of themselves as topline footballers. Bob O'Reilly went to Parramatta before he was 17 years of age — and became the first local junior to play for Australia. Then came Mick Pattison, who was a couple of years older than me and regarded as the star junior player while I was coming through the grades at Guildford. Mick became a regular first-grader and may have played for Australia too if not for all the bad luck that he ran into. When I made first grade in 1980, Patto and the Bear were both in the side.

I went to Sherwood Grange primary school and, although I know a few people will doubt this, I was a pretty good student. When I moved on to Holroyd High School I was still doing pretty well, but by about Year 8 I think my mind was becoming more focussed on sport than studies. I played for the school in rugby league, cricket and basketball — adding those commitments to baseball or league on weekends.

By the time I reached Year 10 I was playing in the centres for Guildford and doing OK. I set my sights on making the team for the Buckley Shield, a statewide competition. But for the first time in my life I could only make it as a reserve.

By this time a lot of my mates were in the senior side and playing in the Amco Shield, which featured some games on television. I thought there wasn't too much I could do at this stage but sweat it out, so I sat on the bench for the Buckley Shield team. I went to all the training sessions after school, did all the right things — but couldn't get a run. Finally I got called on in the second half as a second-rower one day; well, I was the widest running second-rower you'd ever seen. Even Bobby McCarthy would have been embarrassed ... but I'd always been a centre and didn't know any better.

In recent years I have been invited back to Holroyd High School to talk to the students about sport and motivation; I think it helps kids to meet someone who has made something out of himself through sport. In my talks I always bring up the case of a student from the school who couldn't make the Buckley Shield side, but he kept going to training, he kept faith in his own ability, he kept trying. He knew that if he didn't drop his head, he'd make it one day. Then I tell them the kid was me. I hope it gives a lift to all those youngsters who aren't their team's stars.

The next year, getting on TV with the Amco Shield side was a bigger motivator than getting good grades in the HSC. I went on into Year 11. I didn't know what I wanted to do jobwise anyway, so it was pretty convenient to stay at school. Well, the team got knocked out in the first round of the Shield and none of us made it near a television camera.

By then I wasn't the most dedicated of students, although I wasn't a distraction to other class members, and I certainly wasn't a no-hoper. It was just that sport was a priority and study came a poor second. One day the message got through that remaining a school student wasn't the best option for me. I was finishing a can of Coke in class the first period after lunch and let out a loud belch just as the teacher came in. He sent me straight to the deputy principal's office. I'd never had the cane before and I feared the worst. He had a few strong words to say, but fortunately didn't see the need to use the cane. In a fairly stern voice the deputy head suggested it mightn't be the wisest thing for me to return for Year 12. Maybe I'd be better off in the workforce. I took the tip. I couldn't see us having a particularly strong footy side the next year anyway!

I went to technical college for a year fulltime, studying carpentry — but I couldn't get an apprenticeship because I had no practical experience. I needed 12 months' work with someone to complete my apprenticeship, but no one would take me on. Eventually my cousin got me a job at Foamlite, where I stayed until my second season in first grade when Parramatta lined up a job for me in the cellar of the leagues club. It was a long time before I realised the value of a career outside of the football field. I'll never resent the fact that rugby league became my bread and butter and my ticket to a more comfortable life. Without it, I wonder what would have happened to me? Still, I wish I had looked more closely into a second career path back then.

During my first year out of school I trialled for the Parramatta junior representative sides for the first time. At 17 I was invited to try out for the Jersey Flegg (under-18s). I was the only one from my Guildford side to get close to a rep side, although I thought our halfback Bobby Hadfield was good enough. It wasn't until 1985, when he was just too old for under-23s, that I convinced him to come down and trial with the Eels. I always thought he had a lot more talent than he had shown. John Monie actually gave him a big wrap but because he was too old for 23s, and we had plenty of halfbacks at that stage, he didn't get graded. Bobby and I were good mates and when I first made it to grade in 1980, we were coaching the Guildford under-10s together. The first year we had them they won the comp, with one of the stars was a tough kid named Kyle White — the same Kyle White who was playing regular first grade with Wests in 1993. He was a really stocky kid even back then and we used to play him in the centres, sometimes in the second row. When we took the side over, in 1980, we inherited a team which had come last in the under-9s the previous year. Dropping back a division, we went through the first season undefeated; the second year we went up to first division and just missed the semis. By that stage I was playing regular first grade and couldn't fit the kids into an increasingly hectic schedule — so the Ron Massey-Jack Gibson coaching team of the juniors was split up.

There was a kid in that team named George Stanton who really stood out from the rest. A few years later he came down to Parramatta to trial for the under-21s and I thought: how long have I been around? If I ever got to play against Kyle White and he called me grandpa, I wouldn't know whether to laugh — or to try and belt him.

I made the train-on squad for the Flegg side that first year, 1978, but didn't make the final selection. I thought: don't worry, there's always next year. From there I'd hoped to progress to President's Cup.

Next year they selected the Flegg side for summer training and the trials, but I didn't get an invitation to attend. I probably would never have got the chance if it hadn't been for Guildford official Ray Campbell. I hadn't received any letter inviting me to go to training and it wasn't until Ray asked me how I was going at Flegg training that he realised I hadn't even been asked to try out. He rang the coach and selectors and it turned out they had forgotten me; they apparently thought that because I tried out the previous year I was too old.

I finally received a letter and was added to the squad, and then made the line-up before the inter-district competition began. We didn't make the semi-finals and as it panned out I was the only graduate to an eventual first grade career — but it was a valuable first experience in a Parramatta jersey.

For half the season I was playing for Parramatta in the Jersey Flegg competition on Saturdays and for Guildford C grade on Sundays. Occasionally I sat on the bench in A grade but week after week never got called into a game. That was one of the few seasons my side made the semi-finals — although we were knocked out in the minor semi. The A grade side made it to the final and during the week one of the centres dropped out. I got the call-up — to my first match in senior football.

We played Wentworthville and I made a few breaks early, setting up one try and scoring another. I was pretty happy with myself — even though we lost the game — but I realised later that what happened that day was a classic case of a new kid on the block starring in new company simply because the opposition didn't know anything about him. You see it a lot in first grade now, a rookie will come along and have a great first-up appearance, or even first season, but then he doesn't shine quite so much next year because the opposition know what to expect and are looking for him. That was obviously the case in my first full match — and only match as it turned out — in Guildford A grade.

I had my goals set for the next season: having a good year in C grade, getting a few more games in A grade, and making the President's Cup side. I was half-hoping during 1979 that I would have been called up to grade from Flegg. I thought that by the time you got to President's Cup you were too old. But I found out that they did take up players from the President's Cup, so I thought 1980 would be my last big year in the Parramatta juniors; I had to make it count. Then, out of the blue, everything changed — for the better.

4 The Rabbit Who Got Away

I'll let you into a secret. Right through my growing-up years I was a Souths supporter. I used to go to Redfern whenever I could for Souths games — even though it was a fair hike from where I lived at Greystanes. And I'd read every word about them and watch them on TV. In backyard games I was always Ron Coote or Bobby McCarthy or Denis Pittard. Souths were the top side of the late 1960s and early '70s (I was too young to remember much about the great St George era that preceded the Rabbitohs' five successive grand finals). McCarthy, Coote, John Sattler, Ray Branighan, Eric Simms — all those guys were my heroes as I grew up. Even when I'd retired as an international player after achieving all my rugby league dreams it was one of the greatest buzzes in my life when I was introduced to Bob McCarthy and John Sattler after a game on the Gold Coast in 1988. I still thought: "Wow! I used to idolise these guys when I was a kid."

So all of a sudden here I was at Redfern Oval in July 1980, just a few months after graduating from Guildford's C grade to the reserves bench in under-23s, when I got the tap on the shoulder to run on — in first grade! I had sort of stumbled into becoming a winger in reserves, and along with most of the other reserve-graders, I would sit on the sideline during the firsts — hoping to get the call but never really expecting it to happen.

On this day Tony Melrose, playing centre for Parra alongside Mick Cronin, was injured early in the second half. For whatever reason, coach John Peard chose to throw me to the wolves. Against Souths — of all clubs!

I'm lucky in that I retain vivid memories of certain tries I've scored and certain things that happened on the field. But to tell you the truth I can't remember a great deal about that first appearance in first grade — other than how nervous I was and how much quicker it was than reserves and under-23s. I didn't try to do too much and I was lucky that Mick Cronin looked after me. He didn't put me under any undue pressure. He might have passed to Tony Melrose in a certain tight situation but because it was me, he took them on more himself and let me ease myself into the game. I was lucky to make a couple of breaks, though, and one early on led to Lew Platz scoring a try. I was just so relieved afterwards that I didn't make a fool of myself. Tony Melrose had a hamstring strain and I presumed he'd be back the next week, and that I would drop back to reserves.

It was pretty extraordinary that I was at Parramatta at all, let alone tasting first grade. I was picked in the President's Cup side (when it was a junior league representative side, not part of the senior club set-up) and we played a game against some under-23s trialists in February. I must have gone OK and the under-23s coach Ron Fearnley rang me up and asked if I'd like to come down and trial for the 23s instead of playing President's Cup. You don't give up that sort of opportunity, and I said yes.

There was only one problem; I was playing first grade baseball at the time at Blacktown and they played Sunday afternoons. My first trial with Parra was on a Sunday in probably the fourth of the under-23s matches played against Manly at Brookvale. I was asked to sit on the bench in the next game as well and got a run. But I kept thinking I had to get to Seven Hills to play baseball by 3 o'clock. I finished the second game, ducked the showers and hopped in the car to drive across town to Grantham Reserve, Seven Hills — arriving just in time for the baseball warm-ups.

Over the next few weeks I was playing league later and later and things were getting tighter and tighter getting to baseball. Somehow I never missed a match and managed to finish the baseball season. I've never played baseball since.

I was graded with Parramatta and sat on the bench in the under-23s for the first three matches. Finally I got a run as replacement fullback against Newtown. I was chosen as fullback the next week against Cronulla and then finally got a chance in the centres, as John Muggleton's partner against Wests a few weeks later — a game in which I picked up three tries. It was a pretty slick under-23s side, containing the likes of Steve Sharp, Brett Garnon, Paul Taylor and John Muggleton, all destined for better things.

I remember clearly the first time I was in the dressing room before a match and saw all these players disappearing into another room. I thought: "I wonder where they are going" — so I followed them in. They were all getting their ankles strapped. When I was in the juniors you never got strapped unless something was wrong with you but I figured this was obviously the thing to do in grade football. So I joined the queue and got my perfectly healthy ankles strapped. To have your ankles strapped is of course part and parcel of the game now — a preventative thing rather than to protect an injury.

My big break that season came in unusual circumstances at Kogarah in round 11 when we were playing Saints. I played the full game in under-23s and scored a try. When we went into the dressing room after the match I lined up as usual and put my hand out for a can of drink and a towel. The towel came but I was told I couldn't have a drink (of beer). When I asked why not, they said I'd better see the coach Mick Alchin. I thought: "What's going on here?."

I learned that Glenn West, a reserve grade winger that day, had trouble with his car and couldn't get to the ground on time. I had to go straight out after playing a full under-23s game and back up on the wing in reserves. I'd scored a try in the under-23s and subsequently picked up another in reserves. It was the only time in my career I scored tries in two grades on the one day. I didn't try to do anything flamboyant in reserves. For starters I wasn't a winger! I just stuck to my wing, I didn't know the other players very well — I'd never even come on as a replacement in reserves before — but fortunately the play came my way a few times and I was able to make a couple of runs. We won fairly comfortably and I thought that it was a handy experience for a shy 19-year-old learning the ropes but that I'd be back in under-23s the next week. On the Tuesday night they picked me again as a winger — in reserves.

Eventually I found my way into the reserve grade centres. In the team were such blokes as Graham Murray (now Illawarra coach), Graham Olling and a genuine living legend, Arthur Beetson. I couldn't believe it. Six months before, I had been playing juniors; my goal for the year had been to make the President's Cup side. Now I was a reserve-grader — and I count among my memories a particularly valued one of scoring a try off Beetson one day. The big bloke put me through a gap with a fantastic pass.

It all seemed to happen so quickly — from there to first grade, to a match at the home base of "my" team. My expectations after that game at Redfern were not that I would stay in firsts. But the news on Tony Melrose was that he wasn't going to be fit to play, and I got a call from Peardy the next Monday night letting me know he was going to pick me in firsts for the game against Newtown the following weekend.

My parents have kept an extensive scrapbook collection over the years and I get a chuckle when I look back now on that amazing week. Naturally, I'd never spoken to a pressman before in my life but now the phone was ringing. I had my picture in the *Daily Mirror*, alongside a nice story. They had me sitting on a forklift truck — even though I'd never driven one in my life. I was working as a labourer at Foamlite, picking up foam and moving it around the factory. I was quoted in the *Daily Mirror* as saying: "I never thought I'd be playing first grade this season but I don't think it'll last for too long. I'm only in because Tony Melrose is hurt and he could be back the following week." I'm glad my prediction turned out wrong.

The greatest thing about being chosen in firsts was that it meant I was to play alongside Mick Cronin. Even though I followed Souths, Cronin and Steve Rogers were my heroes. I idolised Cronin and Rogers, who were entrenched at the time as Australia's centre pairing and were the perfect combination. Michael Cronin was best known for his strength and skill with the ball while Steve Rogers was mercurial and agile. I thought if I could build myself up like Mick but be as agile as Steve Rogers, it would be a perfect mixture.

Things had happened fast for me. It had been the corresponding match against Newtown in the first round in which I had first been in the under-23s. Only four weeks earlier I had had my first run in reserves. At least I didn't have much time to think about all these good things that were happening to me, or time to worry. I just thought to myself: "Go out and enjoy it while you can." As I told the papers, I really didn't expect it to last.

The team for that game against Newtown was an interesting mix of experienced players with some young blokes like myself. The halves, Peter Sterling and Mick Pattison, had both slotted regularly into first grade towards the end of the previous season; Eric Grothe was chosen on the wing but dropped out with injury and was replaced by John Chapman. Neil Hunt was at fullback; he'd taken the place of Garry Dowling who'd come back from being Australia's player of the tour in New Zealand a couple of weeks earlier but was having problems with some niggling injuries. Hunty was going too well to be dropped. The side was: Hunt, Glover, Cronin, Kenny, Chapman, Pattison, Sterling, Price, Platz, Wynn, Beetson, Edge, Hilditch (c).

I was pretty nervous, and a bit lost in the week before the match. Because I was the new boy on the block the media focussed on me at training. It was all very new. I really didn't know any of the players in the side, other than to say hello to them, and that was a bit unnerving. But the older blokes were really good; Mick Cronin took me aside from the start and made me feel at home. The attitude was a very professional one of welcome and: "You're here with us now, we accept that, let's get on with it."

On Tuesdays at Parramatta all the grades trained together; on Thursdays you did ball work with your own team. I was used to going out to the field at the back of Cumberland; now I had to remind myself to stay where I was, on the main oval. I was a pretty keen trainer by then — believe it or not (some of the current Parramatta players might raise an eyebrow at that). I never cut corners and I did things flat out. I was keen to impress and to keep up.

By the Saturday morning session I had settled down. All the media attention of earlier in the week was gone now, and I was starting to feel at ease with the fact I was a first-grader, for one week at least.

John Peard handed out a typed message to all the players. One section covered the team's performance, the other related to each player individually. It's still in dad's scrapbook with the other clippings of the time. It makes interesting reading:

(July 11, 1980) "To the Parramatta first grade football team: I don't have to stress how important today's match is. We're in a spot. We have to win it, then keep on winning. We were beaten last week by a team not as good as us. But they wanted to win, and they did, because of the sheer enthusiasm of each player. Somewhere along the way Parramatta seems to have lost some of its enthusiasm, some of us have been just going through the motions, just relying on ability. It's not enough. We won't win this competition, we won't even make the five, by just relying on ability. There is an old law of behaviour which is very true in the case of a football team. It goes like this: Performance = Skills x Motivation. If a skill is as high as 10 but motivation is only 4, the performance will be 40. Whereas if skills is as low as 7 but motivation is 10, the result is a 70 performance.

"Our skill as a football team is high, call it nine out of 10. We have some of the best footballers in the world in our team. But our enthusiasm, our motivation, has not been as high as it should be. If we lift our enthusiasm to the same level as our ability, then we are practically unbeatable in this competition. If we don't, then we will be a has-been side, and will have let ourselves and our supporters down in the worst possible way. It's up to us, so let's get stuck into it. Come on, let's be a 90 outfit not a 40 or 50. Let's show ourselves and our supporters that we have what it takes. And let's do it now, today against Newtown. Let's make today the turning point."

Attached was my personal message, words of encouragement and confidence from the coach before my first match in the big time:

"Your form over the past three matches has been great. In that period you haven't missed a tackle, your attacking game has been excellent with breaks, offloads and back-ups. You have loads of ability but you also have another very important thing — enthusiasm. We are going to need that enthusiasm today. You have a 100 percent record in defence over the past three matches. Let's keep that 100 percent record. You have a record of five successful back-ups in the last three matches. That's excellent for a centre. Let's see if you can get three back-ups today. You've earned your opportunity Brett, now take advantage of it."

At the time Parramatta were in some trouble. We had lost the previous two games — 6-3 to Norths and 28-12 to Souths, and another loss could have put us out of the very tight race for the finals. We'd been beaten by Newtown in the first round at Henson. It came down to the fact that we had to win this day to turn things around. Probably the other players felt the pressure more than me — I was on cloud nine just being around them, a young bloke no one had ever heard of partnering the great Mick Cronin in the centres. I didn't sleep well Saturday night, but I was confident I would go OK. I didn't expect to have a spectacular game; just to not make any mistakes and not look out of my depth would be enough, I reckoned.

On match day John Peard organised a team meeting at the leagues club before we went across to Cumberland to watch some of the under-23s and the reserves. My stomach was in knots as I changed for the game and I forced myself to concentrate on the thought of just getting out there and doing a job. I had to keep my defence tight, and back up. When I ran out that day I could hear the racket from my Guildford mates. There must have been 30 or 40 of them, camped on the hill right in front of the press box. Even the newspapers made mention of them next day. Whenever there was a lull in play I could hear them. They made heaps of noise and gave me heaps of support. I'll never forget it. I don't remember that much else about the game other than it was a bright, sunny day and we won well — 37-6 after being behind 6-3 at halftime. The clippings tell the story that Sterlo had a really big game, outplaying Tom Raudonikis who was still playing Tests at that time. One paper called him the "heir apparent" to Tommy's Test jersey. Sterlo and I were involved in five of our six second-half tries; I plucked one of his bombs just after halftime to get us going. But I remember as clearly as anything that Mick Cronin made my debut so much easier than it might have been. He never put me under pressure with the ball and sort of eased me right through the game — plus plenty more after that day!

I held my spot for the following week, against Cronulla. Now I was not only playing alongside Mick Cronin but against my other idol, Steve Rogers! I couldn't believe it.

I had some questions from the media as to what it felt like — the prospect of playing against Steve Rogers, probably the world's best centre at that stage. Maybe they thought I'd say how worried I was but my attitude was more what a thrill it was. I was up against the world's best, with another legend next to me. I was an unknown — what did I have to lose? If I performed well they'd say the kid has a bright future — if I didn't go too well I'd perhaps lose my first grade spot. My attitude was that I had everything in my favour.

Fortunately the game went well. We won 32-7 and Mick put me through plenty of gaps. Again I don't remember a great deal about the match other than the over-riding feeling of how honoured I was to be on the same field as Cronin and Rogers. A glance at *Rugby League Week* 13 years later tells me that I outpointed them in the ratings; Rogers got a 6, Cronin a 7 and I got an 8.

Without the Crow next to me, I'm not sure how I would have survived those first few games. He didn't put me in any tough situations and, being young and fast, I was able to get really deep and pick up those beautiful passes he put on. That sort of dash left me later in my career. It's a cruel thing, age. I remember feeling a lot better about myself after the Cronulla game. I had now played two first grade matches, I knew that no opponent would be tougher than Steve Rogers and I hadn't let anyone down. I was starting to feel a little bit more comfortable with this first grade caper.

Parramatta strung together three wins in a row. Sterlo was killing them at halfback and Neil Hunt, with his big side-step, was being rated as something of a wonder boy at fullback and was keeping Garry Dowling out of the side. And Eric Grothe, once he got free of injury, was starting to make a big name for himself on the wing. Mick Pattison by then was nicely established at five-eighth. With our blend of old and new, plenty of people were starting to think Parramatta would finally win the premiership after making the semis for the previous five seasons, including two grand final appearances (1976-77).

As a new boy I didn't feel the pressures or the disappointment when things didn't go right as much as the others. After all, I was a Souths supporter — I hadn't been waiting around all my life like so many others, waiting for the Eels to break their duck. As a first-season first-grader I had not tasted the anticipation and then the disappointment of the seasons gone by. I was pretty starry-eyed; just to be running around the training paddock with so many stars was all I wanted out of life at that stage.

Yet I still sensed the deep disappointment of the senior players when we missed the semis that year. Winning the midweek Tooth Cup, the club's second title in first grade (after the Wills pre-season competition of 1975) was great. Champagne flowed in the dressing room, we went back to a function at the club after the match, and it was a whole new experience for me. Despite the excitement, that didn't really feel like a dinki-di final to me. My strongest memory of the game is of winger Michael Collins, who never played first grade again, kicking us to victory. Collins was a baby-faced young bloke, plucked from the under-23s, and the commentators kept saying: "They've passed to the ballboy!" He could sure kick goals. We won 8-5 against Balmain at Leichhardt, with Collins scoring all the points from his boot. It was the first time I played without Mick Cronin next to me. Mick had been suspended after having a set-to with Wests' Ted Goodwin the previous Sunday. No more Mr Nice Guy!

In my brief first grade experience I'd played the semi-final and final of the Tooth Cup plus five premiership games — bringing wins against Newtown,

Cronulla and Norths, a draw against Manly and a 34-9 flogging at the hands of Wests the Sunday before the cup final. That day our minds were wandering to the following Wednesday night game. Before that game Parramatta were two points behind Wests at the top of the ladder — but four sides were equal with us.

Ultimately we missed the semis, beaten by Canterbury 15-14 four days after the cup final and by St George 20-11 in the last round. A win in either match would have put us into the semi-finals.

The end of the season meant nothing to me other than that I'd finished in first grade. I'd started as a President's Cup player, a C-grader for Guildford, and finished my season in front of almost 20,000 fans at Cumberland Oval as centre partner to a legend. I was oblivious to any pressure that was mounting on coach John Peard. All I wanted to do was play football and I believed Peardy was a good coach. I will always appreciate what he did — the gamble he took in bringing me into first grade.

I don't know when John Peard was sacked and Jack Gibson appointed for season 1981, but obviously it was a really big thing for a 19-year-old who'd just arrived from nowhere to hear that the guru of coaches was headed our way. Jack Gibson by then had such a reputation, a sort of aura about him.

Like most of the blokes, my first reaction to him was one of some fear. We had the perception of him as a sort of standover man. I had this vision of Jack being the schoolmaster and us the pupils — and it being a case of do the right thing or you're history. Straight up to the office.

The reality turned out to be a lot different. The three years under Gibbo at Parramatta was just a freakish period, with a freakish team ... and success I never dreamed of.

5

The Day I Almost Died

I almost didn't make it past one season of first grade football with Parramatta. Fullback Neil Hunt saved my life one day far from home. I'll tell you the story.

At the end of 1980 the Parramatta first-graders went on an end-of-season trip to The Philippines and Hong Kong. I'd never been overseas before, never been out of NSW in fact, so jetting out with a bunch of experienced drinkers was all new to me. The only football trip I'd ever had was with the Guildford C grade the previous season — to the town of Orange, NSW.

All of a sudden I was in exotic south-east Asia, rooming with Hunty in Manila. We were the babies of the team, and naturally they put us together. It was a real budget accommodation trip; as soon as we pulled up at our motel we could see it was a real dive. It was in a filthy area, with rubbish everywhere. We dumped our bags in the room and discovered visitors in the bath — silverfish. But it didn't seem to matter much. I was 19, a first-time traveller and with a bunch of mates determined to have a good time after a demanding season.

On the second night in town Neil Hunt, Mick Pattison and I decided we'd go downtown on a pub crawl. The first place we stopped at was half-nightclub, half-bar and we settled in for a drink. I thought I'd have a San Miguel beer, which tasted not bad at all. At the next bar I decided that instead of having a beer, I'd have a Tequila Sunrise. That set the pattern for the night — at one bar I'd have a beer, at the next a Tequila Sunrise ... beer then Tequila Sunrise. Before too long we met up with some of the other players and we decided that walking from bar to bar, which were getting increasingly further apart, was not the smartest way to travel. Along the way we discovered pedi-cabs, little motor bikes with a buggy attached to the back, and thought "this is the go". So we hired two drivers to act as our chauffeurs for the night.

Away we went, and before long our cart was way behind the other. We urged our driver to step up the pace a bit and offered him extra cash. The bloke was obviously a frustrated formula one driver — he just took off and away we went ... to we didn't know where. We seemed to be heading out of town, as we chased the other pedi-cab. There were no street lights, it was pitch black and our Nigel Mansell of Manila was on the wrong side of the road, trying to pick up the bloke in front. He wouldn't pull in, just had his foot flat on the pedal in the darkness when we noticed headlights coming the other way. They didn't perturb him one bit, he just kept going. There was a big truck heading towards us, honking its horn, but this bloke wasn't worried. We'd paid him to overtake and that's what he was going to do. A fraction of a second before half the Parramatta backline got wiped out in a head-on collision, he pulled in front of the other cart and punched the air. It sobered us up pretty quickly.

For the rest of the night, these guys transported us from pub to pub, waited outside until we had a couple of drinks (one beer, one Tequila Sunrise for me). Eventually, at some God-forsaken hour they took us back to our motel. There are not too many times in my life that I've felt worse than I did that night. Hunty had more stamina than me and decided to have a drink downstairs with some of the senior players who'd made themselves permanent fixtures in the bar. I went straight to our room to feed the silverfish. In fact, I headed directly for the bathroom and promptly threw up. Next thing I remember was regaining consciousness — with Hunty whacking me on the back.

What had happened was that I had fallen asleep under the basin, with my head down. Some regurgitated food had caught in my throat and when Hunty got to me he reckoned I wasn't breathing. Luckily he was sober enough and smart enough to turn me over, and he then belted me into coughing up the offending substance. Breathing again, I dragged myself off the floor and across to the bed.

Next morning we had organised a white water rafting and canoeing trip. Not wanting to show I couldn't handle a night out, I went right along, and took part. I just hope the river that day didn't provide Manila's water supply; I was crook as a dog.

Our accommodation was so poor that a few of us decided to throw in some money and find somewhere else. We caught a bus to the United States airbase just out of town and stayed at a motel nearby. Although out of town, it was 100 percent better. Table tennis became the game there. It's funny what you learn on football trips away — about life and about the other players. Mick Cronin was my idol, a great player respected by everyone; page boy looks, never a hair out of place. Mick seemed the kind of bloke every mum would like her daughter to bring home. But I learned on that trip that Mick was a real night owl who could outdrink anyone, including the big beer-swilling forwards.

One night, early one morning actually, a few of them were sitting around the bar having a contest to see who could last the longest. Bobby Jay and Ronny Hilditch were there alongside the Crow. Hunty and I called it a night, thinking that these hardened drinkers would make a mess of the Crow. Next morning we got up and went downstairs. Slumped across the bar were four or five bodies. Michael Cronin esq was there as bright as a button, admiring the morning sunshine — a Bacardi and Coke still in his hand.

A couple of days later, we went to Hong Kong. I had not been impressed by the squalor of Manila; in contrast, Hong Kong was heaven. We booked into a modern hotel and the kid from Guildford who'd never been anywhere before had trouble working out what the bloody hell was this plastic card they'd given us instead of a room key. That problem finally solved, I spent the first day around the shops, buying tailor-made clothes dirt cheap and all that.

The next day we took the ferry across to Kowloon and there were some nervous Eels when we came back *under* the harbour, by train. On the train was a kid with an iceblock which he promptly dropped in the middle of the carriage. All of a sudden there was a pool of water on the floor of the train just where we were sitting. Hunty and I looked at each other, and drew the attention of some of the other players to the water. Someone hollered out that the tunnel must be leaking — and a couple of the boys really shit themselves. Hunty and I just burst out laughing. The Hong Kong experience was a great ending to my first year in big-time rugby league.

Despite the long-standing tradition of football end-of-season trips, I only ever went on one more. My marriage to Julie in 1984, and Kangaroo tours in 1982 and '86 meant no trips with the Eels in those years. In the '80s Parramatta started going regularly to Surfers Paradise, but the only time I went along was in 1983. My attitude to things has always been that when something has been achieved or something has been seen, move on. Once I'd been to Surfers Paradise for one trip, I had no real desire to keep going back to the same place. I'd seen a bit of the Gold Coast over the years anyway — my wife's sister Lynne lives there.

One trip I remember well was the 1983 excursion to Wauchope for the annual pre-season weekend on Jack Gibson's ranch, plus a match against the locals. It was always a nice relaxed way to start the season and the run against the Wauchope side enabled us to get a feel of the ball under match conditions before the serious business began. We flew home on the Sunday evening and everything was going smoothly until we noticed that one of the hostesses was looking really concerned. We started to stir her up but then the announcement came that there would be a delay and that we had to circle the airport at Sydney for a while before we could land. Well, we gave it to this hostess even more; the blokes were asking what date it was when the Manchester United soccer team's plane crashed in Munich. Someone else figured out that it was almost exactly the same time of year. There was a quip that we'd all become known as the Parramatta "Angels" instead of the "Eels". The hostess wasn't laughing — in fact, she started to cry. Apparently the landing wheels indicator light wasn't working, and while we were joking away the pilot was preparing for a crash landing. We'd been fuelled by a few drinks and were trying to make light of the situation — all except Peter Wynn, that is. He picked up a napkin and started writing a note to his wife Linda, and asked Graeme Atkins, who was sitting next to him, to deliver it if it happened that Graeme survived and Peter didn't. When we started to descend towards the runway we could see ambulances and fire trucks there, and the glint of flash lights shining up to the under-carriage. The mood by now was decidedly serious.

It was a story with a happy ending. The problem was an electrical fault — the wheels *were* down, even though the indicator light hadn't come on. We landed safely, to be met by reporters summoned there by the "drama". Next day we were on the front page of the newspapers. Our utility man Kevin Stevens "collapsed" when he got off and was taken through the terminal in a wheelchair. Some of us were able to laugh it off ... later, anyway.

So the football trips away of my career were small in number — but eventful. I had a brush with death in Manila, and maybe a glimpse of it as we circled Mascot that day. The football field itself was a much safer place to be.

6 The Witch Was Dead

When Parramatta began the training build-up to the 1981 season, it was the new man at the helm who grabbed the most attention. Many saw new coach Jack Gibson as the Messiah, the man who could bring the club its first premiership. I was a raw rookie, hardly believing that it was all happening to me. Playing first grade (seven games) under John Peard had been a whole new experience for me. He was more professional, and thorough, than any coach I'd ever known. Now I was to experience the qualities of the man they called the greatest coach of them all. This was going to be something special.

It was another "new" name — to me at least — that took most of my attention in the lead-up to 1981. Steve Ella. Not being a Parramatta fan and honestly knowing little about the club before I joined out of the blue in 1980, I didn't know much about "Zip" other than what people had told me — that he was an outstanding player who had missed almost two seasons because of a shocking knee injury. There was a sense of uncertainty about whether he was going to make it back. The fact that he was a centre made me sit up and take notice.

Jack Gibson had coached Ella in the NSW under-18s in 1978 and the coach apparently had no doubts he had the ability to be a pretty special player again. Jack didn't need to see Zip play reserves or under-23s; he knew he could play as long as he was fit and had psychologically beaten his bad injury. Straight away he was treated as a first-grader. But two seasons is a long time out of the game and few people had suffered such a bad knee injury as the one Steve Ella copped. Manly's big centre Steve Knight had wiped him out early in 1979, in Zip's second match in first grade. He spent months in plaster and missed the rest of 1979 and all of 1980. Indirectly his ill-fortune created my opportunity.

Crow missed the pre-season matches of 1981, so Zip and I were chosen in the centres, with Tony Melrose at five-eighth, taking over from Mick Pattison who had left for Souths. The first time I ever saw Steve Ella play was at Wauchope, where Jack Gibson had taken us for our weekend away and warm-up game. We won 53-4 in a cakewalk against the locals, but it was a serious enough hit-out for me to realise Steve Ella was some player and that he had definitely recovered from his knee injury.

We combined pretty well during the Craven Mild pre-season competition, but all the time the thought was nagging away — what happens when Mick Cronin comes back? Crow was right to return for the cup final against Easts and I still vividly remember being extra-nervous on the Monday and Tuesday, waiting to see whether I'd still be in the side, or be the golden-haired newcomer of 1980 who started the next season in reserves. I'd learnt enough about Jack Gibson to know reputations didn't mean much with him. Tony Melrose had been playing well at five-eighth and Zip was killing them in the centres. I figured that I might be the one to go.

Anyway, Gibbo found room for both Zip and me for the match against Easts – – and it was Tony Melrose who ended up being the odd man out, although Tony was brought back to play on the wing for a few matches. Steve switched to five-eighth. I was rapt to be still in the top side.

The game against Easts (which we lost 12-3 in a tight one) began a partnership between Zip and me which proved fruitful for the pair of us and for Parramatta. We were both young, keen and pretty elusive. Next door we had Mick Cronin, wily old Mick, to guide us. And although Zip wore the number six for the first half of the season before I "officially" switched to five-eighth, we alternated throughout matches in a ploy started by Jack Gibson purely for defensive purposes from the scrum — but something that Zip and I took further to a general ad-lib situation.

Jack told us that whenever we had the feed at the scrum, Zip would be at five-eighth because he was quicker on his feet and really dangerous from that set-play situation. But if the other side had the feed, I was told to go into five-eighth because Jack saw me as the better defender. We started that way in 1981, with me sticking to the centres in other situations. But as we got used to each other, we sort of pleased ourselves who went to five-eighth from the scrums and Gibbo didn't have any objections. It really ended up a matter of whoever was closest when the scrum was called. Whoever that was would go to five-eighth. If I was on the other side of the field and couldn't be bothered sprinting 40 metres for a scrum, I'd just wave to Zip and he'd fill in. Although Zip played most of his junior football as a centre (with Eric Grothe as his partner in their Mt Pritchard side), I reckon he fancied himself as a five-eighth, and it was a nice irony that Wigan bought him to replace me at five-eighth in 1985.

The chopping and changing must have been confusing for Mick Cronin — he'd never know who was inside him or outside him. About halfway through the season I started to wear the number six jersey, but nothing else changed. It was one of the great things about those Parramatta sides of the early '80s — the versatility of the backline.

That first year Steve McKenzie ended up at fullback after Phil Mann and Tony Melrose had a few games each there early on. But by 1982 Paul "Tas" Taylor became a regular there, if a fairly unusual fullback in that he was hardly ever in the last line. If we were in our own quarter on the last couple of tackles I used to go back to fullback, to handle the high kick, and Tas would go up into the front line where he was a great low tackler. I used to love following bombs when we kicked, and had the ability to get fairly high, so Gibbo saw this as an advantage in defence as well as attack.

When we were out of our quarter, Peter Sterling often used to drop back to have a spell, and Taylor would again go into the front line where he would drive the opposing forwards mad by chopping their legs from under them, and scurrying out from dummy-half. The tactic gave Sterlo a break and allowed him to avoid using too much energy in defence. Tas loved to tackle anyway and had played most of his football at halfback or in the back row before that season. In 1982 Steve Ella scored four tries playing fullback against Wales on the Kangaroo tour; Sterlo played his first couple of seasons at Parramatta at five-eighth and made his well-publicised first grade debut at fullback in the 1978 semi-final replay against Manly. Our backline versatility was unbelievable really.

When I look at the 1981 side I see a freakish combination of young talent and experienced campaigners under a magical coach. We went on to win three successive titles, four altogether from five grand finals over six years. And I had the pleasure of playing with some of the most naturally gifted footballers of my time, or of *any* time for that matter. Perhaps the Parramatta hierarchy were subsequently lulled into believing that this collection of exceptional talent set a standard that would automatically be continued through the production line of the Parramatta juniors. That was folly, but I'll go into that later on.

Such a gathering of rare talent is once-in-a-decade stuff, once in a lifetime for a single club. It happened when St George dominated in the 1950s and '60s, although many of their players were gathered from other places. To have had players such as Gasnier, Langlands, Smith, Walsh, King, Provan and Raper in the same side at the same time was a dream for the club. Something similar happened at Souths in the 1960s and '70s, with McCarthy, Coote, Sait, Walters, the Branighans, Simms, Stevens and plenty of others all coming through at the same time. Canberra were next, in the '80s, with Laurie Daley, Bradley Clyde, Glenn Lazarus and Ricky Stuart plus players such as Steve Walters and Gary Belcher, who'd never played rep football before joining Canberra. They all came together in a spectacularly successful mix under the leadership of senior statesman Mal Meninga. All of them became internationals.

I still reckon Parramatta had the most special gathering of all over the past couple of decades — in that, in the backline anyway, we all arrived in first grade within a season of each other, were not much more than a year apart in age and were all locals except for Sterlo, who joined the club while still at school. The necessary element of experience came through Mick Cronin in the backs and such tough campaigners in the forwards as Ron Hilditch, Bob O'Reilly, Kevin Stevens, Ray Price and Steve Edge. It was the perfect combination — the older forwards could do the tough stuff and get control, then the young backs could do the fancy stuff out wide.

Looking over some scrapbooks recently I came across a story where Bob O'Reilly had observed, after we had beaten Souths 39-5 in the first round, that Parramatta for so long had had the forwards to win a premiership — but never the backs. The Bear had come through with experienced internationals like Dick Thornett, Brian Hambly and Ron Lynch and the later internationals Ray Higgs, Geoff Gerard, Denis Fitzgerald, Graham Olling and Keith Campbell, plus John McMartin who just fell short of international honours. Other than John Kolc and Neville Glover, who very briefly wore Australian jerseys, the club hadn't produced an international back since Ken Thornett in the early 1960s. In the backline of '81 there were myself, Peter Sterling, Steve Ella and Eric Grothe who all went on to play for Australia, Neil Hunt who played for NSW, and of course Mick Cronin who had been long established as an Australian centre. The pendulum had really swung since the Bear's early days.

Steve Ella scored three tries in that match against Souths and Sterlo and I picked up two each. I value a column written after that match — by Reg Gasnier, probably the greatest centre of all time. He declared that I was the most exciting centre prospect he had seen for years. "Kenny's rate of improvement has been amazing and can obviously be attributed largely to his playing beside Mick Cronin," Gasnier wrote. "I know I certainly appreciated a big bloke called Harry Wells alongside me when I came into top level football." The great centre wasn't wrong; much of what I achieved in those early years I owe to the Crow.

The way the "old" and the "new" at Parramatta blended together so well was the key to our success. And it wasn't just on the field. Off the field, there was never any division, even though the new generation of backs was in many cases a decade younger than some of the forwards. I was a pretty shy bloke and I got close to Eric Grothe at first, then Steve Ella when he came back and Sterlo, Neil Hunt and Paul Taylor. But whenever there was a function or party, whenever the team was together at the after-training barbecues, we all got on extremely well. And not just we players, but our wives and girlfriends as well. A typical example was on New Year's Eve when we always went to Ray Price's place for a party — the "old" blokes with their wives and kids and the "young" blokes with their girlfriends. It was always a night I really looked forward to; it really brought us all together for the year ahead. Camaraderie off the field is often a big factor in success on the field. During the Parramatta golden years that was definitely the case.

All my memories of 1981 are over-ridden by one day — and night — September 25. League history records it as the day of Parramatta's first grand final victory in first grade. It was extra-special for me too in that in all my years of football since the age of eight, I'd never played in a grand final. It was an irony of my career that when I climbed the grades quickly to play firsts in 1980, the under-23s won their grand final. I got a blazer for it because I had played enough games, but it went down as yet another season in which I missed out.

When seasons begin all clubs dream of being at the big ground, on the big day in September. In '81 I was too worried about staying in firsts and pleasing the new coach to make it too big an ambition. As the season went on we were looking more and more like certainties to make the top three and the realisation hit us that we were carrying an army of fans — that just maybe we would be the team to bring them victory for the first time. It probably wasn't such a big thing for me — of having to get the monkey off our back — as it was for men like Bob O'Reilly, or Ray Price or Ron Hilditch. They had been part of the tradition; I was just a new chum. I hadn't gone through the lost finals and grand finals, I hadn't been a Parramatta fan who sat with his mum or dad waiting for the day the Eels were premiers.

It wasn't until the days leading up to the grand final that it really hit home to me what all the excitement was about. For one man above all the others it was extra-special. Bob O'Reilly first played for Parramatta in 1967 and had never made it to a grand final. This finale of season 1981 could be his last game and all he wanted was to win the premiership, to be part of Parramatta's first side to do it. Such an ending would be the ultimate reward for all his years in the game, all the training sessions, all the criticism and the pain of an ankle injury he carried through most of that season. I was almost guilty. Here I was, 18 months out of C grade, and looking at a title straight away.

Much of the publicity leading up to the grand final against Newtown revolved around the Bear (O'Reilly). It was as if the grand final of that year was put on for him. I sat back, a young kid with no such reputation, thinking: well, it's my first grand final too, you know. Coach Gibson had been a veteran of grand finals with Easts and St George and we probably expected him to call us in and say: "Right, this is the way we're going to do it, you're going to prepare for the grand final my way." Instead he called in some of the senior players, some of whom had been at Parramatta for the losing 1976 and '77 grand finals, and asked them what they did in the lead-up those years, and what they learned about it — and what they would like to do this time. In 1976 there had been a big parade in Parramatta on the Thursday night before the grand final when 100,000 people lined the streets. In retrospect, a lot of players were overawed by the occasion and subsequently regarded it as a premature celebration.

In '81 we didn't want anything like that and it was generally agreed we should stick exactly to our normal routine, although there was the heap of media attention to be contended with early in the week. We arranged to get to training an hour early on the Tuesday and get all the interviews and all the photos done. After that, it was business as usual. As much as we tried to play it down as "just another game", the media hype and the excitement of people in the street inevitably made it a brand new experience for me. By Saturday it had sunk in, oh yeah, that this was the game of the season — and the game of the past 34 seasons for Parramatta. We had this sense of security, a sense of unity amongst all of us, and it helped to shut out all the external pressures. I was relieved when I got to training later in the week and there was no-one around but team-mates and club staff.

We'd finished third, dropping from second after our last-round 20-all draw with Manly — a game which ended up being the last ever played at Cumberland Oval. We beat Newtown 10-8 in a dour preliminary semi-final and then minor premiers Easts 20-8 in the major semi-final, to make it to the Big One.

We went to watch the final between Newtown and Manly, and I was hoping Newtown would win. I felt a lot more confident about beating them in the grand final than Manly. So when they got through after a bloody and infamous match I was pretty confident. It might sound off — but I still have the feeling that we mightn't have been premiers if the Sea Eagles had won the final.

But it was Newtown, and I was up against a couple of big rangy blokes in Brian Hetherington and Mick Ryan in the centres. They were strong players without being brilliant, and that suited me. Their prop Steve Bowden was suspended after his now-famous fight with Mark Broadhurst in the final and the other prop Geoff Bugden, who won the Rothmans Medal that year, was out injured. That was another confidence boost.

I'm probably known as being fairly cool and calm about my football, but when I woke up on grand final morning and turned on the TV and could find nothing but talk about the game, it really hit me. It was as if the whole city of Sydney was focussed on just one thing. My nerves came and went all day, although once I got to the club and met the other blokes I was fine. I cracked a few jokes and the mood was nice and relaxed. We got in the bus and, once I stared out the window with my thoughts to myself, the nerves overtook me again. At the ground, the place of battle, I was fine again. A few of the senior players were stopped to do TV and radio interviews on the way in. But the new boys walked straight through to the old dressing room in the Members' Stand. From the annexe, we watched the lower grades. I was fine. I was finally there.

We had all three grades in the grand finals in '81 and it worried me a bit. I thought if we won the lower grades it would be too much to ask for us to win the big one as well. We'd had all three grades in the grand finals of 1977 but only the reserves won (the firsts drew and then were flogged by St George 22-0 in the replay).

When the under-23s were beaten early that spring day in 1981 I was disappointed for them in one way, but glad in another because I thought it increased our chances. Superstitious? Maybe — but it was how I felt. We didn't see all the reserve grade game but when we were told they too had gone down, I was disappointed for the players and the club. Deep down I thought: "You beauty, we must be a chance." It seemed to me that because the two lower grades had lost, it was fate that we would win.

They had the parades and the dancing girls and all the rest of the hoo-hah out on the field before the game. We were oblivious to it all. We warmed up out the back and then it was back behind closed doors to wait. That was the hardest part of the day ... just sitting there waiting. Jack came in and didn't talk for long. He wasn't a ranter or raver or long speech-maker before a game, whether it was a pre-season match or a grand final. He just told us: "You know what to do, you've trained all year for this game, our training has been good all week, nothing's changed, you know you have the ability to win it — now go out and enjoy yourselves." And then he walked out. Someone came in and told us: "Five minutes to go." It was a long five minutes. Just sitting there. Occasionally someone said something, Pricey geeing us up, or captain Steve Edge with a few reassuring words.

Some of the blokes were staring into space, others were tapping their studs on the cement floor. I didn't think it was quite the time to let go with any of my jokes. I tried to crack a few while we were getting changed, but I knew when to talk and when not to. This was a time for silence.

I realise now that maybe I was even over-confident going into that grand final. I was so relieved it was Newtown and not Manly, I couldn't see us being beaten. But when we came in at halftime, leading by just 7-6, we knew there was a lot of work still to be done. I thought Jack Gibson would get right up us at halftime but he came in and, cool as always, just pointed out a few faults in our play — that our defensive line wasn't intact early in the game and our attack had fallen down a little bit. The last thing he said was: "Right, I want you to go out there and just enjoy yourselves," repeating that simple message he had given us before the game. Then he left us alone and the senior players took over, trying to get everyone up and telling us what to concentrate on. Then Bob O'Reilly stood up and sort of looked around and said something like: "If you're going to win this for anyone, win it for me!" We all knew it might be the last chance for the Bear, and I know those few words got me focussed again.

A few minutes into the second half, Tom Raudonikis squeezed over from close out and suddenly we were grouped behind the goal line thinking how the second half wasn't supposed to start like this and we really did need to pull something out now. Someone chipped in: "Stuff winning it for the Bear, how about we just try to do it for ourselves."

The turning point came late, when Steve Sharp was called off the bench and soon afterwards received a good ball from Peter Sterling on the Pat Hills side of the SCG. As Sharpy went to ground he slipped the ball back to Sterlo, who drew his man and gave Graeme Atkins a clear 35-metre run to the goal line. When Mick Cronin converted from wide out, we were back in front and the relief was so evident you could take a photograph of it. From then, we knew we would win. Another try came from quick hands in their quarter, Steve Ella scored in a really slick movement (I was on the left hand side having a bit of a rest!) after John Muggleton gave him a good ball under pressure. That was it, the game was won.

The last try, my second of the game, was inconsequential really — as far as the result was concerned. But a lot of people remember it more clearly than any other I have scored because of the big dummy I threw to Newtown fullback Phil Sigsworth. It wasn't arrogance or a result of any great intuition, it was just that poor Siggy at that stage had no choice but to try to cut off the movement and with a couple of Parramatta players inside, I knew he would have to try to stop the pass. Steve McKenzie had put a little kick over the top. Newtown half Ken Wilson got a hand to it, then Newtown's replacement winger Shane McKellar botched it up by trying to stop the bouncing ball with his boot. Fortuitously the ball bounced up into my arms down the left hand side of the field. I had to tread softly to keep in the field of play but once I got my balance I took off, with Eric Grothe outside me and Steve Ella inside. I only considered the option of the dummy as I approached Sigsworth. I figured he was far enough away to give it a try. If he didn't take it I'd still have time to throw the pass to Zip. If you look at the video, it shows I was miles away from him when I threw the dummy — but Sigsworth fell for it. When he veered inside, space opened up for me and I went for it. I know people thought it was a cocky thing to do, but it just happened on the spur of the moment. If I was in Sigsworth's boots, I probably would have taken the punt as he did. It was late in the game and they needed possession.

As I said, with the game won already, it wasn't such a special try as far as contributing towards the result. But two years later I realised its importance in that it was my second try in my first grand final. I went on to score two in each of the next two grand finals — making it a hat-trick of two tries in our three successive grand final wins. It's something I'm very proud of. I had two tries disallowed in our 1986 win as well, both touch-and-go decisions, but I won't quibble about that.

The fulltime hooter sounded before there was time for Newtown to kick off after my try and much of the attention was on Bear O'Reilly. Our backroom man Joe Joseph was swiftly on the field with a jeroboam of champagne and headed straight to the Bear. There was champagne squirting everywhere and the big bloke had the stuff all over his face. The spraying bubbly hid his tears. It was an incredibly emotional thing for O'Reilly and it hit him straight away. For me, it took longer for the significance to sink in. I was just a kid in my second season. I hadn't realised just how deep the feeling was, how much the club wanted to, had to, win that grand final, had to get the monkey off its back. As Jack Gibson told a packed auditorium that night: "Ding dong the witch is dead."

I was very proud and it was something very special running around the ground toting the J. J. Giltinan Shield. It just took a while to sink in, even afterwards when there was champagne flowing all around the dressing room — most of it being spilled and sprayed rather than drunk. Incidentally, I never swapped that first premiership jumper; I'll never let it go.

The night back at Parramatta Leagues Club was just unbelievable. That's when it really hit home to me what an important thing it was for us to have won — not just for the players and officials and staff, but for the whole *district*. We travelled back to the club on the team bus and we couldn't get within half a mile of the place, the mass of people was so large. Eventually police cleared a path and we were dropped off. Our feet literally didn't touch the ground. We were handed across the top of the crowd to a Hardie's truck, from where we were introduced to the thousands of fans who couldn't get into the club. It was pandemonium. From there, we were carried again by this mass of hands to the club doors. Our feet never touched the ground until we reached the beer-stained carpet of the leagues club.

In a seething atmosphere, we were ushered up to the restaurant to have dinner (with wives and girlfriends) and from there we went another floor up, to the auditorium where we were greeted by another huge crowd — the people lucky enough to get inside the club. I remember sitting in the restaurant below, having a quiet drink and waiting for our meals, and you could see the ceiling moving, literally shaking and bulging. The thought crossed my mind that the floor mightn't take it and that Parramatta's first premiers might finish up as crushed Eels.

One of the officials came down and said the gathering was getting too boisterous and hard to handle. "We've got to get you up there otherwise the place will fall apart," he said. So up we went.

The scene that greeted us was unbelievable. It was stinking hot and stuffy because of the over-crowding, people were sloshing drinks all over the place and I saw a girl faint standing up. There wasn't enough room for her to hit the floor. We made it to the stage. There were speeches and we were introduced to the people. It was just great, and the terrific thing was that we weren't the only winners in the room. These hundreds of people were on top of the world too because of what we had achieved. Eventually we went downstairs and actually had our dinners. I lost all sense of time that night, but I reckon it was about three or four in the morning before we could sit together as team-mates and have a private drink and let everything begin to sink in. We were downstairs when Phil Sigsworth and a few of the Newtown players came in. I thought that gesture — for them to travel up to the winning club — was really something. The sun was up before we walked out the doors to greet our first day as premiers. Premiers? That really had a ring to it.

When we regrouped at the pub of former Parramatta and Australian forward Brian Hambly the next day we learned that we would be premiers with a new home — or perhaps with no home at all. On grand final night I had no idea that a group of fans had headed over to Cumberland Oval and burnt the old wooden stand to the ground. It was no great surprise. There were plenty of people drinking plenty of grog. Anything was possible that night.

As with many things it didn't really sink in until later that we were talking about the end of Cumberland Oval where the Eels had dwelled for so long, and where it had all begun for me. Parramatta Stadium, which eventually was built in the park, is so much more comfortable and spacious — the best ground in Australia to play at. But Cumberland was where I made my first grade debut and our home when we won the first premiership. At least I can say I played in the last match at Cumberland, and later, the first match at the stadium, a 36-6 win over St George before 26,870 people in 1986.

That we played in three grand finals in the "in-between" years, while training at Granville Park and playing at Belmore, showed just how good was the Parramatta side of that time. Of all the premierships and the honours that a lot of us achieved in the following years, that first grand final win sticks out for me ... even if it took a while to sink in to a young five-eighth who was starry-eyed and still learning the ropes.

7 Just Call Me Bert

There are lots of different stories of how Brett Edward Kenny became known to all and sundry as "Bert" — a nickname that has definitely stuck over the years. I can report that it has nothing to do with my uncanny likeness to RoBERT Redford, as some have suggested. No, I am afraid the story behind it was nowhere near as glamorous. In fact the blame lies with Rod "Rocket" Reddy. In fact, it would be fair to say that the irrepressible Rocket could be blamed for a lot of things on my first Kangaroo tour in 1982.

The Australian squad was sponsored that year by Adidas, but something apparently went awry with the deal. We ended up with just a pair of boots and joggers from the company, plus tracksuits and playing gear. Training twice a day in the damp conditions in Yorkshire, we realised those supplies weren't going to last. So Ray Price — typical Pricey — did some sniffing around and organised for us to get some gear from Puma. One day we all lobbed at the Puma warehouse near Leeds and were met by one of their reps who told us to go through the catalogue and identify what we wanted. This done, we waited in a lounge area for someone to bring the gear out. After a while a balding bloke with glasses walked out with his clipboard and started reading out the names, so we could collect our stuff. He obviously wasn't a rugby league follower and got some of the names tangled up. When he got to me he yelled out "BERT Kenny". Rod Reddy was first to catch onto it and almost killed himself laughing. "Bert Kenny," he was yelling, "is Bert Kenny here? Oh Bert are you there?" I told the bloke it was Brett not Bert, but it was too late. From that day onwards, inspired by Rocket Reddy, everyone started calling me Bert. It stuck. A simple slip of the tongue — and I was "Bert" for life.

There were six Parramatta players on that tour. At the first Parramatta training session the next year, John Muggleton came up to me and said: "How are you Bert?" The other blokes in the group of course asked why he called me Bert. Muggo explained and then it was official at Parramatta too. I soon got used to it. This was my third season with Parramatta and until then I didn't have a nickname — I was simply Brett. But from that point on, everyone called me Bert except for my family. Plenty of people no doubt think it's my real name. I've had them come up and say: "How are you Bert?" — genuinely thinking it was my right name.

The most common false story about my nickname is that it came from Jack

Gibson. In one of Gibbo's newspaper columns before the 1982 tour, he made an observation along the lines that, while I might not be the world's most handsome person like a Robert Redford, I was a handsome footballer in the way I played the game. Years later Peter Wynn re-told the story, but added the interpretation that Bert was short for Robert as in Redford. I can hardly take offence to the reference. It seems a very reasonable comparison to me.

The only other nickname I ever had was back in my baseball days. Then I was known as "Rowdy" — and not for the same reason that rugby league's Dale Shearer or cricket's Ashley Mallett were bestowed with the name — (because they were quiet). I copped it because every time I got struck out or didn't hit the ball the way I wanted to, I'd go berserk. If I was struck out at baseball, I'd hurl the bat towards the dug-out, take my helmet off and hurl it into the ground. The other players used to duck for cover. When I was struck out they wouldn't venture from the dug-out until the coast was clear. If I was run out they'd feel a bit safer. I'd toss the helmet in their direction but I would have already disposed of the bat before I started running. I used to get really filthy. If I'd had a punching bag nearby I would have whacked into it. But taking a punching bag to baseball would have been seen as a bit weird.

A former Australian rep in our side, Paul Russell, took it upon himself to give everyone a nickname. After just one glimpse of my antics he called me "Rowdy". Away from sport I was pretty quiet, but on the field, whether it was baseball or rugby league, I'd blow right up if something went against me. Unfortunately, I hadn't changed that much when I became captain of Parramatta. Behind the line I'd go off my head at times — though I'd always cool down pretty quickly. Deep down I'm not as laconic and unexcitable as people believe.

The addition of the new nickname was one of many things which changed for me in '82 during my first extended stay away from home — and only my second trip overseas (after the 1980 end-of-season jaunt to Asia). I had no idea what to expect of a Kangaroo tour. Mainly, I was really nervous about being away for almost three months with blokes I had never met, in a place I had no knowledge of. In fact, I was so nervous the day we departed, I left my official shirts hanging on my bedroom door when I left for the airport. I took the long-sleeved white ones for England with me but when I got to Port Moresby where we were to play a Test, I didn't have the short-sleeved yellow ones that had been issued especially for the tropical heat. So the whole time up there I was stinking hot in the winter clobber while the other blokes stayed cool in their summer gear.

It was great to have Parramatta team-mates Ray Price, Peter Sterling, Steve Ella, Eric Grothe and John Muggleton with me on that Kangaroo campaign ... plus Rocket Reddy. He was by then something of a legend of the game, and a bloke I used to watch when I was at school. I soon found out that Rocket was the life of the tour and perhaps the greatest practical joker of all time. It was a great thing on that tour — how the senior players accepted the no-names like me, welcomed us to any social activities they organised (usually a pub crawl) and never placed themselves above anyone else in the 26-man squad.

The Kangaroo tour experience is a magnificent one for a footballer — although it can be a pretty boring, routine existence at times and ongoing team morale is ultimately important to the success sought. I remember the first day — walking into the Dragonara Hotel in downtown Leeds, Yorkshire, and thinking: "This is my home for 10 weeks." We had the entire sixth floor and life became a routine — of getting up for our morning walk at 7am — a drill insisted on by coach Frank Stanton to obviously walk the grog out of us — then to breakfast, to training, back for lunch, a few hours to kill before afternoon training, then when there wasn't a match on to organise something to do at night. There were a couple of electronic games machines installed in the sixth floor hallway, and after the first week a dartboard appeared. Then someone got a cricket bat and tennis ball; we had some good cricket Test matches in that hallway. I was waiting for someone to be put out of a (rugby league) match with concussion because they weren't alert at silly leg in our cricket "Tests". The days rolled one into the other and much of the time we were looking for something to do to break the boredom — the only release was in playing football and going out at night. The football was what we were there for and I tried to be the model tourist by doing everything right on the training side, and not having too many late nights.

I have some varied and happy memories of life off the field. Plenty of them surround Rocket and his pranks — and one of the most notable is of the morning my room-mate Mark Murray, current Eastern Suburbs coach, went within a whisker of copping the wrath of "Cranky Frankie" Stanton at a time when the coach would have been in the mood to send someone home.

"Muppet" Murray went away as third-string halfback behind Steve Mortimer and Peter Sterling and played only 10 matches on the entire tour. His Queensland mate Greg Conescu was another relaxed tourist, with just nine games. Muppet was a great bloke who was always happy and who loved a drink and a good time. Playing only 10 matches in 12 weeks in England and France, half of them as reserve, encouraged him to concentrate studiously on the *social* side of the tour.

Frank Stanton was strict on discipline and although he was seen as a cranky bloke at the time, a bloke who never let up on us, I can look back now and say he was the perfect tour coach who realised the value of keeping the hammer on us all the time. In that regard he was a lot different from his successor, Don Furner (1986). There came a time in the '82 tour when the coach was concerned about fading discipline. There had been a few late nights and lots of frolics, and he'd read the riot act. He would often have a team meeting during the day and if anyone was late they'd be fined.

One particular morning I couldn't rouse Muppet out of bed. He had had a very late one the previous evening; he opened his eyes and mumbled something, then his head crashed right back on the pillow. I said: "C'mon Muppet, you've got to get up, we've got a meeting." But he wouldn't (or couldn't) stir. Time was running out and when you've got a coach like Frank Stanton, it's every man for himself; there's no time to be worrying about anyone else's fate. I gave Muppet one more almighty shake and screamed in his ear. He opened his eyes and looked like he might be coming to. The time was up and I rushed out, leaving the door open. Well, Muppet must have fallen straight back to sleep.

When we gathered for the meeting "Biscuits" (his other nickname) Stanton checked around and did a quick head count. "Right, everyone's here," he said sternly. What? As Frank moved into his address blokes were whispering to me: "Where's Muppet?" The first thing I thought of was — how the hell Stanton had counted wrong? Then I realised he must have included our trainer Alf Richards, who was sitting with the players instead of the other side of the room with the officials. Next I thought: "What if Muppet wakes in a panic and rushes downstairs halfway through the meeting?" Luckily, when I went back upstairs, he was still dead to the world. I had to memorise everything that was said at the meeting so he wouldn't be caught out next day. The same Mark Murray is now a respected, ultra-organised first grade coach. I'm sure this yarn won't be lost on any of his players who happen to read this book. Sorry Muppet!

When I look back on my two Kangaroo tours it is very special to realise that they were the two historic ones, The Invincibles and the Unconquerables (or the Unbeatables). Neither team lost a match. But they were so different — for me at least — those two campaigns. In 1982 I was no more than a naive 21-year-old away, surrounded by players I'd idolised when I was a teenager. I had no idea of what to expect of England and France; I wasn't deemed a Test player and my expectation was to be in the B-team and play the club matches. The thought of being in the Test side never entered my mind. As it turned out I had a wonderful tour, shocking everyone including myself by making the Test team and getting a lot of publicity as a result — mainly because I happened to be taking the place of the tour vice-captain (Wally Lewis). It was a tour on which Peter Sterling, Eric Grothe, Wayne Pearce and I cut our teeth in Test football. Mal Meninga had played just one Test previously, against New Zealand that year.

In 1986 I was a more senior player and had finally established myself in the Australian side, as a centre. I was married now and Julie was pregnant with our first child. The campaign of 1986 was my third trip to England after 1982, and my 1984-85 stint with Wigan. The Test side — and the backline particularly — was very settled. I didn't have such a stunning tour this time, although I wouldn't say I played badly either.

The coaches were vastly different. Discipline was very tight in 1982 under Frank Stanton, but much more lax under the easy-going Don Furner in 1986. Yes, they were two very different tours united by a strong thread — that we didn't lose a match during either.

It was a couple of years after the 1982 tour before I realised how good a coach Frank Stanton was. He might have seemed like a school master at the time. But looking back I could understand the things he did and why he did them. He would rant and rave at times to get a point across; at other times he would be softly spoken. I remember Steve Roach, who played under him at Balmain, said years later that he needed the Stanton-style approach to bring out the best in him. It didn't seem important to me. I'd nod my head, but basically it went in one ear and out the other. That was just the way I was — fairly laid-back without the need for "revving up". Tactically, Frank was good, he always had the opposition worked out, and could get across to his players very well what he wanted.

He was very different from Jack Gibson. Jack's approach was a quiet one — he wasn't a complex tactical coach; he simplified things. His line was: "We'll work to the centre of the field and from there we'll go this way or that way" — then leave the option to us. After a match he'd point out where we went right or wrong and that would be the end of the story. There was no shouting or retribution. Frank was a more iron-fisted coach, but perfect for a tour.

Don Furner was different again. He wasn't the disciplinarian, or motivating type like Frank Stanton aimed to be. He was much more easy-going, and not particularly in-depth tactically. But Don had a strong understanding of the game. His motto was to play it in the opposition's territory. Don was a great bloke but I wouldn't rate him up there with Jack Gibson or Frank Stanton when it came to analytical coaching. Some of the players on the 1986 tour used to complain about having to be out of bed and on the team coach at 9am for training. We'd tell them to stop their whining — that they should have been there in 1982 when we were out in the cold at 7 o'clock every morning.

It was because Frank Stanton was so tough that getting away and having some outrageous fun was important in '82. It was akin to sneaking out of school, throwing off your tie and feeling free until the bell went the next day. Also life in a hotel for 12 weeks can be pretty wearing unless you make the effort to amuse yourself. Underneath the hotel was a casino and a lot of blokes spent a lot of time there. I caught the bug too. I lost a lot, won a bit, lost a lot during the tour, and it rammed home the message to me that gambling doesn't pay. I don't have to spell out the names of the blokes who spent most of their time there, such as the little fella who played with me at Parramatta. When I went back in 1986 and we stayed at the Dragonara again, I was much wiser. If I was on my way back from being somewhere with the blokes, I might have 10 pounds in my pocket and I'd pop in, get two five pound chips, go to the roulette wheel and put them on two numbers — 36 and 21. Win or lose, I'd walk out. A lot of times we'd call in because you'd get a free meal. There was a big smorgasbord you could pick from. It just had to look a little bit like you were betting. One night Graeme Hughes, who was over with the Channel 10 team, was playing the roulette wheel, and had been for some time. I sat next to him, put my two chips down and, believe it or not, number 36 came up. I picked up 175 pounds. Hughes asked what I was going to do now, what number I was going to put my money on, and I told him I wasn't. I walked out and went to bed. He couldn't believe it. A lot of blokes couldn't walk away.

One night in 1986 Peter Sterling, Royce Simmons and Gene Miles had an eight-hour shift at the casino. Every time one of them was down in money, another would help out. Then he'd win, pay the money back and by then someone else might be in trouble and he'd come to the rescue. I don't know if they ended up winning or breaking even, but it was a long session. I couldn't stay interested that long. I played the tables a lot more in 1982 than '86. I was going with the flow, being a young bloke on tour doing his best to fit in. On the way over on that tour I was very quiet on the plane and probably a bit oblivious to all the shenanigans that went on — like the famous moment of Rod Reddy shaving off one of Max Krilich's eyebrows. I sat next to Eric Grothe. We had just a couple of quiet drinks and kept to ourselves. It took a few weeks after we arrived before we really felt at ease with all the other blokes.

The Parramatta players stuck together much of the time, and although there weren't any distinct groups or barriers between any of us, the Queenslanders also tended to keep together. After a while Steve Ella and I started to hang around with Gene Miles. We hit it off together and became terrific mates. Gene was a bit like me, a little quiet and laid-back, but he still enjoyed a good time. Outwardly, even before the biggest match, he never appeared nervous and was always a bloke I could throw a joke at. He wasn't in the Test side in 1982 but by 1984 we started to play regularly together in the Australian team. By the time we went back in 1986 we'd become great mates and had a terrific understanding on and off the field. It was an interesting development at a time when interstate rivalry was at its fiercest that a Queenslander, Geno, was the bloke I got closest to of all my representative team-mates, outside of my own club. In '86 I became particularly friendly with Queenslanders generally. Both my room-mates on the Kangaroo tours were Queenslanders, Mark Murray in 1982 and Mal Meninga in 1986. Greg Dowling was another I got on very well with. He went on to play with Wigan the season after me, along with Steve Ella.

There was a big contrast in how I started the 1986 tour compared to 1982. It was one of the few times I overdid the "few quiet drinks" on the plane. In fact, the difference was pretty marked by the time we got on the plane. In 1982 we had to wear our official uniforms on the flight to Papua New Guinea, and then from PNG to England. In 1986 we waved goodbye and had photographs taken for the press in our blazers and ties. As soon as we were out of sight it was into the T-shirt, shorts and joggers. It was another reflection of a different management approach. When we were about to land in Manchester, back went on the official gear. Unfortunately, I wasn't in the best of shapes. I thought I'd have a few beers on the flight, but I then switched to Bacardi and Cokes. They'd give you a cup of rum, a cup to mix the drink in, and a can of Coke. Well, let's just say I proved to be something less than an expert on what proportions rum should be mixed with Coke. After a few hours I had the sick bag out just in case — and before long I needed it.

Worse was still to come before I could retreat into the safety of slumber. I got up to go for a walk to sober up and Gene Miles was at the back of the plane, standing up. I started to talk to him then he pointed up and said: "Look Bert, what's that thing hanging down from the ceiling?" I said: "Don't worry, I'll put it back up." So I proceeded, in the middle of the movie, to clamber over a couple of people and push the projector screen back into the ceiling. I then walked off and collapsed into my seat. The people on the plane just sat dumbfounded, obviously thinking what boofheads these footballers were. A hostess appeared and safely retrieved matters. I slept all the way to Bahrain, where I gingerly headed out for some fresh air. I was much quieter on the last leg of the tour.

I'd like to think that was the only time when I fell below the standard of my 1982 behaviour. I was a lot smarter in day-to-day living by '86 — knew about the washing and ironing and all that stuff. I suppose I can thank Mr Organised, Mark Murray, for that in 1982. Many a night he'd go out with some of the boys and I'd stay put, just watch a bit of snooker or darts on the TV and do my ironing. He used to look at me puzzled and off he'd go. One or two days a week a big group of us would bombard the local laundromat with our washing. All finished, I would get my gear and throw it straight into a plastic bag. I used to watch all the other blokes folding their clothes neatly and meticulously, stacking them up in a perfect pile. I thought: "What a bunch of wankers, what a waste of time, you've got to iron them when you get home anyway." I didn't realise until a little later that they didn't have to iron their clothes at all, just pick them off the pile. They were good enough. So while they were having a good time, I'd be in my room ironing away. I took the tip and, in 1986, never went near an iron.

The pranks in 1986 weren't much different from the 1982 version, which were probably the same as 1978, 1973, 1967 etc. In '82 Rocket Reddy was always the ringleader. It was traditional after a Test match to gather in someone's room the next day, about 9am. We'd be given a day off training, and would sit there all day drinking and laughing. After the second Test in '82, Rocket suggested we should go out into the countryside for a barbecue instead of staying indoors. Yeah, good idea, everyone thought. So we've all met in the morning, arranged for the driver to bring the coach downstairs to pick us up. We all filed downstairs, dressed for the occasion in tracksuits and sweatshirts or jackets, and all of a sudden Rocket turned up — in a pair of shorts and singlet, declaring: "It's a barbecue isn't it?" We headed off but it started to rain lightly, so someone suggested we pull up at a country pub and have a feed there instead. And that's where we spent the day with some locals who I'm sure didn't know what hit them. There was one bloke who'd had quite a few under his belt who wanted to join in our party games. So we tried the one where you roll up a newspaper into a funnel and stick it down your shorts, put a coin on your forehead and try to bow your head and get the coin in the funnel. Of course after a few tries, out comes a a jug of beer which a Kangaroo pours down the funnel. Luckily the bloke didn't get aggro; he just laughed his head off. In fact he came back for more. He wanted to join in the wooden spoon duels, where one bloke is blindfolded, puts a spoon between his teeth and has to try to hit the other bloke kneeling in front of him with the spoon. The local yokel put on the blindfold and he hit Rocket a few times, and thought he was great. Then we decided to switch the game and we blindfolded both and give them a rolled up newspaper each and they had to try to hit each other. You could imagine the scene of a pub full of Aussies with a few locals. The gathering provided a rowdy audience as Rocket and the brave Yorkshireman went into battle. Of course, Rocket would slip the blindfold down and belt his newspaper into this bloke like there was no tomorrow, and when time was about up, he'd push it back up and the bloke was none the wiser. It was a party trick that did the rounds more than once in 1986, with skipper Wally Lewis the new ringleader.

I have many funny memories, including the Green Hornet, the bomb of an Austin that Sterlo and I bought at the motor auctions in 1982. It lasted about a week. We ran out of petrol one day about 15 minutes from base, and we had to walk a mile to get some fuel. We got the beast home that time and finally decided it just wasn't worth the uncertainty of whether it would get us from A to B.

Someone else in the team, who shall remain nameless, borrowed it one day, decided not unreasonably that it was a complete bomb and abandoned it ... a few metres from the front door of the Dragonara Hotel! The management asked us to move it, which we did — to the back of the building where it stayed until a moving last-night ceremony — of throwing all the team bombs into the River Aire (a canal really) at the back of the hotel. The trouble was that the Green Hornet decided to come to life for a fleeting moment that night and as it was about to sink like the Titanic its lights flashed on, sparking the attention of some hotel residents. Dressed in our green blazers, we simply waved to the police who turned up to see what all the commotion was about.

A vivid memory that remains of Rocket is of somewhere in France, as he strolled through the streets to the team bus sporting a plastic moustache and a nose which looked more like a penis, and tipping his hat to everyone who walked past, bidding them "bonjour".

France just wasn't my cup of tea. I disliked being there and I reckon it should be dropped from future tours or at least made into a one-Test whistle stop en route to England. Rugby league there has become a farce. The 1982 stay was bad enough, but in '86 it got worse. We went to more obscure places and the motel we were put in near Perpignan was a shocker. We were stuck in this place out of town, in the middle of paddocks and flanked by a huge new car depository. We had to catch a bus to town to have a good feed, which was a difficult assignment to organise anywhere in France. One night we were playing table tennis about 7pm when we were asked to stop because the residents were complaining about the noise. Another night a match had to be put back half an hour because our coach driver got lost on the way to the ground. The whole thing was Amateur Hour, and the French "leg" should be scratched off future tours.

At least in '86 we were able to get to Monte Carlo on another "Snookel Tour", organised by Michael "Snookel" O'Connor. In 1982 I didn't get around anywhere, just stayed in camp. In '86 when we were given a couple of days off after the first Test, I thought I should get out and see some of the place. We got up at some ungodly hour of the morning to catch a train to Monte Carlo and on arrival booked into the cheapest motel we could find. We went for a tour around, waited for Princess Stephanie to come out of the palace and invite us in, then took a taxi down to the harbour to see the Onassis cruiser, followed by a circuit of the Monte Carlo Grand Prix course. We found a pub run by a couple of Englishmen who asked who we were and what we were doing there. They'd had some West Indian cricketers drop in there a few months before and gave them a free round of drinks and wanted to repeat the gesture. No problems. Well, out came some sort of liqueur which we had to scoff down and follow with a beer. Whatever it was packed a real punch.

We didn't have dinner suits so we couldn't get into the casino, and a few drinks at a nightclub cost us around $100 so we beat a tactical retreat back to our rooms. Next day, after all sorts of hassles getting across the border, we headed into an Italian town, ordered a pizza each, then went straight back to interpretation hassles at the border. From Monte Carlo we hopped the next train back to French rugby league territory. At least I can say I've been to Italy!

8 The King and I

People often ask me if I resent having played in the shadow of Wally Lewis. The simple answer is "no". Sure, there were times when I thought I should have been considered ahead of him as Test five-eighth, in particular after we'd won the Origin series 3-0 in 1986 and it was generally agreed that I had won the duel. And sometimes I puzzled over why it was me who had to be switched — to the centres — for Australia when Wally could just as easily have been switched to lock where he played much of his early football. But looking back I reckon the selectors were right. Wally would not have been as effective at lock, and the fact was I had more room to move outside him as a centre and combined well there with Gene Miles.

I don't consider Wally Lewis took the shine off my career. I'm happy to concede Wally will go down in history with much more kudos than me. He was Queensland's first super-hero and many people will nominate him as the best player they've ever seen. But I'm happy with just about everything I did with my career, and when I'm retired I know I'll sit back and look at photos and press clippings and videos and think "yeah, well I did a lot too". We were two very different types of five-eighths who happened to play in the same era. Each of us achieved a fair bit of success in our own right. I certainly feel fortunate that I played with him in Australian sides — and against him in State of Origin. He was the greatest opponent I faced. The called him the King, the Emperor, Mr State of Origin — and he deserved all that idolatry. My career was in a lower key. I just played football to the best of my ability and enjoyed every minute of it. How people judge us is out of our hands, so why worry about it?

It wasn't until I sat down to write this book, though, that something hit home that I had never really considered. I was the only player ever to knock Wally out of a Test side during his international career. That's pretty special, I guess. Yet the controversy of beating the 1982 Kangaroo vice-captain to the Test five-eighth's job really went over my head at the time. I was just a young player on his first tour trying to do everything right, a bloke generally over the moon about wearing the green and gold. Being embroiled in what was later regarded as one of the great tour controversies didn't sink in with me.

I'd heard the name Wally Lewis for the first time in 1981. State of Origin didn't mean a great deal to me then, it was still in its trial phase, but this guy Lewis was thrust into the headlines as the new star from the north. He became Australian vice-captain virtually overnight for the series against France. Even then, he seemed to be disliked in NSW — whether it was because they felt an unknown Queenslander didn't have the right to be in the Test side let alone vice-captain, or whether they were dirty on Queensland dominating those first couple of Origin matches, I'm not sure. I felt sorry for Wally at times — for the bagging he got. In '81 I had no idea that our names would be thrown into conflict within 12 months.

While Wally had become an international and was being hailed as the best thing from Queensland since bananas and pineapples, I'd hardly thought of representing. I'd made the City Seconds along with Peter Sterling (a reserve) in 1981, which was a nice surprise, but we knew selectors liked to blood a few youngsters in the seconds just to show they were looking at us. It was a long way from there to NSW or Australian selection. And I had a few five-eighths in front of me south of the border. I'd switched permanently to five-eighth for Parramatta, but Terry Lamb had switched there from half with Wests, Mick Pattison was in top form for Souths, and Robert Laurie had played City Firsts in 1981 and won the Dally M player of the year trophy a season earlier. And Alan Thompson was still seen by many as the top dog ahead of all the young up-and-comers. I was picked as a centre in that City Seconds side in 1981, but with Mick Cronin and Steve Rogers established as the best centres in the country, there didn't appear much opportunity to go further there either

Mick Pattison was chosen as NSW five-eighth for the 1981 Origin match (after the first two interstate games had been played under the old residential set-up) but had to withdraw on the day of the game because of illness. Terry Lamb was rushed up to Lang Park. Looking back now, it's apparent the NSW spot was in fact pretty open, but I kept thinking it was a bit early for me just yet.

Playing for Australia had been my ambition since I first pulled on a Guildford jumper and I never lost sight of that. NSW selection, when it came — whether sooner or later — was the first big step towards that goal.

In 1982 I missed the City sides altogether. Cronin and Rogers were the City Firsts centres and Pattison got the five-eighth spot, with Sterlo at half (Steve Mortimer was injured). Peter Mortimer and Brad Izzard were the centres in the seconds and Thompson was five-eighth. I thought to myself: "Don't worry your time will come."

Patto had the misfortune to bust *both* his shoulders in the City-Country match, played in Newcastle, which was tragic for him after he had been forced out of the NSW side the year before. My family and I followed Mick's career closely because he also came from Guildford. We were all disappointed for him but I remember my mother ringing up next day and saying that it might be the break for me to make the NSW side. My own thought was that Alan Thompson would go in.

Origin football became the "real thing" that year — a full three match series. Mick Cronin and Steve Rogers were the centres and Alan Thompson five-eighth as I expected. Brad Izzard had arrived as a whiz kid from Penrith and got tossed straight in as a reserve, with Souths centre Ziggy Niszczot picked on one wing. For the second match a week later, Crow was out with a corked thigh. Brad Izzard went into the centres and I was chosen to make my debut from the reserves' bench. There were rumours that Crow knew I was the shadow player in the backs and that convinced him not to take any risks with the injury and drop out to give me a chance. I've never discussed that with him but the suggestion got back to me and, frankly, I wouldn't have put it past him. He was (and is) that sort of bloke.

To be picked for NSW was a huge buzz — although I admit to being a bit scared about it; not so much playing in the match but going into camp with blokes I hardly knew. I felt a bit overawed by that prospect at that stage of my career.

When we arrived at Lang Park, I didn't know what had hit me. It really is an awesome place — and it's worse when you're a reserve sitting on the bench seeing and hearing every big hit as well as being so close to the crowd. You could *taste* the tension. It was like nothing I had ever experienced, a vast step up from club football. I really just tagged along the whole night, standing there mute in the dressing room, not game to say anything and just absorbing the whole experience.

Late in the game I got my call to go on when Steve Rogers was hurt. It's hard to get thrown cold into a game at any time, to have to pick up the pace instantly, without a settling-in period. My main recollection of that night is of the speed, another three gears higher than a club match ... including grand finals! We were down 11-7 when I went on and the score didn't change. Welcome to State of Origin!

The Origin phenomenon wasn't quite in place then. There were only 19,435 at Lang Park — nowhere near the guaranteed full houses they got in later years — but it was still like another world to me.

For the third match of 1982, the first scheduled for Sydney, I was picked at five-eighth in a NSW side that underwent plenty of changes. It was the first time I faced Wally Lewis. Yet the match is remembered for one incident — the Phil Sigsworth-Phillip Duke mix-up. Duke was a Country Firsts winger from Moree who looked overawed in his first big match in such exalted company. Siggy ran a Lewis kick out from his in-goal but passed to Duke before he cleared the goal line. The winger dropped it, Lewis came through and dived on the ball for a try — and Queensland went on to win 10-5. Wally was chosen as man of the match for the first time and Queensland won the first-ever series 2-1. The fact that it was the first Kenny-Lewis contest didn't make a splash — although our duels would receive a fair bit of publicity in the years ahead.

The Origin series was completed in June and it hadn't registered with me that there was a Kangaroo tour at the end of the year and that I might have a chance of going on it. I thought my time would be further down the track. It wasn't until we looked like we were headed for the grand final that the possibility started to creep into conversation around Parramatta. People were pointing out that the premiers often gained at least half a dozen spots in the Kangaroo squad.

I was sitting down to dinner after Parramatta won their second premiership on September 26, 1982, when I learned I'd become a Kangaroo. That triumphant grand final night, the names were read out over the loud PA system at the leagues club — Ella, Grothe, Kenny, Muggleton, Price, Sterling. Mick Cronin would have been there too but he'd made himself unavailable for representative football at the end of that year's Origin series. Ronny Hilditch might have made it too if he hadn't been injured late in the season.

Everyone was congratulating us and I thought: Wow, I've made it! But at the same time I sort of felt uneasy. I'd been going out with Julie for a couple of months and I thought: Geez, I'm going away for three months. I don't know any of the blokes outside of Parramatta. My feelings were definitely mixed ones.

Sterlo, Zip and I pretty much accepted we were going away as the young blokes who would just play in the club games for experience. Muggo had played the Tests against New Zealand that year and Pricey was the Test lock. Guru was by then rated as a great chance to make the Test side. Once it sunk in I'd become a Kangaroo the plan formed: "Right, I'll go over and get the experience — and come back and start pushing to become a permanent member of the Test team."

As it turned out I played in the Test against PNG (classified as an official Test match) on the way over and when we arrived coach Frank Stanton used all the Parramatta players for the first match against Hull KR — mainly because we were match fit, having played in the grand final just two weeks earlier. I got knocked out during the game and couldn't remember much of it afterwards.

Sterlo and I combined pretty well in the early club games, against sides that were really below par. I trained as hard as I could and did everything by the book. I never complained. Like anyone selected for Australia for the first time, I wanted to make a good impression. Wally was the reigning Test five-eighth and tour vice-captain, and in everyone's eyes a certainty for the Tests. When he looks back I'm sure he'll admit now that he took a few short cuts early on that tour. He probably didn't see the need to over-extend himself before the Tests.

It was at a team meeting in the hotel one morning that the side for the first Test was announced. I was sitting on a bench at the back of the room when Frank Stanton started to read out the team. Brentnall ... that's right, Grothe ... great, all the reporters were saying he'd make it, Rogers ... of course, Meninga ... yeah, they can't handle the big bloke over here, Boustead ... naturally, Kenny ... what?????? I sat there, stunned. Sterling ... fantastic!!!

I didn't hear any more names after that. I didn't jump up in the air or show much emotion, but, oh boy, I was shocked, and excited. Sterlo said to me later that as soon as he heard my name announced, he knew he was a chance. It set the pattern for the second and third Tests; neither of us assumed we'd be there again, even though we won each Test comfortably. It was a matter of just playing as best we could and waiting to see what happened. I can see now that the fact we replaced the Test vice-captain and the reigning, experienced Test half in Steve Mortimer, was a story and a half for the press.

Wally was one of the first to congratulate me. The pair of us never had a problem personally. I hardly knew the bloke before we left and wasn't particularly close to him during the tour. But I can honestly say he never held any grudge towards me. He would have been hurt that first Test week, 1982; he wasn't even picked on the bench. Steve Ella and John Muggleton were the reserves.

My fair dinkum rugby league Test debut came at Hull City's soccer ground, Boothferry Park. It was to be the last league Test match played there. I'd actually become a "Test" player in Port Moresby on the way over but I didn't really consider that quite the real thing. At Hull, we smashed the Poms, 40-4, and I picked up my first Test try. Notwithstanding the thrill, and the glory of winning the first Test of the series, I was disappointed with the match. The Poms were pretty awful. I had memories of watching Tests on my black and white TV as a kid and seeing Bobby McCarthy and Ron Coote and Bob O'Reilly playing in really tough games in England. Here I was in 1982 finally making it to that standard — and the British side were soft as butter. Sydney first grade was tougher.

We won the second Test at Central Park, Wigan, 27-6 and the final Test at Headingley, 32-8 — so it was an easy Ashes victory for us. I was up against a different five-eighth in each Test. In the first my opponent was John Woods who was a very skilled player, then in the second I faced Ken Kelly who I don't think ever played another Test. For the Third Test the Poms brought in David Topliss as five-eighth and captain. I knew he'd played in Sydney for Balmain and Penrith and wasn't that young, so I felt pretty confident against him. As it was I did a rib cartilage in that Test when Topliss' knees caught me as I was tackled.

Wally had started to put some good games together and was on the Test bench. In fact he came on and set up a try for me in the third Test — the second try he created in two minutes. When we got to France, Wally was in the first Test side at five-eighth and I was in the centres. I returned to five-eighth when Eric Grothe came back from injury, and Mal Meninga went back into the centres.

That '82 tour has its special place in history as the first in which the Kangaroos went through undefeated ... and to a lesser extent for the fact that Sterlo and I kept out Wally and Steve Mortimer.

In 1983 there was a complete role reversal between Wally and me. I came back from the tour as reigning Test five-eighth but didn't get a look in with the selectors. Wally went straight back as Test five-eighth after the Origin series and I missed out altogether. There were no headlines of "Kenny Dumped". My swift exit was just accepted.

It was probably the first time that Origin form became the be-all and end-all of Test selection. Queensland won the series and had nine players in the first Test against New Zealand at Lang Park. Although I was the Aussie five-eighth, I was picked at centre for NSW, with Steve Ella at five-eighth — until Ted Glossop pulled a late and somewhat notorious switch with Alan Thompson. Ella, belatedly was left on the bench — and the reasons behind it took some working out.

Frankly, it came down to the fact that my form wasn't good enough in 1983. Maybe I felt a little smug after the tour. Maybe I was a little stale as well. I thought I only had to play reasonably well and I'd be picked — you know the old line about it being harder to get out of an Australian side than it is to get into it. Wally was playing better than me; he got two man-of-the-match awards in three Origin games — and he got the job. I couldn't complain.

Wally had a huge push going for him too — orchestrated by the Queensland administrative strong man Ron McAuliffe. I think the Maroons were smarting that I had got the jump on Wally in England and there were moves afoot to make quite sure that wasn't going to happen again now we were back in Australia. Wally got man of the match in four of the six Origin games in 1983 and '84. I'm sure he would have been embarrassed about at least a couple of those.

Wally Lewis was captain of Australia by 1984, succeeding Max Krilich. It seemed as if the NSW selectors quickly gave up on me ever beating Wally to a Test spot, because I was chosen in the centres for the first two Origin games of 1984.

My record against Wally when we opposed each other as five-eighth was: eight wins, three losses from 1983-87 (8-4 overall, taking in the game in 1982). When I played centre and Wally was five-eighth the score was: Queensland four, NSW nil. It's a statistic that few people realise — including me until Mick Cronin brought it up during my testimonial year in 1992. I don't know how much you can read into it, but it's a fact.

Wally and I actually didn't come into contact that much in Origin matches. I tended to hang back on him in defence and tried to grab him ball-and-all if he ran. It was fatal to rush him.

By 1984 it was plain that if I was to play for Australia it would be in the centres. I pretty much resigned myself to being a five-eighth with Parramatta but a centre anywhere else. I always thought, though, that my chance of being chosen for NSW was stronger at five-eighth, because with Gene Miles and Mal Meninga as Queensland centres and with lots of good big NSW centres around, I never felt confident of being picked at centre. So it was basically a feeling of: I hope I get picked as NSW five-eighth, but that the Australian selectors see me as a centre. And that's often how it worked out.

NSW won the Origin series in 1985 and '86. We won five out of those six games, and I played five-eighth in every one of them. Once during that period, the Wally push really got to me. We took the series at the SCG in the second match of 1985 and I scored the match-winning try and thought I'd finished better than Wally on the night. Yet Wally was named man of the match — from the losing side. There were loud boos from the crowd when his name was announced before the end of the game and later some of the press blokes came to me saying they couldn't believe it. I was walking to the car with Julie after the game when we bumped into Channel 9 commentator Darrell Eastlake. Julie couldn't help but ask him how the hell Wally could be man of the match when Queensland lost and she and a lot of other people thought that I had played better. Darrell muttered something unconvincing and we left it at that.

It was about then that I started to think that if I outplayed him on the night, or during the series, why was it taboo for me to be even considered as the Test five-eighth? Was Wally above all the rules which applied to everyone else? It wasn't that I reckoned Wally shouldn't be in the Test side somewhere; he was too good a player to be left out. But he could play lock. Pricey had retired from Test football and Wayne Pearce could play second row. Ray Price wrote a *Rugby League Week* column saying exactly that. Why was it out of the question? The question was never answered. I was picked at centre, Wally at five-eighth and it never changed for the rest of my international career. After that time it never worried me. I accepted my lot and looking back now, I'm happy and proud to have played as many games for Australia as I did. Also it was a joy to play outside Wally Lewis.

He was a superb captain, he seemed to know exactly when his team needed a lift and he was often just the player to supply that lift. He was always a step or two ahead of everyone else on the field. If it hadn't been for Wally's leadership skills, we may not have gone through undefeated for the second time on the Kangaroo tour of 1986. Before the third Test at Central Park, Wigan we were flat — and we played that way. The Ashes had been won fairly easily in the first two Tests and the Poms had made a heap of changes for the last match. We led narrowly at halftime, 12-8. In the dressing room coach Don Furner was talking to us but wasn't getting through; I don't know if it was because it was a long tour and we were tired, or whether we were being genuinely tested for the first time. No one seemed to respond. Then Wally got up in the dressing room and said his piece. Straight away I could sense everyone lift. We went out in the second half and GB promptly scored to level at 12-all before Royce Simmons set up a try triggering our second half surge. It was Wally who scored. From then we were never going to lose the Test match, and we got home with a comfortable enough advantage, 24-15.

I can't remember exactly *what* he said at halftime that day, but it reinforced the message that there was no way we were going to lose a Test to a British side which wasn't as good as us. Wally pushed the point too that there was no way history was going to slip away from us with a loss on the last match of the English leg of the tour. His few words hit the spot; I recall Greg Dowling saying to me later that he just couldn't get himself going until Wally spoke out at halftime.

Wally and I became good mates in later years. It wasn't that we did much together or were on the phone to each other every week, but in Test team situations we got on well and had plenty of respect for each other. The Kenny v Lewis thing inevitably became a big part of Origin discussions and the League co-opted us for a major promotion in 1986 — putting out a poster of Wally and I having an arm wrestle. We'd always have a laugh and swap a few jokes and I would think, he's not a bad bloke, we should be ignoring all this Kenny v Lewis stuff.

In the end I've got to pay compliment to the Australian selectors. I remember during the great debate that Jack Gibson was asked who he would chose as Test five-eighth and he replied that he would find room for both of us in the side no matter where we played. When you consider what Wally could do with the ball, the incredible vision he had and how he set up his outside men, I think those talents would have been wasted to an extent at lock. I was more a running player and I could play that role more effectively outside Wally in the centres. He was always a step ahead of the rest and there's no doubt he made me look good in the centres at times. I am proud to say I played for Australia at both five-eighth and centre and played a bit of fullback in one game in 1982 too. When I look back, 1983 was the only season I could say that having Wally Lewis around cost me playing a Test match. The truth of that year was that while my form was OK, it probably wasn't as good as it needed to be for me to play for Australia anyway.

It's not until a player reaches the end of a career, and in my case particularly when I sat down to research this book, that he tries to put into perspective what he has achieved, or failed to achieve. I am very fortunate. I played in four premiership-winning sides, five grand finals, won and lost State of Origin series, went on two undefeated Kangaroo tours, won 16 of my 17 Tests, won at Wembley where I won the Lance Todd Trophy, captained Parramatta and won the Adidas Golden Boot as the world's best player — probably my greatest honour.

Wally Lewis was King of Origin, captained his club, state and country, played 33 Tests and also won the Golden Boot. Yet he didn't have the good fortune of winning a Winfield Cup, although he won plenty of titles with Wynnum-Manly in Brisbane. He was embroiled in plenty of controversy, while I was pretty quiet on that score. We were very different. Yet I'd like to think we were both big achievers and we shared a mutual respect that will never fade.

9 Take a Holiday Son

I never played reserve grade from the day I made my top grade debut midway through my first season with Parramatta in 1980. I'm proud of that. But in 1983 Jack Gibson made it clear that was *exactly* where I was heading unless I took a break from the game. I was an international by then, but my status didn't worry the coach one bit.

One day at training that year I was given the message that Gibbo wanted me in his office, a little room specially constructed in the old wooden stand at Granville Park — where we were forced to train for four seasons after Cumberland Oval was destroyed by fire on the night of our first premiership win.

I'd just arrived at training and got changed and we were mucking around before we headed out for some conditioning work when I was summoned to see Jack. It was never a good feeling; it reminded me of school days, of being called to the principal's office. You knew it could only be bad news. I sat down with Jack and we discussed how I was playing — which wasn't very well. I'd lost my Australian spot after returning from a successful Kangaroo tour, although I'd still made the NSW side for all three games. Apart from a brief patch mid-season, my club form had been ordinary.

Jack didn't rip in and say I was not doing this right and that wrong. He just gave his opinion that my problem was a mental one. Physically I was fine, but he felt I'd had a lot of football over two years and just wasn't right mentally. As soon as he said it I thought, well maybe he's hit the nail on the head. Some of the spark had gone; I wasn't getting nervous before games, I wasn't getting involved in matches. There were times when I felt tired and lethargic. But I was only 21 and supposedly had the world at my feet. I realise now that I probably thought I just had to go through the motions and I would regain my Australian spot. Now my club coach was telling me I was battling to keep my position at Parramatta!

Jack told me he didn't want me to play that weekend against Wests, who were running last. But I hadn't missed a match since I came into the under-23s side in early 1980 and it was a record I was proud of. I told him I wanted to play, that I didn't want a rest. Then he hit me with it — the message that if I played, it would be in reserve grade! To use Jack Gibson's words: "If you play you'll be starting at 1.30pm."

Well, for sure, that was something I didn't want to do. It would have been some sort of humiliation — the young star who beat Wally Lewis for his Australian spot a few months earlier, playing reserve grade. So I copped the tip and stood down. Then Jack told me he didn't want me near the place until the following Tuesday. He told me to stay right away — from training and the match and not to go near a football. Go away and have a rest, he said. So that's what I did. It was the strangest feeling I've had in football. Going to training and the weekend match was such a fixed routine with me that I felt sort of useless sitting around. I'd get home from work and watch a bit of television, and generally be lost. But it sure beat playing reserves.

In two years I had played 54 premiership games, 14 games on the Kangaroo tour, 10 KB Cup and rep matches in Australia. If my maths are okay that's 78 games. I'd played 72 games straight for Parramatta since making first grade. I was mentally stale.

Parramatta beat Wests 39-0 without me and I was back in the side for the following weekend's match against St George. We won 33-4 at Belmore and although it wasn't an instant cure that produced a "blinder", I certainly played a lot better. The great thing was I got the butterflies in the stomach before the match! I felt keen again — after just one week away. I have wondered at times what would have happened to me that year if the coach hadn't ordered me to have time away.

Maybe it was then that people started to say I was a hot and cold player. That I could look totally uninterested. My own view was that I was very consistent. Certainly in my later seasons, I don't think I blew hot and cold. Significantly my two worst seasons came after Kangaroo tours — 1983 and 1987. And there was one other time when I felt jaded mentally, in fact got to the stage where I almost couldn't care less about the game. That was after I came home from Wigan and Wembley in 1985.

Back in 1983, though, I didn't know what was happening. I didn't know what was wrong with my game. In hindsight, I took too many things for granted — I even *expected* to stay in the Australian side. When we returned from the Kangaroo tour we were given a month's break from training, to freshen up for the 1983 season. It was a new experience for me, coming back to Sydney in December after 10 months of continual football. I thought I'd have a break and then things would automatically fall into place and I would continue on where I left off from the Kangaroo tour.

There were significant differences in this off-season and the one before. I'd done a lot of sprint training before the 1982 campaign and was good and sharp. This time I did none. And the fact we started the season matched against a lot of sides who weren't expected to challenge for the semi-finals didn't help. We had easy wins over Newtown 54-14, Canberra 46-16 and Penrith 46-8. I probably went into games with a fairly relaxed attitude, thinking things were going to just happen for me on the field. When the games became harder, I was still going through the motions and not adjusting. It all came to a head in the weeks leading up to my visit to the boss's office.

Notwithstanding my only-fair form, I was disappointed when I was chosen in the centres in the City-Country game. For some reason I was also shifted to the centres at Parramatta, with Steve Ella switched to five-eighth. That's the way we finished up for NSW, too. Steve Rogers missed the first Origin match and I thought I was a chance for the centres in the Test team, alongside Mal Meninga. But Rogers was chosen despite missing the Origin match and I was on the outer. Steve Ella got the nod ahead of me as Test reserve.

I had taken over Wally's role from the tour — I couldn't get a look in. It took a while to realise I couldn't complain; although I ended up having a fair Origin series and Zip and I were the only NSW players to play in all three matches, I wasn't playing well enough.

In the wake of the Kangaroo tour I had set myself the goal of playing Test football in Australia. The dream was rapidly slipping through my fingers.

The first interstate match in '83 will go down as one of the most controversial in Origin history — for two reasons. It was the night Les Boyd wiped out Darryl Brohman at Lang Park, as a result of which he earned a 12-month suspension. But before we had even kicked a ball the NSW camp was thrown into turmoil. Our coach Ted Glossop amazed all of us on the day of the game by sacking chosen five-eighth Steve Ella to the bench and bringing in Alan Thompson.

That team had a strong Parramatta influence — with Geoff Bugden at prop, Ray Price at lock, Peter Sterling at half, Steve Ella five-eighth, me in the centres and Eric Grothe on the wing. It was healthy for the combination of the side; most people believed this would be an advantage for NSW.

Zip trained at five-eighth right through the week, with reserve back Thompson filling in at times to get used to the pattern. None of us could believe it on the day of the game when Glossop told us he was starting Thommo at five-eighth. In 1981 when Terry Lamb was called into the NSW side to replace Mick Pattison who was ill the day of the game, apparently coach Frank Stanton hadn't wanted to start Lamb but was overruled by the selectors. Two years later I don't think the selectors were even consulted by the coach.

The shock move certainly didn't help our cause. If Glossop had decided to make the switch he could at least have told the side and run Thommo at training, asking us to keep it quiet. But to throw the switch at us a few hours before the game was extraordinary. I suppose his thinking was that Alan Thompson's experience in a fairly young backline was going to be a plus. Balanced against that was that he was breaking up the Parramatta connection which was one of our strong points. As it turned out, we were well beaten. When Steve Ella came on he scored a try almost instantly.

For the next match the selectors obviously disagreed with Glossop's judgment and Thompson was dropped. I went to five-eighth and we finished up with a record eight Parramatta players in the side, including Stan Jurd on the bench. The backline was all Parramatta — except for fullback Marty Gurr: Neil Hunt (who was called in to replace the injured Brian Johnston), Mick Cronin, Steve Ella, Eric Grothe, myself and Peter Sterling — with Ray Price at lock. We won 10-6 at the SCG with all points scored by the Eels — Hunt, Ella tries; Cronin goal. Sterlo was man of the match.

So we headed into the final match with a chance of winning the series but with Sterlo, Pricey and Guru (Grothe) injured, we were under-strength and were flogged 43-22. Wally Lewis received the man-of-the-match award for the third time in four games.

I missed the first Test side to play against New Zealand — with the team picked the night of the first Origin match. Steve Rogers and Mal Meninga were the centres and Wally Lewis the five-eighth. Australia won 16-4 in Auckland. The second Test side was picked the weekend after the second Origin game and Steve Rogers was out injured. I thought I might have been a chance this time after NSW had won the second Origin match via our large Parramatta contingent. But this time Gene Miles was chosen to make his Test debut alongside Meninga. I missed out on a reserves spot too, with Steve Ella replacing Mark Murray as reserve back.

Australia went down 19-12 at Lang Park — the first time the Kiwis had won a Test in Australia since 1963 and their first Test win over us since 1971. Indicating how State of Origin football had influenced selectors in such a short period, there were only four NSW players in the starting line-up — Eric Grothe, Steve Mortimer, Ray Price and skipper Max Krilich. The Queenslanders revelled in the fact that they had nine spots — including fullback Colin Scott and prop Brad Tessmann in their only matches for Australia.

I might have won the first battle with Wally when I took his Test jumper in 1982, but I was to lose the "war". I made it back into the Australian side the next season (1984) against the touring Poms, but never played five-eighth for Australia again. I learned a hard lesson in 1983, and it was only the last few premiership rounds and the weeks leading up to our third grand final win that made the season worthwhile.

Emerging from the relative disappointments of 1983, I finally achieved my dream of playing a Test on home soil, on the Sydney Cricket Ground in June 1984. Soon afterwards I found myself studiously trying to get *out* of a Test match. It's a startling admission, I know, but it's true. The story of why I tried to miss that Test is one I'll tell a little later on.

10 Big Mouths

Fans and critics alike were casting serious doubts on Parramatta's chances of winning a back-to-back premiership in 1982 when Manly thrashed us 20-0 in the major semi-final. We had finished eight points clear of them at the top of the competition ladder, but 20-nil is something of a drubbing, and the Sea Eagles had beaten us three out of four times that year, including a KB Cup clash. They were the side I feared most. What I remember most of all about that semi-final loss was the continual mouthing off by the Blake brothers, Michael and Phil.

Phil Blake had hit the scene that season as a 19-year-old try-scoring freak. His two tries in the semi-final took his tally to 29 in all grades. He was playing halfback and was fast, elusive and had a great chip-and-chase. Michael, who was briefly a Manly whiz kid the season before, was slower, but a tough, solid centre.

When Phil scored his first try, he ripped into us verbally. He gave us heaps, really rubbing it in. Older brother Michael joined in the chorus, and the sledging increased as the match went more and more Manly's way. We increasingly slid behind on the scoreboard and there was nothing we could do but cop it. I was taught at an early age that sort of stuff is not on, particularly when you're new to the game. Phil Blake had only come into first grade, in his first year out of school, midway through that season. He won the Dally M rookie of the year award, and a Mazda RX7 car in the KB Cup golden try award. People were talking of him as a bolter for the Kangaroo tour, and the player who was going to win Manly the grand final. He was running hot, physically and verbally ... but every dog has his day.

Sledging has never been my go. I resented it from other players and I resented it from the Blakes that day. It really got to me. My firm philosophy was never to goad your opponents when you happened to be on top because, sure enough, one day you'd be on the other side of the ledger, and it would all come flying back in your face. I was hoping like mad that would happen to Phil and Michael Blake next time we met. But I didn't say anything, not a word.

I'm sure Phil Blake learned. In later years the sledging caper was no longer part of his game and when I met him, he came across as a real good bloke. It was a demonstration perhaps of how young blokes thrust into the headlines can get carried away with it all. That season Blakey was a genius — but he never did play for Australia and in fact only played the one game for NSW. For some reason he never quite turned out to be the superstar everyone thought he would be.

After the thrashing by Manly we had to beat Easts in the final to get another crack at the Sea Eagles. We did that pretty convincingly — by 33-0 on a soft surface. But in the meantime we lost our tough prop Ron Hilditch with a serious knee injury, giving Chris Phelan his chance in our grand final side.

You wouldn't want to know — Phil Blake scored after just two minutes of the grand final after diving on his own bomb. In the left-hand corner, Neil Hunt had fumbled a difficult kick. Yep, and you've guessed it — straight away he was giving us a gobful again. Blake was really pumped up with Manly getting such a dream start to the grand final. It was the worst possible start for us, and especially for Hunty, but Mick Cronin had a quiet word to him and got his head up and Steve Edge did a good job settling everyone down and re-assuring us that if we stuck to our match plan and didn't panic, everything would come together.

It did. We recaptured our composure and in the 10 minutes before halftime we ran in three tries to lead 16-3 at the break. I picked up one try, Neil Hunt squared his account by getting one and Eric Grothe got a gem after quick hands across the backs. I remember going into the dressing rooms, saying to Steve Ella: "We've got these blokes; we've only got to hold them and we've won." Well, we did it comfortably, running out 21-8 winners.

For us to beat Manly was like a dream come true for our supporters. Manly, the "Silvertails", had become our arch-rivals over many years and I remember supporters at the club that night were ecstatic that we'd "stuck it up Manly". That meant as much as us having won our second successive premiership.

The rivalry traced back to the year the clubs joined the premiership together, 1947. It intensified in the late '70s when the Sea Eagles stopped Parramatta winning our first grand final — in 1976 — and then knocked us out in rather dubious circumstances in 1978. Even in 1981, I thought Manly were our biggest threat, though they finished the competition proper in fifth spot.

Over the next couple of years every Parramatta-Manly match was on TV. Our rivalry dominated the back pages whenever we met and it became almost automatic that the experts would tip either Manly or Parramatta for the premiership.

We finished eight points clear of them at the top of the ladder in 1982. The next year they finished eight points clear of ourselves and Canterbury. Bob Fulton was now coach and he bolstered the ranks with the signing of Kerry Boustead, Noel Cleal, Dave Brown and Ian Schubert — all from Easts. The Sea Eagles were now thoroughly installed as the "Silvertails" and no one was more crooked on them than Parramatta and Wests supporters; Wests fans maybe hated them even more than ours did, because of Manly's pillaging of Les Boyd, John Dorahy, John Ribot and Ray Brown. Manly also signed up the man of the match from the first two Origin games, Chris Close, from Queensland, Phil Sigsworth from Newtown plus Bruce Walker from Norths and Paul McCabe from Easts. They already had international players in Terry Randall, Graham Eadie, Alan Thompson, Geoff Gerard (who left Parramatta at the end of 1980) and Paul Vautin. In later salary cap days they would never have been able to assemble such an array of stars.

Personally I never held any extraordinary feeling of rivalry or "hate" for Manly. I played representative football with many of their players and seven were chosen in the 1982 Kangaroo squad, along with six Parramatta players. A lot of us became reasonably good friends. I enjoyed their company and enjoyed playing against them because I respected them as footballers. But I often had Parra fans come up to me, asking me did I hate Manly, virtually *willing* me to develop a deep dislike for them.

No doubt, though, there was a feeling of "us and them" over those years. It was no surprise when we came up against them again in 1983 in the major semi-final.

Jack Gibson always told us it was harder to stay on top than what it was to get there and we had that in our minds through 1982. Having so many experienced players around who had been in grand finals before helped us younger players keep our feet on the ground throughout that season. It turned out to be an even better year than 1981.

The next year, '83, was definitely harder. We had six players returning from the Kangaroo tour and had already won two premierships. Was the desire there to win a third? Manly were stronger with the addition of Fulton, his three Easts players and Sigsworth. Canterbury were also a good side, who liked to throw the ball around under the open coaching style of Ted Glossop. Their defence was a bit suspect under pressure though, and you always felt you could get a few points back on them after they scored. Canterbury actually beat us twice during the season, each time on the week before we played Manly. In the first round, we finally clicked as a team when we played Manly at Brookvale in front of 24,000 people. We beat them 24-6 and again 26-6 in the second round (at Belmore), two of only four defeats they tasted all season.

We had to beat Canterbury to play Manly in the major semi-final and we did it 30-22 in a game most remembered for Eric Grothe's amazing try. In what has been rated one of the most outstanding tries ever seen at the SCG, the Guru beat five players in a 50-metre run up the midfield. I'm not sure it was the greatest try Eric scored, some of the ones in England in 1982 were unbelievable, but it is *the* single Eric Grothe try that people will never forget. He received the ball from Steve Ella and headed back infield, beating John Coveney, Geoff Robinson, Garry Hughes, Steve Folkes and Chris Mortimer before diving over in Steve Mortimer's tackle.

Eric Grothe was quite an enigma. I don't think he ever realised how good he was — and he definitely didn't play as many Test matches as he should have (he played eight between 1982-84). He only ever ran as fast as he had to, and he mucked around at training. He just never seemed to take himself or his amazing ability that seriously. Eric had a dry sense of humour and was great company, but will openly admit he was lazy. He seemed to be injured much of the time, and probably didn't treat his injuries well enough because of his easy-going approach. I remember one time we were playing a match at the SCG and we'd been out the back in the car-park warming up. As we came back into the dressing room, Eric slipped on the concrete and injured a knee. He always had dicky knees. The medicos were working away frantically trying to ascertain how serious it was when we ran out with 12 men. We played that way for five minutes or so before the coaches realised he wasn't going to come good and sent on a replacement.

But on this semi-final day at the SCG in 1983, he was hailed as a genius with the try that broke Canterbury's spirit — and put us into another showdown with Manly. I had very different fortunes in that match; I finished the game sick as a dog, stretched out on the strapping table, the legacy of a pretty heavy Chris Mortimer tackle. I was knocked cold and staggered back to fullback for a time.

Trainer Alf Richards ran on and I told him I'd be OK, I'd just try to stay behind the play and clear my head. Canterbury had the ball and were threatening out wide. I weaved across field on legs that were like jelly.

Luckily nothing came of that burst and I quickly decided I'd be better off in the dressing room after all. I felt sick for hours after the match and spent the next day in bed trying to get over it. The fact we were up against the old enemy Manly again was enough to have me at training by the Tuesday.

Manly were first into the grand final after beating us 19-10 in the major semi-final. That year I'm sure they thought: "This time we've got them." They led us 11-0 midway through he first half in a match in which neither of us played too well.

Again we had to win the final to get another crack at Manly and we did it convincingly (18-4 over Canterbury). But Manly were the hot favourites; they were clear-cut minor premiers, had beaten us in the semi-finals, and we lost both our props in the final, Geoff Bugden and Ron Hilditch, with injury.

I think the hearts of all our fans went out to Ronny Hilditch. It was the second grand final in a row that he had to miss because of injury suffered the week before. The medical report read: knee, 1982, shoulder 1983. Ron had decided to retire before the 1983 season because his knee injury was giving him trouble but he was talked into coming back and was an integral part of our side. They called him the "Hit Man" because of the toughness of his defence and he was a great bloke to have alongside, on and off the field. Ron was never the most naturally talented bloke and he won't take offence when I say he really didn't have the natural ability to play for Australia. But he made it because he worked so hard on improving his game and because of his unbelievable competitiveness. In later years I always used Ron Hilditch as an example to younger players when talking to them about working on their games. I tell them if Ron Hilditch had relied on ability alone, he would never have played for his country. It was through sheer dedication that he got to scale the heights.

In '83 the majority of the pundits thought Parramatta had met their match this time in a Manly side that had only one player — Blake — who wasn't, or didn't become, an international. Their side was: Graham Eadie, John Ribot, Chris Close, Phil Sigsworth, Kerry Boustead, Alan Thompson, Phil Blake, Ian Schubert, Noel Cleal, Paul Vautin, Paul McCabe, Ray Brown, Geoff Gerard. Our team was: Paul Taylor, Eric Grothe, Steve Ella, Mick Cronin, David Liddiard, Brett Kenny, Peter Sterling, Ray Price, Steve Sharp, Peter Wynn, Paul Mares, Steve Edge and Stan Jurd. We had seven internationals.

History records that the critics got it wrong again. Maybe Manly thought their all-star side only had to run out to win. The roles were reversed from the 1982 grand final; this time we got the early break when Paul McCabe tried to pop a ball up to Chris Close — but didn't realise I was right between them. The ball went straight into my arms about groin height. I almost bombed the try when, after seeing Alan Thompson coming across in pursuit, I passed to David Liddiard near the line. After watching the video I came to the conclusion that Thommo hadn't had any real chance of tackling. Luckily Liddiard got the ball back to me on the line as the cover picked him up and I took Kerry Boustead over. That was 6-0 after eight minutes (tries became worth four points that year) and five minutes later

Eric Grothe scored a try which typified his strength. The ball travelled out along the backline and I did a run around with Mick Cronin, stepped outside John Ribot and passed to Eric on the inside. He beat Phil Blake and, when confronted head-on by the massive Graham Eadie on the line, just took him over with him. I doubt there would have been anyone else in rugby league who could have done that to Graham Eadie. It was 12-0 after 13 minutes and Manly were fumbling and bumbling; no one seemed to want to take the ball up; no one was stepping forward to dig them out of the hole.

Two minutes into the second half I picked up my second try — from a call gone wrong. Peter Sterling was setting himself for a bomb with 19-year-old prop Paul Mares at dummy-half. Maresy fancied himself as a kicker in general play and Jack Gibson had told him that if he was in the position where he thought he could get in a good kick, to have a go. Sterlo had set himself and we were ready to follow his bomb, when Maresy lofted it instead. The ball bounced between Graham Eadie and Phil Blake, right into my hands. Eighteen-nil ... thank you linesmen, thank you ballboys. Manly scored three minutes later but we closed it up from there and finished 26-6 winners. We had completed the hat-trick!

Reporters quizzed me in the dressing room later about my feat of scoring two tries in a third successive grand final. The fact honestly hadn't registered with me. These days I'm proud to look back on that achievement. Two of the tries came from bombs, one from a miss-kick off the side of Steve McKenzie's boot, one from a dummy-half play, one from an intercept and one from a Ray Price break from the scrum. None of them came from any magical Brett Kenny-initiated breaks, but what the hell! If any one of them stands out, it was the second try in the 1981 win against Newtown — the one in which I threw the big dummy to Phil Sigsworth. It probably sticks in my mind the most because of the dummy. These days I get mixed up with the four I scored against Manly in '82 and '83. I've got to think twice before I'm sure which try came in which grand final.

To win three grand finals in three years was beyond my wildest dreams. The first, 1981, will always be the standout — because it *was* the first, for me and the club. But to bring up the hat-trick in 1983, against such a star-studded Manly side who were such hot favourites, was probably the most impressive victory. We were an enormously closely-knit unit during that magic period. Jack Gibson deserves the credit for that. He encouraged unity off the field and really took time to be interested in our families and our other activities. When he announced at a function a few days after the grand final that he was standing down as coach, it was a shock to all of us — even though we knew he'd never stayed more than three years at the one club. He'd never won three premierships at one club before either. I'll never underestimate his influence on me and on all the young players who developed under his guidance.

The next year we had a new coach — and a new arch-rival in Canterbury. Grand finals, and the game as a whole, changed dramatically. When 1984 arrived there were obviously some doubters who thought we wouldn't be able to stay at the top without Jack Gibson as coach. John Monie, an ex-player who had been beautifully schooled in the lower grades during the Gibson era, was promoted from second grade to take over. We were all comfortable with that. John had the benefit of knowing exactly what we were used to, how we operated and had a good knowledge of all the players. Maybe it doesn't happen enough now that young coaches are automatically promoted through the ranks. Instead, clubs seem to want to go for big names from outside.

While we felt we really only had to leap the hurdle of Manly during the previous two years, 1984 presented new threats. Warren Ryan, who coached Newtown into the grand final in 1981, had taken over at Canterbury, and he took some good players with him, including Phil Gould and Peter Kelly. At the same time, St George were building a strong side which included my boyhood idol Steve Rogers who had joined them after a decade with Cronulla.

Ryan toughened Canterbury's approach and they were an entirely different proposition from what they had been in the recent years. Instantly successful under his coaching, they finished with the minor premiership, four points clear of St George and Parramatta. We played a good part of the season without Mick Cronin who suffered a serious knee injury, and without skipper Steve Edge who'd suffered a detached retina of an eye during the 1983 grand final. Manly were still in the hunt, in fourth spot. Already people were saying we weren't tough enough to beat Canterbury when the heat was on. Right through the next three seasons the Bulldogs felt they could steamroll our forwards and beat us. That's the way they played us; most times I felt our forwards stood up to them; sometimes I admit they got on top of us. But never in a grand final.

We started 1984 with an 18-16 loss to the Bulldogs. St George beat us mid-season before we won nine games out of 10, including turning the tables on Canterbury (16-6).

In the preliminary semi-final we scored two tries in the first eight minutes against St George but relaxed and found ourselves 16-10 behind, before recovering to 16-all at halftime. The second half saw a great improvement in the defence and only one try was scored — when a Peter Sterling bomb hit the crossbar and Steve Ella snatched the ball to score — and give us a 22-16 win.

That meant we were up against the "new" Canterbury in a semi-final for the first time. We had a great start to that game when Ray Price scored from a Peter Sterling bomb. Things were going well but maybe we underestimated the spirit Canterbury had built that year. Mick Potter scored down the blindside, despite a great last-ditch effort from Eric Grothe, then their prop Peter Kelly, of all people, hoisted a bomb. I was back at fullback as I often was in our own quarter, but Chris Mortimer beat Steve Ella and me to the ball, putting us 12-6 behind at the break. We got back to 12-8 and I reckon it was only the great cover defence of Steve Mortimer from there which stopped us from winning. Turvey mowed down Eric Grothe and later Steve Ella with magnificent tackles when we thought they were certain to score. It was Mortimer again who stopped another try when he took Peter Wynn head-on. Turvey was actually knocked out in the tackle but was able to trip Wynn as he went down.

Mortimer was akin to Eric Grothe in that they both made their names through brilliant attack — but I never saw a better cover defender than the little Canterbury No.7. Eric was a genius at that too; some tackles he made for

Parramatta had to be seen to be believed. He had no right to even get anywhere near the players he pulled down.

It was replacement forward Darryl Brohman who made the decisive break that sealed the game for Canterbury. Steve Folkes ploughed over from dummy-half from the resulting play-the-ball. We went down 16-8 and again the cry was out that Canterbury had the wood on us.

We had to beat St George in the final the following Sunday and all week the talk was about how it was Steve Rogers' last chance to get into a grand final and win it. He'd had two attempts at Cronulla and gone close but, as he neared the end of his career, this could be his last chance. Even I felt that it would be wonderful for such a champion to go out a winner. But there was no room for sentiment. We wanted a fourth grand final. Rogers put St George in the position to win the game and was then put in a desperate position of trying to save the game — and for an instant I even felt some guilt that I played a part in ruining his fairytale.

We needed two mighty strokes of luck to get us into our fourth grand final. The press called it the "Great Escape" when we snuck home 8-7 with a try to Eric Grothe three minutes from time. We led 4-0 at halftime that day, with no tries scored despite some end-to-end action and big hits. In the second half Steve Rogers, who was doing most of their kicking, set as if to kick deep, but instead popped one over the top and winger Steve Morris flew through, scooped up the ball and ran away to score. Steve Gearin converted and all of a sudden we were behind. Rogers then picked up a field goal after we held off him, waiting for the bomb. We now needed a try to win it. I thought it was on when Eric Grothe broke through from our own quarter, but a great trysaving tackle by Brian Johnson stopped him. Johnson then came up with a great take from a bomb. Time was ticking away and we were starting to get a little worried.

In direct contrast to Canterbury the week before, St George seemed to want to lift the pace and score again. They were silly tactics. We were in our own quarter and getting tired after our second tough game in a week when Steve Gearin put a chip into the in-goal and flew through after it. The ball rolled dead fractionally before he got there. That meant a 22-metre tap, and our last chance. After a couple of plays Ray Price made a long break which gave us the field position to put something on. Things just rolled our way from then. We got a couple of penalties (which St George disputed) — one against Craig Young for holding on, one for a high tackle by Robert Stone on Paul Taylor. We also got a line drop-out when Saints claimed they should have got a 22m tap after there had been a scramble for a bomb in the in-goal. Saints reckoned Peter Sterling knocked on.

We were able to keep play in their quarter and Saints were anticipating a bomb from Sterlo on the last tackle. I called to Mick Cronin to put on an "A" move. I'd run across field and Mick would come inside me at an angle. Out the corner of one eye I could see a small gap, so I dummied to Mick and went for it. It was the last tackle and as the gap snapped shut I glimpsed Eric Grothe on the far right in open space. The St George defender hit me around the waist and my arms were free. As I was going down I desperately flung the ball over for Eric — hoping ... praying it would find him. It did, about 15 metres out from the corner. Rogers did brilliantly to get across and threw himself at Eric. But not even the genius of Rogers could stop the unstoppable and he scored — with three minutes to go. We'd won. I'll never forget the vision of Steve Rogers slumped desperately on the ground, completely heartbroken. I really felt for him.

That last gasp meant we had another crack at Canterbury. We had no doubts about how they were going to play us. We also we knew the game was going to be so close that one mistake, one mis-tackle could win it or lose it.

Our lead-up to our fourth straight grand final was no different from the previous three, except that on the day of the game we travelled to the Sydney Cricket Ground with our wives and families or girlfriends — all together rather than the players going by bus and everyone else by car. When we got there we had time to get families and partners seated and settled before we headed to the dressing room. The hardest part was always the waiting.

As usual I cracked a few jokes, tried to laugh things off — it was my way of coping with nerves. I had to know who to muck around with and who not to. Pricey was one I never tried to lighten up. He was so intense before matches, I've never known anyone to be so focussed.

It's a strange reality of the game that the teams are usually out the back of the stand or across the road when all the pre-match hype goes on. It was in those years that the League really started to get into all the razzamattazz. We never had a clue what went on ... until we watched the game on video the next day or the next week.

Canterbury had the bigger pack and we knew that they would try to run over the top of us. Most people pinpoint the key moment of that desperately close game as the one when their hooker Mark Bugden scored, running from dummy-half and scoring while Pricey was down hurt and we only had one marker. But to me the crucial moment came after just seven minutes — when Steve Ella had to be replaced because of a knee injury. Zip was such an elusive runner, such a potential matchwinner that it was a devastating blow for us so early in a grand final.

Canterbury reacted straight away to us being down one of our main attacking forces and they threw the ball around a bit more than we expected. Luckily for us Peter Mortimer was called back for a forward pass after he "scored". We had our own bad luck as well when Eric Grothe dropped a relatively easy pass in "Glover's Corner" — that end of the ground where winger Neville Glover dropped a pass which cost Parramatta the 1976 grand final.

But we were able to capitalise on a dropped pass close to their line. Straight afterwards Sterlo elected not to put up the bomb on the last and instead found a small hole for Mick Cronin who scored a try — just two minutes before halftime. Mick missed the conversion, which wasn't from all that wide an angle, but at the time I didn't think it would be particularly costly. The thing was we were handling Canterbury's aggression; we knew our forwards wouldn't fold. But one swift moment in the second half won Canterbury a premiership. Bugden's score decided the future home of the Winfield Cup. The game presented *the* classic examples of the danger of those periods just before and after halftime. We had a grand final with just two scores — an unconverted try two minutes before the break and a converted try three minutes after it.

There was plenty of time to go when Bugden scored and we knew if we stuck at our plan, we'd win. I'll never forget John Monie's prophetic words at halftime that the first 10 minutes of the second half could tell, they could decide the premiership. Unfortunately he was right.

There were near misses for both sides from that point onwards. With about five minutes to go, we were awarded a penalty for Canterbury "holding down". It was well within kicking distance for the Crow and I said to myself: "Get your breath – – we're going into extra-time." That goal attempt is still vivid in my mind — from the time it left Crow's boot it looked like it was going over the black dot but suddenly it veered away and just shaved an upright.

It was a strange feeling to lose our first grand final, very hard to take. For the first time in four years, we weren't going to be celebrating at the club that night. My after-match memory is of standing near the sideline and watching the Canterbury players receiving their medals and picking up the J.J. Giltinan Shield and then heading on their victory lap ... the "wrong" way (they went clockwise instead of anti-clockwise). And they walked instead of jogging. One of our trainers Joe Joseph said he thought what they were doing was wrong, that it was arrogant. I told Joe they'd won, not us, and they could do as they pleased. I suppose walking instead of running let them soak up the atmosphere for longer. We stayed put, and waited until they completed that slow lap of honour; then we shook their hands as they walked in towards the Members' Stand. It was the thing to do — to be sportsmanlike, to wait for them and to congratulate them and concede they were the new champions. That night I still felt proud; we'd made four grand finals, which was quite a feat. There was no shame in losing — but it still hurt.

A year later the feeling was even stranger. For the first time in five years we didn't make it to the grand final. It felt like someone had taken away something that was rightfully ours.

It was a season in which we had seven players in England (Sterling, Muggleton, Grothe, Hunt, Phelan, Taylor and myself), all of us returning well into the first round. And it was the first year without captain Steve Edge, with Pricey taking over the reins. We finished fourth and for the first time didn't get a second bite of the cherry in the finals. When we returned from England, the "second-stringers" had played that well that the team was placed second on the ladder. At full strength we promptly slumped to fourth. We cost ourselves the valuable third spot in the second-last game, against Easts. It was one of those miracle results – – we led 20-4 five minutes into the second half and got beaten 22-20! We had been equal third with Canterbury until that stage.

Into September and the semi-finals we had comfortable wins against Penrith and Balmain. It was Penrith's first time in the finals and, psychologically, they may have played their big game in beating Manly in a play-off on the Tuesday. We beat them 38-6 after leading 22-0 at halftime and I guess I had a lucky day. The press reports relate that I scored a try and played a part in six others, although some of them were just the old quick hands trick across the backs.

I remember saying in the dressing room after the match that all we had done was proved we were the fourth-best side in the competition. Now we had to prove the next week against Balmain or Canterbury that we were the third-best, and then week by week we had the chance to prove we were still the best team. We didn't have the luxury of even one slip.

Canterbury beat Balmain after extra time on the Sunday which meant we played the Tigers, who we'd beaten 40-8 only a few weeks before. But finals are different, past wins count for nothing. Balmain seemed to share the same opinion as others — that we were suspect in the forwards, that we weren't big enough or strong enough to contain them. They kept it tight and tried to hammer their way through us. We led only 10-4 at halftime. Luck often counts in big matches and we had it four minutes into the second half when Balmain got a touch to a Mick Cronin kick and Ray Price, already downtown, was then onside and got the ball. Three passes later Mick Cronin scored. That made it 16-4 and the Balmain spirit was broken. We ran away to win 32-4.

It was two steps down, two to go, and we faced the prospect of Canterbury or St George in the final. I wanted to play Canterbury, I was looking forward to facing our toughest rivals before grand final day, getting them out of the way and then taking on St George. I got my wish.

I was confident, I knew it was going to be a tough one — but I felt good. Canterbury got a start they could only have dreamed of when Peter Tunks barged over from dummy-half in the 12th minute. Then for the second year in a row we lost Steve Ella through injury — this time with a badly corked thigh. It threw us gain, but at halftime we were still only 4-0 behind. We were angling to play them in the backs while they were trying to bulldoze us in the forwards. We were hanging in well. The few minutes to have a talk and get ourselves re-organised at halftime was all we needed, I thought.

Things didn't quite go to plan. Four minutes after the break David Liddiard dropped a bomb from Andrew Farrar and their young winger Matthew Callinan scored. Six minutes later David Gillespie scored. Suddenly we were 14-0 behind. The grand final dream was fading. We didn't panic but we could sense Canterbury's confidence lifting. With 20 minutes to go we were 20-0 down and with no other option but to throw the ball around. The tactic forced errors, and we kept turning the ball over. The game slipped from our gasp bit by bit and we went down 26-0. The run was over — and by a wide margin, 26-0. They weren't as convincing as that scoreline indicates, but in the history books it appears a flogging.

That loss was extremely hard to take. Our routine was out the window — we were signing off a week early. We sat there in the dressing room for a long time after the game trying to fathom why things didn't work for us. Why were we beaten this time 26-0? There was no easy answer — that was the hard thing to accept. I felt that if *we* had got the break early in the second half, we could have done to them what they did to us. There was little between the teams. Instead, Canterbury went on to beat St George in the grand final and we sat at home watching on television.

It's a sudden ending. You're sort of still in shock and players start talking about what they're going to do next year to turn it around. Some said they were going to get fitter, as if that was the reason we fell down. I felt, at that stage of the year, we couldn't have got any fitter. Others said they were going to get lighter or stronger, Paul Taylor popped up and said he was going to drink more! We all did a fair bit of that later that night, knowing we had to live with defeat ... and that the grand final we coveted was going to go ahead without us.

11 Battles With Bulldogs

Season 1986 started in the most tragic way for Parramatta, with Mick Cronin almost being blinded in one eye in our first trial — at Cessnock in February. Then it looked as though his career may be over. But instead the season turned into a happy story with a fairy-tale ending. In September Mick Cronin's two goals won us the only tryless grand final in league history.

Well, it was tryless according to the record books. But I saw it differently — and I still do. By chance I was involved in the three most controversial plays of the 1986 Parramatta-Canterbury grand final — and two decisions by referee Mick Stone cost me the record of scoring two tries in each of Parramatta's four grand final wins. Later in the game I was the player Phil Sigsworth hit in a high tackle, leading to him becoming the first player sent off in a grand final since St George's Billy Wilson in 1963.

After all these years, I'll come clean. I definitely scored one try but I have to agree that Mick Stone got it right on the other controversial call. And to this day, I don't reckon Phil Sigsworth should have been sent off.

My first "try" came with the score at 0-0 after 17 minutes. Peter Sterling put up a bomb which bounced past Sigsworth. I followed through and leapt in the air over the top of Sigsworth's head; I grounded the ball as I came down. But the force of the impact caused it to bounce away as I hit the ground. Referee Stone ruled I knocked on. I'll never agree with that decision and the replays show I'm right. A lot of people asked me later that if I was so sure it was a try why hadn't I disputed the decision with Stone, instead of just running back into my position. The fact was that the referee had made his decision and awarded a 22m tap. The Canterbury players quickly tossed the ball to the 22m line for a quick re-start. There was no way I could stand in the in-goal arguing the toss. I had to scurry back to get into position. Anyhow, who wins by arguing with referees?

Three minutes into the second half, Canterbury were a man down, with Peter Kelly in the sin bin. We reckoned it was a chance to catch them out wide. We did just that and Eric Grothe was tackled brilliantly by Steve Mortimer, a few metres from the line. Grothe managed to get the ball away to me, and just as I took it Steve Folkes hit me in a tackle. As I hit the ground I reached out for the line. Try? This time Mick Stone ruled a double movement and after looking at the replay over and over again, I reckon he got it right. I was short of the line and moved my arm out after my progress had been stopped. The close decision wasn't what disappointed me the most. When I looked at the video I realised that one of our props, Terry Leabeater, had arrived on the inside and if I'd only looked I might have been able to squeeze a pass out to him. It would have been a certain try.

With 13 minutes to go Canterbury kicked through at a time when I had dropped back in defence while fullback Paul Taylor was in the front line. I took the ball, with Phil Sigsworth flying through. As I stepped away from him, he flung himself at me, and in a reflex action, caught me high. It didn't hurt and there was no malice intended but unfortunately for him (and fortunately for us because it relieved a lot of pressure!) he was sent off. There were far worse incidents in that game than that. I thought he was unlucky. He didn't deserve to go off.

Ray Price and Mick Delroy copped much worse tackles than the one I took from Siggy. Delroy got hit high and late by Andrew Farrar early in the match on our left wing. To the disbelief of the Parramatta players who saw it, Farrar didn't even get penalised. Pricey came in for extra "attention" throughout that match and also in the semi-final against Canterbury, which we won 28-6.

Farrar was at least penalised for a high tackle on Pricey later and Peter Kelly was sin-binned for the same offence. It looked like they thought they couldn't beat us by playing football.

We led 2-0 at halftime, through a Mick Cronin goal. A Terry Lamb goal, after Peter Sterling was penalised for knocking Steve Mortimer down while charging a kick, made it 2-2. Canterbury tried anything they could to unsettle us — and it was a sweet irony that the winning of the match came from another illegal tackle on Pricey — this time from their replacement forward David Boyd. After the match Canterbury were complaining about Pricey's "dying swan" performance, claiming he went down too often. They would have been better looking at themselves. It was their pre-occupation with belting him that went a fair way towards costing them the game.

Steve Mortimer was the one Canterbury player who tried to do something out of the ordinary in attack. He made some breaks through the middle of the rucks from dummy-half and tried a few chip kicks; apparently this didn't please Warren Ryan. Mortimer worried us more than anyone else; he was the one player I feared could win the game for them.

As it was, Terry Lamb had the chance to draw level with a penalty shot from fairly wide out with two minutes to go. Our cover defence had been outstanding during the second half and we seemed to have six or seven players there everytime they made a half-break. It showed just how much we wanted to win, how desperate we were to win — certainly for ourselves but also for Pricey and the Crow who were retiring. Lamb missed the goal and Canterbury came at us in one last big effort. They piled on the pressure and we concentrated on not missing tackles. I'll never forget the frantic last play. Their hooker, Mark Bugden, tried to scramble over from dummy-half and was tackled a metre out. We had a few players lying on him, slowing down the play-the-ball, when the hooter sounded. Every Parramatta player was screaming at Mick Stone: "It's fulltime! it's fulltime!" but it was so noisy we didn't think he'd heard the siren. Anything could have happened if Bugden had played the ball, and I'll forever be thankful that the hooter didn't go three seconds later, and that Mick Stone *did* hear it.

It was a genuine fairy-tale ending for Pricey and the Crow. They couldn't have asked for anything more — except better vision in Mick's right eye. After the slowest victory lap we ever had, champagne was flowing everywhere ... except into glasses.

The season was a mighty one for Parramatta — just when people were starting to doubt whether we could get back to the top. General opinion was that we had begun to slide in 1985. But in '86 everything fell into place. We opened the spanking new Parramatta Stadium, the best league venue in the country, with a 36-6 thrashing of St George and then went on to average crowds of more than 20,000 at our new home throughout the season. We won the Panasonic Cup, the minor premiership and the club championship and this time went straight into the grand final with a 28-6 win against Canterbury — our best victory over them during those years. Then we sent Pricey and the Crow out winners on grand final day. For Sterlo and me there was more glory — in being part of the NSW side that became the first to win a State of Origin series 3-0. We also played for the Australian team that beat New Zealand 3-0. It was the best season of my career.

Canterbury under Warren Ryan went from Entertainers to Intimidators. Along the way they changed the face of the game, relying on their brutal defence stopping the other side from scoring — rather than setting out to create opportunities themselves. They set a trend that was to come under a fair bit of attack by the critics. Consider the scores in the grand finals they played in; there was a meagre total of *four* tries scored in the 1984 (v Parramatta), 1985 (v St George) and 1986 (v Parramatta) games.

At Parramatta we were well aware of the need for tight defence, but with the available talent in our backline we liked to throw the ball around and create things — even from deep inside our own territory. Canterbury no doubt felt they intimidated us, even scared us with their physical style, but the record of those three seasons proved that we stood up to them very well overall. Our record over the three years (1984-85-86) was seven wins to five losses (including a Panasonic Cup game). In 1984 and '85 we lost all three big end-of-season games at the SCG but we beat them in twice in the final series of '86. That year their forwards never at any stage got any momentum against us. I don't think our forward pack ever got enough credit for that. Canterbury made their intentions clear in both end-of-season games in '86 — they obviously thought if they stopped Ray Price, by any means, they would stop the Parramatta forwards. Pricey copped a battering, but Canterbury conceded a few costly penalties. They also under-estimated Pricey's toughness. I don't think I've seen any player get so much attention from opposing forwards as he did in those two games in 1986, the last two games of his Australian career. I'm aware, though, that he copped a similar battering in the 1977 grand final replay against St George. Plenty of times in '86 he was down in backplay and some people reckoned he was play-acting. He wasn't. He got belted time after time, particularly by the props, Peter Kelly and Peter Tunks. But we had the last, sweet laugh — we won the premiership thanks to a foul on Ray Price.

The thought that we couldn't send Pricey and the Crow out losers was in our minds in those last desperate minutes in 1986. Crow only returned a few weeks before the finals, and under difficulties, but just having him on the field made us feel more confident. It seemed right and proper, after all he had done for us earlier in our careers, that we could repay the favour by nursing him through. Mick had only 20 percent vision in his right eye. Pricey was an inspiration to everyone who played with him and he had a burning ambition to captain Parramatta to a premiership. Both men had done a lot for me over the years. Of the four grand final wins, I'd have to place the 1986 second on the list. Nothing could ever beat the first-ever in 1981, but to give Pricey and the Crow a fairy-tale send-off ran it pretty close.

Back at the leagues club that night, it was just like '81. They couldn't fit all the fans in the club, so we were again placed on the back of a Hardie's truck outside the club, hoisted above people's heads from the team bus to the truck, and one by one introduced to the crowd. Then it was inside to the auditorium, where the atmosphere was just unbelievable.

Until that day, John Monie had lived to some extent in Jack Gibson's shadow. But in 1986 John strode to centre stage by winning a premiership and a midweek cup, a feat only achieved by one man before ... Jack Gibson (with Easts in 1975). By 1993 John Monie had gone on to become the most successful coach in the history of the English game with his Challenge Cup and championship feats during his four years with Wigan, which built on his double success of 1986 with Parramatta. No other coach has ever had anywhere near that success on both sides of the world. I'm sure he'll do very well in his next challenge, with the Auckland Warriors — a new challenge in which he will start a team from scratch.

I don't think the domination of Parramatta and Canterbury (eight of nine premierships between 1980-88) will ever happen again — because the salary cap and other circumstances made the Winfield Cup much more even in the 90s. To consider that Parramatta and Gold Coast were the only sides *not* to have made the semi-finals in the first five seasons after the 16-team competition was introduced in 1988 is quite extraordinary. I regard Parramatta's record from 1976-86 as the greatest feat of any modern club, outside St George's 11 straight premierships from 1956-66. In 11 seasons we made six grand finals, and only missed the semi-finals once. No other team had such consistency during that time. Manly were arch-rivals from 1976-78, then in 1982 and '83; Canterbury made grand finals in 1979 and '80 and then came back in 1984-86, but throughout all that time Parramatta were up there. I consider myself very fortunate to have been able to cut my teeth in such an exciting era.

Both Manly and Canterbury bought big to try to beat us, but there was great contrast in the way these two keen rivals approached the game of rugby league. The scorelines in our four grand finals from 1982-86 show the difference: 1982 v Manly 21-8 (seven tries), 1983 v Manly 18-6 (five tries), 1984 v Canterbury 6-4 (two tries), 1986 v Canterbury 4-2 (no tries).

It's sad to think how quickly we faded from that high point of 1986. Injuries decimated our side in 1987 and from then on Parramatta have never been the same. But success comes in cycles. Parramatta will be back, provided a few changes are made in attitude, and I'll be watching in pleasure from the comfort of my retirement.

12 Wonderful Wembley

It was a casual conversation with Parramatta team-mate Neil Hunt in 1984 that led to the most unexpected, most memorable day of my career. That was the day I played in front of 97,000 people at London's famous Wembley Stadium.

Hunty had decided in mid-1984 he was going to play an off-season with Leeds in England. Julie and I were pretty close to Neil and his wife Donna and one day when we were sitting around talking he threw in the suggestion that we should go over to England too, and play with Leeds. I had no inclination whatsoever to play club football in England; the thought had never crossed my mind. But over the next few weeks Neil and Donna kept on at us. "Come on — come over ... it'll be great".

Julie and I were to be married the following October and after a lot of thought and a lot of talk we decided it wouldn't be a bad way to spend a honeymoon. I'd been to England for the 1982 Kangaroo tour but didn't really know too much about the place. I knew the grounds, I knew that it was nearly always grey and cold, and I knew that Australia had the better Test team. We reached a decision — if something came along, we'd give it a go and join Neil and Donna.

Local businessman John White, who managed Ray Price's and Peter Sterling's affairs for a few years, had lined up Hunty's stint with Leeds, and I asked him if he could get me a start there too. But Leeds weren't interested — they didn't need anybody in my position — but they just said "no thanks". So John White got onto Wigan who were looking for a back with a bit of speed, a player who could give them some thrust. John told me that I could get a fairly good deal there and that they'd made it to Wembley a couple of months before, after being in second division three years earlier.

There was only one problem. I hadn't re-signed with Parramatta and for the only time during my career, I'd received genuine interest from another club, Manly. Manly were talking far better money than I had been getting at Parramatta.

One day I went over to Manly and was taken to lunch by coach Bob Fulton and club secretary Doug Daley and was given the real red carpet treatment. They were very impressive with the way they did business. We talked about the beaches, and they told me how they'd look after me and that they'd win the premiership. I really was interested. Then I dropped it on them — that I wanted to go to play with Wigan in the off-season. Manly weren't too keen on that. I explained that I was about to be married and that Julie and I thought it would be a good experience to travel over there and play football and see some of the world while we had the chance. I told them that we'd just bought a house at Greystanes and didn't have money for an extravagant honeymoon, and we decided it would be a good opportunity. Manly's answer was to offer to send Julie and me to Hawaii for a honeymoon in the summer! It was an incredible offer.

I did the right thing and told Parramatta I had received another Sydney offer, and also the offer to play with Wigan as well. Denis Fitzgerald put some figures together for me and although he wasn't too keen on me going to England, said he'd allow it — but I'd have to re-sign with Parramatta for three years, within a week. In those days there was no deadline on Australian players returning from stints in England and Fitzy knew I could miss the first two months or more of the 1985 season.

I took all the details to John White, and we discussed what the Manly offer was worth. The Sea Eagles also wanted an answer within days so we had to work through the whole thing as quickly as we could. I'd decided that I really didn't want to move to the Manly area because we'd just bought the house. When we went through everything, and included the cost of travelling from Greystanes to Brookvale three or four times a week, the Manly offer wasn't worth much more than Parramatta's. So I decided to stay an Eel — and become a temporary Wiganer.

I had no real idea where Wigan was in relation to Leeds; we played them in 1982, but I wasn't in the team that night. I didn't know anything about the place at all — other than the news a week or so later that Easts winger John Ferguson was going there as well. To me it was going to be an experience; I'd earn some extra money and we'd provide the Hunts with some company. In Australia then the Challenge Cup final at Wembley wasn't such a big deal. It was replayed here on TV late at night a week or two after the event — unlike now when it is shown live, and draws a large audience. So I couldn't even say that the chance of playing at Wembley was the motivation for me going to England, which is the case for most of the guys who go there now. I just thought it would be something different, a bit of an adventure with some friends.

By the time we left, half of Parramatta's side seemed to be going in the same direction. Eric Grothe joined Hunty at Leeds, Paul Taylor was going to Oldham with Chris Phelan, and Peter Sterling and John Muggleton were going back for their second stint at Hull.

Wigan were happy for us to not arrive until early December, as long as I could stay until the end of the season. "Chicka" (Ferguson) was going over pretty much as soon as our season finished but he had to return in early March. We jetted out on December 1, on a warm, sunny Sydney day and arrived in Manchester on December 2, an overcast, freezing morning, with everything grey and damp. Welcome to England.

Wigan had played Neil Hunt's side Leeds the day before, and Neil and Donna were at the airport to meet us, along with the Wigan coaches Colin Clarke and Alan McInnes. We were taken straight to our house near Wigan, a semi not unlike the ones in Paddington, Sydney. There was a living area downstairs, bedrooms and bathroom upstairs, a little yard at the back with a pond in it, all in a nice quiet cul-de-sac. It was small but quite comfortable, very different from what we were used to in Australia, but compared to the accommodation most players had it was quite nice. Paul Taylor, at Oldham, used to have to put 20 pence coins in a meter to keep the central heating going. We had a modern heating unit and, as we learned a few weeks later, we needed it.

Neil and Donna stayed for a while and then headed back to Leeds — which I presumed was just half an hour up the road, but which in fact was over the other side of the Pennines and a good hour and a half away. Jet-lagged, Julie and I dozed off. When we woke up, it was pitch dark. The Wigan people had organised some food for us, so Julie decided she'd cook us tea. We hadn't checked the time but figured it was pretty late. We sat down to eat, turned the TV on ... and realised it was 4.30 in the afternoon!

The next day Graeme West, the former New Zealand captain then playing at Wigan, came over with Maurice Lindsay, the club's driving force and the man destined to be chairman. They took us down to pick up a sponsored car, then it was over to Central Park, the club's home ground, then a look at downtown Wigan.

I didn't know what to expect when I got to training that first night. I wondered what the reaction of the English players would be towards me. John Ferguson and another Australian, Mark Cannon, were there so I linked up with them and they introduced me around. Everyone was fine — I certainly didn't sense any animosity. It was a funny set-up in that although we played at Central Park, which was a very good ground, we couldn't train there. It was a case of arriving there, doing weights or something indoors — then everyone would pile into their cars and we'd drive a couple of miles to a training ground where we'd do ballwork on synthetic turf. Then it was back into the cars and back to Central Park for a shower. The club was reluctant to use the ground for both training and playing, because of the wear and tear factor. It wasn't until right near the end of the season, when it became warmer and dryer, that we were able to actually train on the main ground.

We were still acclimatising to our new home when I made my debut for Wigan the following Sunday against Warrington. It was a real eye-opener. I kept thinking all week that they'd give me some gear soon. I had a tracksuit, but what about shorts, socks and a jumper? They kept telling me everything would be there on Sunday. Then they asked me for my boots and promptly took them away; I didn't know if I'd ever see them again. It was explained to me that they would be cleaned for me and waiting at the game on Sunday. For years I had a fixed routine of having a shower, getting dressed then packing my bag on match days. All I had to do at Wigan was take a shave bag with a razor and tooth paste. When I got to the ground — Wilderspool Stadium, Warrington's home base — there was my jumper, shorts and socks all hung up, with my boots neatly placed underneath the seat, number six in the chain of 15 meticulously placed around the dressing room. It was very professional, and very impressive.

On the way to the ground in the team coach, the English players were telling me that this was a real grudge match. The teams were arch-rivals and there was normally trouble between spectators. On the paddock, they said, Warrington were a pretty tough mob. The first time I ran with the ball, I made a small break. I was heading across towards the the sideline and passed inside. I'd no sooner got rid of the ball when a Warrington player came across, hit me in the back of the head with an elbow and knocked me down. I thought: "This is a nice welcome to English rugby league!" That day it was tougher *off* the pitch; there were fights all over the ground as we won 22-8.

We won our next two matches comfortably against Leigh and Hunslet and were scheduled to play on Boxing Day and New Year's Day, certainly something new to me. On Christmas day all the Parramatta crowd travelled across to Hull for a get-together — the Hunts, Paul Taylor, Chris Phelan, the Kennys, Muggo and his wife Jan, Sterlo's sister. For me it was a return to the place where I played my first Test match in 1982. It was a great day and naturally we all felt a bit homesick. That day it also hit home to me that everything in the north of England wasn't as close as I presumed. Hull was more than two and a half hours' drive for Julie and me. I realised that getting together every second day with the other Aussies wasn't going to be as easy as I thought. But in the weeks ahead we tried to catch up with them every fortnight or so — weather permitting!

It was a pretty quiet Christmas, with all of us having to back up next day to play. Wigan were scheduled to play St Helens in the traditional local derby. It was a Boxing Day tradition of many decades and beforehand I had no idea what it meant to the locals. I took me a while to catch up with a whole lot of things over there. I'd just missed the John Player competition, but by December we were playing in the championship one week, the Challenge Cup the next, then the championship, then back to the Challenge Cup. One game would be super-important because of tradition, and there would be extra urgency in the players, the next would be just a normal game. When the cup games came, we'd be on big financial incentives to win; the next week we were back to regular match payments. The Boxing Day local derby rated pretty close to the top of the pile. Saints headed the ladder and had beaten Wigan in the Lancashire Cup final in late October. They had my 1982 Kangaroo team-mate Mal Meninga, who had been braining them. It was a season which featured a proliferation of Australians in England, about 50 I'd guess, with Mal getting most of the publicity. He had quickly become a superman for St Helens.

The game was played at Saints' ground Knowsley Road and it was packed. We won 30-22, a considerable achievement away from home. It was as if Christmas had come twice for the Wigan fans. They were delirious. Then we had to back up on New Year's Day against Warrington, which guaranteed a quiet New Year's Eve, spent with a couple of friends from the office at Wigan plus Shaun Edwards who was then a teenager in his second season of first grade at Wigan. After a quiet toast at midnight it was off to bed to get some sleep for the next day's match. My mind strayed to Ray Price's place back home, where everyone would be just warming up for a big night.

The New Year's Day game had to be called off because of frost and we finally ended up beating Warrington easily again on January 3 — before the big cold set in. People kept telling me it looked like being the worst winter for years and that it might snow. Julie and I thought "great". We'd never lived in snow before, although we'd been down to the Snowy Mountains skiing now and then. A few days after Christmas, down it came. It was beautiful, all the rooftops and trees covered in white; the pond in the back yard was frozen solid and we could walk on it. We went straight outside and built a snowman, it was wonderful — for a while ...

Apart from a brief let-up which allowed us to play the New Year's Day match against Warrington two days late, it snowed almost constantly for three weeks. The really cold snap had hit before the snow, which meant the ground underneath was frozen and the snow acted as a blanket which kept the cold in. We couldn't train outdoors or play for nearly a month. We became idle Aussies in a foreign country, worried about even driving on the roads because of the snow and the menacing black ice. The motorways were closed at times, and even getting out of our street was a bit hairy. The only trips we made were to do the shopping, to the video store (I reckon we watched every movie on the shelf) and to training which normally comprised of a game of basketball at a local school, or weights at Central Park. It was 27 days before Wigan saw any further action that snowy winter. It was a tough time for us; we'd never been so idle, never been forced indoors for such long periods. The days meant just seven to eight hours' light and it was too depressing outside to do anything much anyway. It wore us down, particularly when my only outlet — playing rugby league, the reason I was there — was taken from me for almost a month. Some people enjoyed the pub scene but that really wasn't our go. A scotch with coke off the shelf (not the fridge) with no ice, or room temperature beer, wasn't too inviting.

A couple of weeks after we commenced playing again I was in the club one day when Maurice Lindsay came up and said: "You know we should have sent you and Julie over to Europe for a couple of weeks while it was snowing." Great, *now* you tell us! Probably we should have taken the opportunity to travel and look around more, but I felt I was there to play football and to train with the local players. I didn't want to take liberties. I didn't want to be seen as an Aussie who just dropped in when it suited him; I was a footballer, not a tourist.

On January 30, we finally hit the playing field again, although England was still in the midst of a shocking winter. We beat Widnes and then played regularly through February. From my first match we went 15 straight games without a loss (including a draw against Halifax) and were moulding into a good side. Wigan then was far from flooded with internationals the way the side is now, but there were some good players there and plenty of good blokes. The spirit was great. I started to settle into a foreign style of play, where keeping the ball alive was everything, and to a new role where I was expected to call the play as much as play on instinct. John Ferguson was in great form on the wing and had become a real crowd favourite at Central Park.

Steve Hampson, who cemented himself as Great Britain fullback for many years, had come back from a broken leg and was in reserve grade, Henderson Gill, the flamboyant black winger, was a real character and a good player. He used to turn up to training in his black Celica and you'd hear the music blaring out from the car radio way before he reached the carpark. I didn't realise for

Classical pose ... Kenny in space against Canterbury in the 1983 finals at the SCG.

Above left: "It wasn't me, mum!" Four-year-old Brett looking rather guilty. Above right: "Bert" the toddler, born to be a baseballer. Below: The star of Guildford Under-9s, the handsome one (fourth from left) in the back row.

Right: "Make room in the trophy cabinet, dad." By age 10, it was obvious Brett would follow in Alan's footsteps — in another sport.

Below: "Rowdy" Kenny the baseballer. He may well look composed here but team-mates knew to hide if he was struck out.

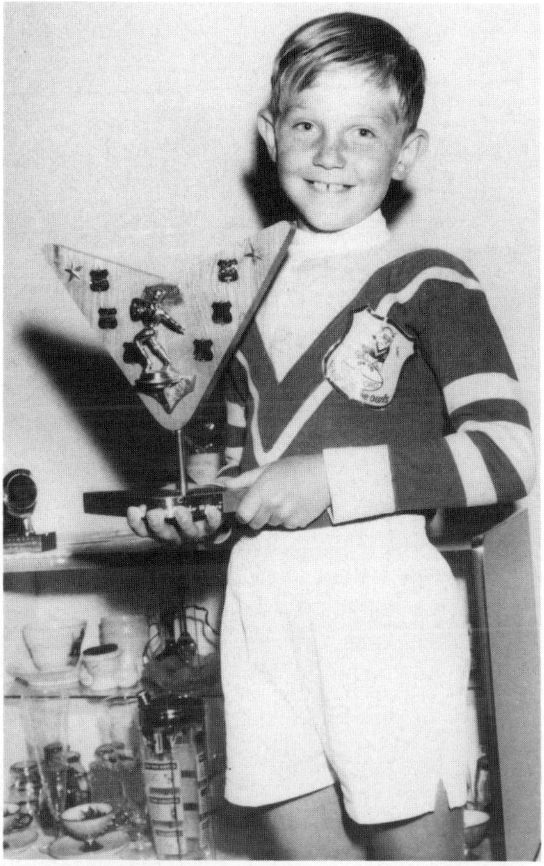

Above: Versatile sportsman at Sherwood Grange Primary School. Brett (front row, third from left) played cricket the way he did baseball. He was only interested in big hits.

Above: Adversaries from 1980-93 and great survivors of the modern era. Brett trailed by Terry Lamb, then a Magpie, in 1983. They made their first grade debuts five weeks apart in 1980. Lamb is rated by Brett as second only to Wally Lewis as his toughest five-eighth opponent.

Right: A boyhood hero who became a team-mate, Mick Cronin. He had enormous influence on the Kenny career.

Above: Bob "The Bear" O'Reilly putting a young Kenny into a gap, 1981.
Left: Mick Cronin (left) and O'Reilly.
Below: The old and new — O'Reilly, who made his debut as a 17-year-old in 1967, surrounded by Steve Ella and Peter Sterling 14 years later.

Right: Steve Ella — injury stopped him from becoming one of the greatest players in the game.

Below: Jack Gibson — "I expected the old school-master but got a kind, generous man," says Kenny.

Above left: Parramatta's "on field Gibbo" — skipper of four Eels' grand final teams, Steve Edge. Above right: Paul "Tas" Taylor, who once turned up for a 10km run straight from a big night out ... and beat everyone home!

A sleek Kenny slips past Jim Walters during the semi-final against Newtown in 1981.

Left: A Kangaroo before his time. Brett had no thoughts of making the 1982 Invincibles until around grand final time.

Below: The joker responsible for the nickname "Bert" — Rod "Rocket" Reddy.

Above: In his cherished NSW No.6 jersey in 1983. His amazing record when opposing Wally Lewis at five-eighth is eight wins to four!

A magical moment from 1985. Kenny, Sterling and the hooker who loved to celebrate tries with a hug, Michael Moseley, after a touchdown against Balmain in the semi-final.

Left: Halted by Poms David Topliss and Brian Noble (No.9) in the third Test, Headingley, 1982. Veteran Topliss left his mark on Kenny — rib cartilage damage via some wayward knees.

Below: Sleeping beauty Mark "Muppet" Murray, Kenny's room-mate during the 1982 Kangaroo tour. On the tour Muppet overslept one morning but was saved from a fate worse than death (the wrath of coach Frank Stanton) by trainer Alf Richards.

Right: Good friend Neil "Guilty" Hunt. If it wasn't for Neil and his wife Donna, Brett would never have become a Wembley hero.

Below: Speeding away from Manly's Chris Close in 1982. Close was one of the many big-name imports signed by the Sea Eagles in their bid to beat the Eels in the early 1980s.

Left: A try against Canterbury, who, in the mid-1980s, replaced Manly as Parramatta's chief rivals.

Inset: Ron Massey, perfect right-hand man for Jack Gibson 1981-83.

Above: An historic photo. The Eels' record seven NSW reps for game two, 1983: (from left) Ray Price, Peter Sterling, Brett Kenny, Mick Cronin, Steve Ella, Eric Grothe, Neil Hunt.

In search of an opportunity at Belmore, the Eels' home away from home from 1982 to 1985.

Left: Proud but lonely, Wigan hero "Bert" is lost in the vastness of Wembley, torn away from his team-mates during the victory lap.

Below: Great mates, but great rivals on English league's greatest day. Wigan's Kenny slips past Hull's Sterling at Wembley in 1985. The British bookmakers only had two players in the market to win the Lance Todd Trophy — Kenny and Sterling.

There could only be one winner. Exhausted Aussies, Bert and Sterlo, sought each other out immediately after fulltime at Wembley. Each put in a phenomenal effort in the big game.

Above: Mr and Mrs Kenny, with wedding guests Eric Grothe, Mick Cronin, Paul Taylor, Ray Price, Stan Jurd (obscured), John Muggleton and Neil Hunt.

Left: The Kenny children, Mitchell, Joshua and Nikolah.

Below left: Julie and Brett Kenny.

Below: Proud parents Marj and Alan.

months that he was married to a lovely little Scottish girl. He was so much one of the boys who enjoyed life to the fullest. I was amazed he had a wife.

Ian Potter, who went on to play for Great Britain against the 1986 Kangaroos, was a good forward and the hooker Nicky Kiss was a tough customer. Prop Brian Case had been around for a while and was a wily player. Mike Ford was at halfback and he too went on to play for Great Britain, as did centre David Stephenson. Shaun Wane was also a good prop and Colin Whitfield, who had a season with Canterbury later on, was the goalkicker when he was in the side; otherwise David Stephenson kicked. I'd only been there a few weeks when the club sold the Aussie Mark Cannon to Barrow. Mark had been five-eighth the previous season when Wigan went to Wembley, but there were no hard feelings between us. We developed into a pretty good side at a time before Joe Lydon, Andy Gregory, Ellery Hanley, Andy Goodway and Dean Bell bolstered the team to such an extent.

We played second division Batley in the first round of the Challenge Cup and beat them 46-8. What I remember most was that the game was taken to Bolton Wanderers' soccer ground because of the weather and it was the first time I'd seen an English soccer stadium. It was great, really compact with stands on both sides. It wasn't until we played Warrington the next week in the second round of the cup that I realised what a big thing this Challenge Cup was to the Pommy players. Our only cup back home, the midweek cup, played a poor second fiddle to the premiership. In England the guys wanted to win the Challenge Cup more than anything. It was the big one. And they knew if they went well, that's where the money was.

We beat Warrington 24-14, which took us into the third round against Bradford Northern at Odsal Stadium. It was the first time I ever opposed Ellery Hanley. He was the up-and-coming superstar of Britain, their answer to Wally Lewis, and a prolific tryscorer. To be honest I had barely even heard of him. That was probably good because I didn't feel any extra pressure coming up against him. We won 7-6 and I learned that Ellery was a very strong player indeed, with a good fend and with a lot more pace than in his later years when he was the top dog of English football. Neil Hunt was in the crowd and he commented later how tough it was, and how he thought we were lucky to get away with the win. Henderson Gill scored the only try of the match and Mike Ford kicked a field goal to give us the win.

Now, we had to beat Hull Kingston Rovers in the semi-final to make it to Wembley. By now I had the Wembley "bug" too. I realised what a fabulous experience it would be to get there. The semi-final was played at another soccer ground, Leeds United's Elland Road, and it was fantastic. The grass was as if it had been manicured.

On that day I nearly cost Wigan the chance of going to Wembley. They would have kicked me out of town if it hadn't it been for a bloke named Mick Scott, a borderline first-grader who was on the paddock only because one of the forwards was injured. In the second half I threw a bad pass on Rovers' quarter which was intercepted by winger Gary Clarke. Clarke set off, looking certain to score, but Mick Scott came from nowhere and ran him down in our own quarter. We were leading 12-11 at the time and there were about 10 minutes to go. Had they scored we would have been behind 17-12 and under real pressure. As it was Henderson Gill scored in the last couple of minutes and we were off to Wembley. Apparently I wasn't too sweet with the wives in the stand after my wild pass, especially with Mrs Scott, who was bagging me savagely, but at least I was able to face my English team-mates after the match.

So we were off to Wembley — in six weeks' time! That was the unbelievable thing about English football, the chopping and changing from one competition to another. Because of the lost month in January, we had a fixture bank-up which meant that we played 12 games between the semi-final and the final of the Challenge Cup. Unbelievable! We beat Oldham three days later, they were an ordinary side that year, but then we lost four straight — because our blokes had their minds on Wembley. It was hard to switch off Wembley and back to the championship, especially when we were playing twice a week to make up for lost time.

By this time John Ferguson had gone home to Eastern Suburbs, but once we made the final they organised straight away for him to come back for the Wembley game. By then they were calling Chicka the new Billy Boston; every time he got the ball he brought the crowd to its feet and he ended up scoring 24 tries in 25 matches. I wouldn't say we had a great natural understanding, me being in close at five-eighth and Chicka on the wing, but we certainly knew what each of us was capable of, and we learned to anticipate when one might make a break. Off the field, I didn't see a lot of him. Chicka and his wife Cheryl lived right across the other side of town with their two kids. He was a quiet bloke, but I was sure glad he was there. On the field he was a sensation.

Everyone in Wigan was focussed on Wembley. I'd walk down the main street and people would be patting mc on the back, and telling me they'd bought their tickets and arranged their coach or train or lift to London for the big weekend. Everyone wanted to talk about it. Although Wigan had gone to Wembley the previous year, with Mark Cannon, Wayne Elvin and Kerry Hemsley as their Aussie imports, they hadn't won the cup for 20 years. They all believed this was going to be their year. It was my first experience of the one team-one town situation. In Wigan they followed the club with a passion. The week before the match there was a real grand final atmosphere. All the shops were decked out with cherry and white streamers. The aura that surrounded this game was really starting to get to me by then.

The lead-up showed the professionalism of the Wigan club; they were well ahead of the Sydney clubs at that stage in things they did off the field. Our playing gear was completely looked after by the kitman and we had shoes, pants and shirts made for us to wear down to Wembley; we'd already been given a tie and blazer. We really looked the part.

Just a week before playing Hull in the final, we had to play them in a premiership match — which is the final series for the top eight clubs. First past the post — the championship — was the next best thing to Wembley and Hull KR won that with St Helens second. We ran third. Hull had made the Challenge Cup final after surviving a semi-final replay against Castleford — an infamous match in which Malcolm Reilly made a comeback and had a run-in with Sterlo, who subsequently accused him of gouging. At one stage the dispute between the pair looked like heading to court.

Since arriving the previous December and playing 27 matches, I hadn't lined up against Sterlo and John Muggleton. Now I was facing them twice in a week. We flogged Hull 46-12 in the premiership play-off, and we left that game pretty confident of repeating the dose at Wembley.

It was springtime now, and the weather had improved. Life was much better; it wasn't getting dark until close to 9 o'clock at night, and my parents had arrived from Australia. In a generous gesture, Wigan offered to fly them over for the match, along with Julie's mum. But Julie's mother decided she didn't want to fly. We managed to squeeze my parents into our tiny house for two weeks and it was really special to have them there for such a big occasion, so far from home.

We travelled to London a couple days before the game and booked into a hotel not far from the ground. On the day before the match all the wives and girlfriends and families went down by coach and were installed in a nearby hotel. After the game the players were allowed to swap to be with their families.

On the Friday before match day we went down to Wembley to get a feel of the place. It was my first glimpse of the magical stadium, and I wasn't disappointed. The turf had the look of a bowling green. It was awesome to look up at the huge stands. It sort of reached out and touched you even when it was empty and I thought: "I wonder what it's like when it's full." We weren't allowed to train on the pitch but we took a ball out anyway and started mucking around until the penny dropped and we were hunted off.

We trained on a nearby park, and didn't see Wembley again until the team coach turned in there the next day. Our dressing room was the biggest and most luxurious I'd seen in my life. The team bath was the size of a diving pool, the tiles immaculately polished. You could have used the place for a function room. Once the gear was in we stuck to tradition and headed out to inspect the playing field. We reached that along the longest tunnel you've ever seen. Then it was over the dog track and onto the turf. The stadium was about a quarter full at that stage, but even so the noise the fans made as soon as we appeared was pretty impressive. There were flags everywhere, but I still wasn't prepared for what hit me when we walked out the tunnel the next time.

We were briefed of the formalities we had to go through before the match. Both teams came out of their dressing rooms at the same time and marched down the tunnel, on opposite sides. In front of the main stand we were introduced to the League hierarchy and the special guest, this year the Earl of Derby. I told the blokes I was disappointed it wasn't Princess Di. Then we peeled off one by one and headed across the pitch, to toss the ball around for a couple of minutes before kick-off. It was ritualistic and very new to me. In the four grand finals I played in, it was just a case of running out onto the field and then — the whistle sounded and it was on.

I'll never forget the arrival at the end of the tunnel after the long walk that day. The cheers that greeted us were literally deafening. All this was exciting to me because it was so new and so grand — but to the Poms it was more than that.

It was what they played the game for. To be at Wembley is heaven on earth for a league player in England.

We had tracksuit tops on and I like to stay as calm and relaxed as I can before a game. So I put my hands in my pockets as we strolled slowly to the line-up to meet all the big wigs. Without me realising it, that's where my hands stayed. If I hadn't, I would have probably put my hands behind my back. But I just did what came naturally — I didn't think it was any big deal. Then Maurice Lindsay headed down the line and, one by one, introduced us to the Earl of Derby and another dignitary. Maurice told him I was an Australian and he stopped for a brief chat. I pulled one hand out of my pocket, shook the Duke's hand and he moved on. Well, apparently the BBC commentator Ray French was insulted because I kept my hands in my pockets and looked uninterested in the whole thing (which I wasn't!), including during the playing of God Save The Queen. Former Great Britain international Brian Briggs was quoted in *Rugby League Week* as saying: "It was an insult to the occasion, I thought he showed arrogance of the worst kind ... it was bloody disgusting." The issue of my "casual" behaviour really blew up in the press in the days following the match. What I had done, or failed to do, just wasn't the done thing, especially at the 50th final at Wembley in front of some of the game's greatest players who had paraded before kick-off. I had no idea what all the fuss was about. It was no big deal at all to me — but it certainly was for the English. In the same *Rugby League Week* story, journalist Ian Heads probably summed things up well when he explained: "Kenny did virtually nothing different from what he does in Sydney on grand final day. Kenny switches off, never runs onto the field and walks around seemingly engrossed in his own thoughts."

Fortunately, I redeemed myself during the match, which many people now claim was the finest Challenge Cup final ever played. I was one of 10 overseas players in the game — four Australians and six Kiwis — and it was the first time the match was telecast live to Australia. I can remember every try and most of the match because I've seen it on video plenty of times. We had a bad start and Hull led 6-0 after just 11 minutes. Sterlo handled twice to set up a try for their winger, Kevin James. I let my opposite five-eighth Fred Ah Kuoi stand in a tackle, and then I followed fullback Gary Kemble across too far, leaving Henderson Gill stranded. Kemble flicked a pass inside to James and they scored. It wasn't the best start to my big day at Wembley.

Six minutes later we hit back, and I had a hand in it. I saw a small gap but got caught going through. I was able to stand and flick the ball out the back to Ian Potter who sent Chicka Ferguson in for a try. About 10 minutes later we hit the lead for the first time when I cut through to score a 50-metre try after getting a good, long ball from halfback Mike Ford. I just found the gap ... and kept going; I was looking for Henderson Gill but couldn't find him so, with Hull's fullback Kemble coming across, I thought I'd better go for it. I just snuck in at the left corner.

We led 16-8 at halftime and three minutes into the second half Shaun Edwards scored, from a pass which I reckon was slightly forward from me after I twisted out of Sterlo's attempted tackle. We led 22-8 — and we thought it was all over.

We'd won at Wembley! Well, we hadn't — but we relaxed. What we forgot was that a champion named Peter Sterling was in the other side. Single-handedly he almost led Hull back to the biggest shock win of all time.

A couple of minutes after we had got to 22-8 Sterlo made a great 35-metre run and flung a ball inside for their centre Steve Evans to score. 22-12. Then came the strangest of tries. Chicka Ferguson was down getting treatment on his leg and I noticed him hobbling for a while and thought he'd go off. The next thing Hull were attacking on their left and the ball went out to their winger Dane O'Hara who stumbled and fell just as the pass got to him. Up sprung Chicka; he picked up the ball, got rid of the wobbles and ran 50 metres to score. We had two goalkickers that day; Henderson Gill kicked from one side of the field, David Stephenson from the other. Gilly kicked the conversion and with 29 minutes remaining we led 28-12. This time we didn't relax straight away and with 16 minutes to go, the score was still the same. Surely now there was no doubt; get the champagne ready.

Hull by now had brought on Gary Divorty and Garry Schofield as replacements, both whom I thought would have been in their starting line-up. There was a big controversy about Schofield being on the bench. He was about 19 then and had been in great form in the centres, but for some reason their coach Arthur Bunting decided not to start him. Both were on the field when Hull scored a typically English try. John Muggleton was allowed to play the ball sideways, despite having a Wigan player marking him at the play-the-ball. He passed to Sterlo, who found Divorty and then James Leuluai used a shepherd to get away and score. It was 28-16, and still no great no cause for alarm. Unbelievably, we then let Hull in for two tries in two minutes and thank God neither was converted, because the scores would have been level! I couldn't believe it.

I was pretty quiet normally but after the second try which brought the score to 28-24 with a kick to come, I blew up for the first time since joining Wigan. Graeme West was trying to rally everyone and I just told them that I would have thought they'd learned from losing the previous year. "If you want to do the same thing again, just keep going on like you are. You've just dropped your bundle and relaxed, the game's not over yet," I snapped. The intensity had dropped right off and instead of having a comfortable lead, we were in trouble. Our centre Steve Donlan said to me after the game he couldn't believe I went off like I did. No one expected it, but he said it was the best thing that happened because, having always been so quiet, it hit home. Well almost.

We kicked deep and got in Hull's quarter and contained them well when they had the ball. But when we got possession Mike Ford received a pass, and hesitated, before trying to get a pass to me. I could see it happening as if in slow motion. James Leuluai came through and intercepted and I thought: "This is it, he's going to go all the way and score." But luckily he was run down and we were able to keep them at bay for the last couple of minutes. I got the ball and kicked it into touch just to waste some time. A few tackles later it was all over.

As soon as the hooter went our blokes were jumping up and down but straight away I looked for Sterlo. I really felt for him. He was on the ground when I went over to him to shake his hand. He was shattered. Without him, I reckon we would have won by 20. By now the field was just a sea of bodies; all the players and support staff had come off the bench and there were supporters everywhere. I finally found Muggo and shook hands, then joined the rest of the Wigan players for the long climb up the steps to receive the trophy. The fans were singing, and the scene was unbelievable. Almost 98,000 people (97,801 in fact), twice as many as we fit in at a game in Australia, can sure make some noise. When I got my medal and it was my turn to hold up the cup, I didn't know what to do. The players in front of me had held it aloft, and kissed it. I sort of just grabbed it, held it up for a second and gave it to the next bloke.

As we walked down someone told me I'd won the Lance Todd Trophy awarded to the player of the match. I didn't even know they had an award! And when I found out later I was the first Australian to win it, I was chuffed, to use a good Pommy expression. *Rugby League Week's* Ian Heads was there covering the match and he told me in the dressing room afterwards that people bet on who was going to win the award, and that Sterlo and I had been the favourites. All the publicity before the game was about Parramatta team-mates Sterling and Kenny being the key players and the odds were pretty fair that one of us would go close to winning it. I wish I knew there was betting, I would have had a punt! It was actually months after I'd returned home before I got the miniature replica of the trophy. It now holds pride of place at home.

Once we went down the stairs it was off for a victory lap, English-style. It was a long way around the dog track and so many people came out to congratulate us. I managed to get separated from the rest of the players. It was lonely really, it took so long and for most of it I just walked around by myself. But the way the people sang and chanted and cheered for us was incredible.

Nothing could compare to the next day when we got back to Wigan, though. I've never experienced anything like that in my life.

We stayed the night in London and had a dinner with our families. Next morning we were up for the coach trip back to Wigan — about a three-hour drive. As we got close to Central Park there were people lining the streets, and when we got to the car-park, the police had to clear a path to get us through. We slowly made it from the bus into the clubhouse and from there were ushered into the boardroom overlooking the ground. People were climbing on top of each other to touch the window. When I looked out I couldn't see a blade of grass, a seat in the stand or a metre of cement on the terrace. Central Park officially held about 37,000 then and it seemed like there were double that number of people at the ground to welcome us home. It was absolute chaos. Even The Beatles surely wouldn't have had this sort of reception in their heyday.

We couldn't stay long that day because I had to get my parents to the airport. But when we walked out to find the car, there were people walking over the top of it! It took 15 minutes just to get the 50 metres to the car, but from there, there was no way out. Luckily, someone from the club saw what was happening and the police stepped in and gave us an escort out of town. They stuck with us halfway to Manchester airport. After saying goodbye to mum and dad, Julie and I went home. What was going on at Central Park was overwhelming, and I doubt we would have made it back to the clubhouse anyway.

The whole experience is something I'll never forget. It remains vividly in my mind: the fact we won and the fact I was the first Australian to win the Lance Todd Trophy. Chicka Ferguson and I were the first of the new breed of Australian players who went across and won at Wembley after the international ban was lifted in 1983. It was just magic, and to have experienced it means the world to me. It was the wrong message if people got the idea that I didn't get a buzz out of the whole thing, because of the way I sauntered around the field before and after the match. That was just me ... my way of handling extreme nervousness. I wouldn't swap the memory of that day for anything.

And if it hadn't been for Neil and Donna Hunt wanting some company ... it would never have happened.

The fairy-tale ended there. The trouble was that we had to back up against St Helens three days later for the premiership semi-final. Can you imagine a team winning the grand final in Sydney then having to play a semi-final of another competition three days later? I couldn't come to grips with it. Unfortunately, after the triumph of Wembley, the very next Tuesday became perhaps the most controversial day of my life in football ... the day I was accused of throwing a match.

13 They Said I Didn't Try

The match against St Helens was scheduled for the Tuesday after Wembley. Our celebrations after the Challenge Cup win ended sometime late Monday. Perhaps you can imagine the task we faced. But we had no choice — the game was on, and we had to play it, and play it at St Helens' home ground to make things even tougher. The reality of this peculiarly English competition was that we had one, possibly two more games to play after winning the greatest prize of all. I'll admit I had difficulty getting "up" for the match and I don't think there's much doubt it was the same for the rest of the team, considering the way we played.

We were thrashed, comprehensively, 37-14. Mal Meninga scored a try and did a tonne of the damage for St Helens. I had a very quiet match just three days after being the toast of Wembley. I learned later that Wigan fans were yelling out "C'mon Kenny" and "Get into the game, Kenny" — comments I didn't hear at the time. I didn't think I was *that* bad, but after being hailed as a hero just a few days earlier, I certainly didn't live up to the fans' expectations.

The club had booked some tentative flights for us to return home. One was on the Thursday if we were beaten by St Helens, the other the following Monday in the event that we made it to the final. Julie and I had been a long time away from home; Parramatta were getting anxious for me to return and I'll admit I was looking forward to going back. But I refute completely the whispered rumour that I didn't try in that semi-final against the Saints.

We left on the Thursday, dropping our car down to Central Park and hitching a ride to the airport with a couple of the players. It was a happy farewell — but there was a lot more yet to be heard of that great anti-climax of a match that followed Wembley.

The following September, four months later, with Parramatta into the semi-finals of the 1985 season, *Sydney Morning Herald* reporter Tony Sarno came to training to do a feature article on me. He started the piece by harking back to my stint with Wigan, and mentioned my casual approach to all the formalities at Wembley. Sarno then turned his attention to the match against St Helens. I was quoted (wrongly from my point of view) as saying that at one stage in the match I pulled up after making a break and purposely lobbed the ball over the head of my support player so it went into touch and the movement broke down. According to the *SMH*, Julie was supposed to have been waiting outside the ground with our bags packed, ready to go straight to the airport, so keen were we to get away. It made me look like I wanted to lose the match and skip the country as soon as possible.

I saw red. Neither contention was true. I did make a break during the game and, with a St Helens player in between me and my centre, I had no choice but to throw the ball over the top. It missed him and went to ground. That was the only incident I can recall I could have spoken about to the reporter. I admitted I didn't play well and wasn't particularly keyed up for the match, considering it was three days after Wembley. I was actually taken off in the second half after copping a whack on the head which left me pretty groggy. I told him that we lost the game, and it was disappointing, but I'd won at Wembley, so losing to St Helens wasn't going to be something I would be dirty on for the rest of my life. That was how I felt then and still do.

Any suggestion that I threw the game because I was so keen to return to Australia was mischievous and plain wrong. Furthermore, we weren't due to fly out until two days after the game, so why would I say Julie was waiting at the airport? In fact, she was at home. The people next to us had a radio and often listened to the Wigan games. You could hear the radio through the wall and that day Julie actually listened in to some of the match at home. That's how she knew we lost. We'd been in England five months; why the hell would a couple more days have made any difference?

Rugby League Week followed up with a story from their English correspondent, who asked Wigan coach Colin Clarke if he remembered the incident. Colin responded by saying he had nothing but praise for my efforts for Wigan and couldn't remember any such incident in the match against St Helens. But then Don Furner, the then Canberra Raiders coach, had a go at me in his *Sunday Telegraph* column. He said virtually everything but that he wouldn't like to have me in his side. He wrote:

I couldn't believe a statement attributed to Brett Kenny that he deliberately threw a pass over the head of a fellow player to lose a game in England to ensure he would make his flight back to Sydney. I have to admit I didn't think anyone would make such a statement but as I haven't read a denial I take it that the statement was correct. Even if Kenny did throw such a pass why would he want to admit it — to be shown to be letting down his team-mates and his employer. It must really gall the players who were in that team knowing that such a champion player had let them down.

Don was unaware that I hadn't had a chance to deny the story and that I was already taking legal advice on the matter. Nor had he been at the match to witness the supposed "incident". The irony was that a year later he was my Australian coach!

Wigan coach Colin Clarke said in England the next week:

We are well aware of what Kenny has been reported as saying. If it is true I find it totally amazing — unbelievable. In the five months he was here his attitude was superb. He was a model player and a coach's dream.....none of us can remember an incident in the St Helens match like the one he describes.

Clarke went on to make some comments about Julie — about her not trying to settle in and that situation putting pressure on me. I thought they were unfair comments from the coach 'though he added: "But it never seemed to affect his attitude on the field".

When I got to the Sydney Cricket Ground the following weekend some of the press guys quizzed me and I told them I didn't say the things I was alleged to have said — that the *SMH* had got it wrong. They suggested I should take legal action and when I thought about it later, I decided they were right. I'll stand accused of being casual and outwardly unexcitable — but *never* of purposely trying to lose a football match. Jack Gibson steered me towards a solicitor and I took action against the *Sydney Morning Herald*, *Rugby League Week* and the *Sunday Telegraph*. I was told it could be a long drawn-out process, which it was. In the end the *Sunday Telegraph* settled out of court and I decided to leave it at that. I'd copped plenty of good and bad press over the years, but that was the one time when I felt I had been really dudded. I became sharper at knowing who to talk freely to and who to be wary of or to avoid altogether in the press.

To be honest, I've got very few complaints about the media over the years. My attitude is that if you don't play well you've got to cop the bad press just as you accept it readily when you're getting all the wraps. Other than that one occasion, what has been said about me in the media hasn't concerned me too much one way or the other.

When I returned to Wigan with the 1986 Kangaroos 15 months later, I wondered what sort of response I would get at Central Park. We played Wigan in the first match of the tour and I was keen for a good game to show that I was still a good player and thoroughly worthy of returning to Central Park as an Australian Test player. When the Australian team coach pulled up at just about the same spot where we battled to hop into our car the day after we won at Wembley, I was swamped with autograph-hunters. It was great to be back. After we put our gear in the dressing room a bunch of us decided to head out into the middle to check the conditions.

I was talking with Wally Lewis as we walked along the tunnel from the dressing room, then I started daydreaming I suppose as we walked out. I thought Wally was just a pace behind me. Little did I know that he told all the other players to stay where they were, so I ended up walking out onto the field by myself. Well, the crowd let out this huge cheer and started chanting my name — I didn't know what was going on. Then I looked around and saw Wally and the others laughing their heads off back at the end of the tunnel. They'd set me up, but in hindsight, it was a nice gesture, and a great way to break the ice. The Wigan people remembered me for the good things I'd done in '85 — not for that last game against St Helens.

I was determined to have a good game — good enough anyway, considering we hadn't played for a couple of weeks. I expected a tough game but I didn't expect any extra treatment from the Wigan players, and I didn't get any. We won 26-18 in front of more than 30,000 people. I had a pretty fair game, and realised that Wigan were still the major force in British rugby league. It was hard for even me to believe, having experienced the professionalism of the place, just how much they would dominate in the next few years.

We went back to Central Park for the third Test, and it was the toughest match of that second undefeated tour. I knew then I'd never go back. I took a good long look around the ground at fulltime, breathed the place in. Central Park and the people of Wigan will always signify good memories for me — well, mostly. Now and then there had been times when the weather was at its worst and we were in the depths of homesickness and I would have been happy to take the next plane home. But we humans tend to remember the good times rather than the tough times a few years down the track — and that's certainly how it is with Wigan and me.

But there was never a chance I would go back — even when Ray Price bounced the idea off me when he was at Wakefield Trinity four or five years later. The Wembley win of 1985 was an impossible act to follow ... and I wasn't even going to try.

14 The Reluctant Blue

When I got home from England in June 1985 I was tired and stale — both physically and mentally. I had played 25 games for Wigan, the last 15 in five and a half weeks. I landed on a Friday and it was planned that I would have the weekend off to "freshen up". But when Steve Ella was a late drop-out from the match against Manly, I was asked to play. I touched down on Friday, trained on Saturday and played on Sunday. Parramatta were in the middle of an injury crisis, although nicely placed, second on 14 points from eight rounds, a point behind St George. Manly were just a point behind us, and I agreed to play because it was such an important match. It was a funny feeling, a bit uncomfortable. I hadn't played with the Parramatta players since the 1984 grand final; the pace and style of the Sydney game was very different from what I had been used to up to the previous Tuesday. I played accordingly, i.e. not too flash and we went down 14-10. John Muggleton and Peter Sterling were still on their way home.

That night the City and Country sides were picked (it was the second season Country were allowed six Sydney-based players). In the lead-up there had been a big fuss made by the Australian Rugby League and the representative selectors that anyone who returned late from England could not expect to be picked in the representative teams. Frankly, I didn't expect to be chosen. The Australian clubs weren't happy with the situation of players trickling back from England where they had picked up some extra cash, and that certainly went for Parramatta. Eric Grothe and Neil Hunt had returned just a week before me, Paul Taylor and Chris Phelan a couple of weeks earlier, and we were still waiting for Sterlo and Muggo.

ARL Supremo Ken Arthurson was in Paris for an International Board meeting and the day I arrived home there was an article in the paper suggesting that Australian players would be banned from playing for English clubs in future unless they returned before the start of the Australian season. It looked as though I was one of the last of the breed to go north for a full season, then be allowed back in to the Winfield Cup. Within a few weeks the ARL softened their stance and declared players had to be back by March 31 (a month and a half before I'd returned). This rule remained until 1989 when the date was brought forward to February 1. The change has meant that few topline players have gone to English clubs since. I guess I was lucky to get the English experience that I did.

I was interviewed by the *Telegraph's* Phil Rothfield at the airport minutes after I'd put my feet on Australia soil, and this is what I told him: "I loved the football and the experience but to be honest I really don't fancy going back. Even for the Kangaroo tour next year I'd have to give it a lot of thought." On the possibility of playing for the City or NSW side: "I know I'd be dirty if I'd been playing in Sydney all along and they picked someone ahead of me who had been playing in England."

When I got home, the last thing I wanted to do was play representative football anyway because we'd just moved into our first home, I didn't have a job and I was so tired mentally that I didn't want to contemplate the thought of any extra matches. It's not a great opening line when you're looking for employment to say: "By the way, I'll need time off every few weeks to play for NSW or Australia." Peter Sterling and Mal Meninga were the only regular rep players who returned from England later than me that year. The City side was chosen the night I played against Manly and the NSW and Queensland teams were scheduled for a week later. I never gave selection a thought.

I was thankfully overlooked for the City and Steve Ella was chosen as five-eighth, Andrew Farrar and Michael O'Connor in the centres. Sterlo captained Country the year before but this time Steve Mortimer got his spot, plus the captaincy, for the match which became infamous for Mortimer's dubious tackle on Michael O'Connor — a tackle made just a few weeks after Jim Comans had warned Mortimer: "Football will be a memory to you" if he found himself back in the judiciary room. Turvey escaped with a warning and went on to captain NSW to their first Origin series win.

A week later, Parramatta beat Easts 34-8 and I won the Dally M points as best player. The week's rest had certainly helped. But I couldn't believe it when I was chosen for NSW, particularly after being overlooked, and rightly so, for the City team. I was sure I wouldn't have been considered; I'd only just unpacked my bags and played two games in Australia. And what happened to the big warning about players going away not having the right to expect to be picked straight away? To be honest, I didn't think it was fair to the blokes who had been going well in the Winfield Cup, even though I'd received a lot of exposure by playing at Wembley.

I have always set goals throughout my career. Once achieved, I would look for more goals. I knew I couldn't get out of playing for NSW without being stood down for Parramatta matches because of the strict rule of the time. But the more I thought of it, the more I realised that the one goal I *hadn't* achieved was winning a State of Origin series. So, as unexpected as it was, I thought it was an opportunity to latch onto. I headed down to the medical to be confronted by new coach Terry Fearnley and captain Steve Mortimer who was unbelievably keyed-up to beat the Queenslanders.

My selection at five-eighth was at the cost of Steve Ella, who was relegated to the bench. I virtually apologised to Zip, who too often seemed to be made a reserve for representative matches.

The great irony about me being in the NSW side against all the odds in 1985 was that it turned out to be NSW's first win — and that I ended up scoring the try that wrapped up the series.

It was only the second year that the NSW players were stood down from club matches and thus were able to match the preparation of the Queenslanders. I'm sure it was a major factor in the win. The spirit of Steve Mortimer was a bonus, too.

Turvey was so passionate about NSW winning and his attitude rubbed off on a lot of players and went a long way towards creating good team morale.

Terry Fearnley was an excellent coach in that situation too. There isn't time to worry about any fancy, complex tactics in Origin matches, and Terry decided to stick to the basics of us kicking deep and keeping the pressure on Queensland. He was spot on in predicting what to expect from certain players. He'd worked out that every time Wally Lewis went to first receiver we should rush him because it meant he was going to kick; when he was second receiver we shouldn't charge him because he was going to run or pick up a player outside. The tactics worked well. Terry was also the first coach who wanted me to kick in general play — something that had always been done by Mick Cronin or Peter Sterling at Parramatta. One play we used was that on the first scrum of the match just inside Queensland's half, I'd kick deep and try to get the ball into the in-goal. They'd be up flat and not expecting it; the chance was there for a try or for us to pin them in the in-goal or on their line. Everytime I tried it at training the ball never went where it was supposed to go, but from the first scrum in midfield at Lang Park I put the kick in and it was spot on. Queensland got caught behind their line and we had possession back in great field position from the line drop-out.

Terry Fearnley had given Steve Mortimer a brief to "gee up" the players and Turvey was free to talk tactics without the coach being around. Turvey is one of the most emotional blokes I've ever met and he wanted to beat Queensland real bad. He seemed to always be at us; there were meetings in his room throughout the week. On the way to Lang Park for the first game he got the driver to stop the bus and talked about how all these Queensland supporters were coming to watch us getting beaten and how we had to spoil their party. Before the match he patrolled the room, speaking individually to all the players. His keenness did rub off — although not as much on me as some of the other blokes. I'm just not into group rev-up sessions or shouting and crying. I just listen and nod my head — then do my own thing, go back to my own world. A lot of other players were super-inspired by Turvey Mortimer, but not me — although I appreciated how pumped up he was.

We beat Queensland 18-2 at Lang Park in that first game, with Michael O'Connor scoring all our points in his debut match (two tries, five goals). It had been raining all day and rained for much of the match but we played with good control, and purpose. Knowing the second match was to be at the Sydney Cricket Ground, we were confident of winning our first series.

But I was really feeling jaded. I'd had no break from football for a long time, and had been pitched straight back into club football then rep football as soon as I got home. At that time there were no split rounds, so you backed up from the Tuesday Origin match and played for your club on the weekend. I had the additional worry that I still didn't have a job. When I was chosen for the second game, I actually asked to be rested from it — and from all other rep matches for the rest of the season — because I didn't think I could do justice to the teams. I was worried I would let someone down because I had lost the desire to play football. But Terry Fearnley took me aside and told me he wanted me in the team, and I finally relented. There were no problems about me wanting to win for NSW, it was just that I felt lethargic all the time. I wasn't getting nervous before games. I just felt, subconsciously, that I'd had enough football.

As it turned out it was my try right on fulltime that sealed our first-ever Origin series victory, in the second game at the SCG. We had led the game 12-0 early; Steve Mortimer put up a bomb which I regathered and then he hoisted another one from dummy-half and his brother Chris scored. Then Benny Elias went over after one of his big dummies. But Queensland struck back to lead 14-12 early in the second half. A goal and then a Michael O'Connor field goal got us back to 15-14.

Late in the game I took a pass just inside the Queensland quarter. I saw Wally Lewis on my right, sold him a dummy, and was able to squeeze between Dave Brown and Tony Currie to score. Steve Mortimer must have been backing up because the first thing I saw as I looked up was Turvey flying over the top of me. He sailed straight over me and then starting kissing the ground. He knew we'd won — that it was too late for Queensland to get back into the game.

Turvey had announced to us in the days leading up to the game that this would be his last series for NSW. In fact it was his last match in the famous blue jumper. I've never seen a bloke so happy to win a football match.

In between the second and third Origin games there was an Australian tour of New Zealand. Although I was reluctantly prepared to play for NSW, I just couldn't afford to play in the Tests against the Kiwis, one of which was to be held in Brisbane and the other two during a two-and-a-half-week tour of New Zealand. The third Test wasn't until July, which meant I would have been back in Sydney almost two months without the chance to even look seriously for a job, or without having spent barely a day getting the new house organised. Additionally Parramatta would have seen almost nothing of me until the last six rounds of the premiership. So I wrote to the Australian Rugby League and asked if I could be excused from the tour on compassionate grounds. When the news got out that I was going to try to miss the tour, the media had a field day. The contention about how a player should never turn his back on playing for his country was flung around by former Test players, by media experts and just about everyone on the street.

I'll talk more of the "other" side of representing later but this time it was purely a personal decision. I simply couldn't afford to be away from home at that stage of my life. I know I upset a lot of people by saying at the time that I didn't care if I didn't get to play for NSW and Australia again, but the fact that I said it showed just how drained I felt. I knew that in that frame of mind in a Test match, I wasn't going to help my Australian team-mates much. I realised my actions may have stopped me playing for Australia again, that selectors and influential officials may well hold a grudge. It was a risk I had to take.

The ARL granted me my wish and so I wasn't chosen for what ended up the most controversial tour of New Zealand ever, with huge drama surrounding Terry Fearnley's dropping of four Queenslanders — Chris Close, my '82 Kangaroo tour "roomy" Mark Murray, Greg Dowling and Greg Conescu. It wasn't a bad tour to miss. I was good mates with a lot of the Queenslanders and I sure didn't regret not being around when all the unsavoury business blew up.

The Queenslanders hadn't forgotten the events of New Zealand when we headed back to Lang Park for the final Origin match. Their fury, plus the fact referee Barry Gomersall gave us a hard time from the start, made it pretty obvious we weren't going to win the series 3-0. Chris Mortimer turned around after one early penalty and flung up his arms in frustration. I just told him not to worry about it, it was going to be one of those nights. Queensland didn't want to lose 3-0 and Gomersall wasn't going to do us any favours. The Maroons came out like men possessed, obviously fired up and ready to show Terry Fearnley a thing or two after the events in New Zealand. I was caught in the middle of it all — and it was a bit hard for me to come to terms with, being oblivious to what went on over there. We copped a caning in the penalties plus the full brunt of the Queensland players' aggression and went down 20-6. But the series had been won and it didn't bother me too much. I had played a part in an historic "first". Looking back I'm obviously glad I didn't get my wish to be stood down from the series.

The next year the Blues had a change of coach, with Ron Willey stepping in. Ron and Terry Fearnley were like chalk and cheese. Terry was quiet and calculating, very reserved by nature. Everything he said made sense, and had obviously been thoroughly thought out. Ron was more of the "old style" coach. A jovial bloke, he'd say things in a more general round-about way. He didn't seem to me to be the type of coach who sat for hours studiously analysing things.

At training one day Ron told us that when we ran with the ball to realise that our opposing backs were only going to worry about the man they were individually marking. He reckoned the Queenslanders were so intent on getting over the top of their opposite numbers, and into the Australian side, that they'd stick with their own man. He suggested we use decoys to confuse the issue. It worked pretty well.

Ron also made his well-recorded famous speech about chipping in our own quarter — the one in which he told a long yarn about a mate of his who was now one of those down-and-out blokes you see sleeping on the park benches around Woolloomooloo. I was scratching my head, not knowing what Ron was going on about, until he came out with the punchline that the bloke was so down-and-out because he had the nerve one day to chip in his own quarter! Ron Willey also reckoned all games were won by physical intimidation up front, and NSW were pretty well covered in that area with Wayne Pearce, Steve Folkes, Noel Cleal, Peter Tunks, Royce Simmons and Steve Roach plus David Gillespie, a pack that was unchanged in all three games.

I reckon we won the 1986 series 3-0 because of the confidence we gained from 1985, plus the fact that we had a pretty hot side. I played in some great NSW teams in earlier years but the outstanding difference in 1985-86 was that we didn't have to play for our clubs the Sunday before the Tuesday Origin match.

Steve Mortimer had talked on the subject of "mateship" and suggested that players before 1985 didn't really care too much for the NSW cause. I didn't agree. Sydney was the centre of world rugby league, boasting the toughest competition in the world — and it was embarrassing to be beaten by a Queensland side which had a heap of its players based in the lower-standard Brisbane competition. In the early Origin years our preparations were always unsettled. We'd play for our clubs 48 hours beforehand and go to the medical on Monday morning. Generally there'd be two or three blokes drop out with injury or someone given the benefit of the doubt only to drop out the day of the game. You'd hit the 60-minute mark of an

Origin game and fatigue would set in. There was certainly no lack of effort or pride within the NSW ranks — it was more that the make-up of the team kept changing and too often we ran out of steam thanks to the previous Sunday's club football.

We won the first match of 1986 20-16 at Lang Park in a match I remember most for the try by Royce Simmons from dummy-half which brought us from 16-12 behind to 18-16 in front. It was the try that virtually won the match. There was some luck attached to it, in that Peter Sterling was calling for the ball for a kick and the Queensland markers shot out so fast to stop him that the space just opened up for Simmo and he had no option but to go for it himself. It was the game in which Simmo was in "Disneyland" early, weaving like a drunken sailor after taking a knock. Royce Simmons, who took over from 1985 hooker Ben Elias, was a tough, reliable player and to be honest I preferred him in my side rather than Benny because he played the percentage game better. Benny had more tricks in his repertoire but he was inclined to go by himself or try some fancy play when you had something else planned.

In Singapore on the way home from the 1986 Kangaroo tour we had to draw a name out of a hat and buy a tour mate a Christmas present. Don Furner drew Benny and bought him a Mickey Mouse doll, announcing he picked that because Benny always wanted to try the Mickey Mouse plays. That probably summed him up, although I would never deny that he was a fine and talented player.

We won the second match, 24-20 at the SCG and I recall that Barry Gomersall gave us the best run of penalties we ever received under him in State of Origin football. We completed the clean sweep with an 18-16 win at Lang Park, the match ending with me forcing a grubber kick in-goal — then the ball slipping out from under, and Dale Shearer storming through and claiming a try. I would have tried exactly the same thing if I had been Rowdy but there was no doubt I'd forced the ball. That was the only time I won an Origin man-of-the-match award and I think it was my best series all-round — with Sterlo and me combining well throughout. We got a lot of wraps for our performances that year.

I obviously preferred Sterlo as my halfback partner in Origin because I knew his play so well. Steve Mortimer was a great player but I found him a bit difficult to play with. I was only alongside him for two matches in 1985 and I'd reckon it would take a bit of practice to get a sense of what Turvey might do. He'd often dart himself and you'd just lose him; he was hard to follow. Other times he'd go for a run, see that he wasn't going to get through, and then fire out a pass when you least expected it. I'd be caught flat-footed thinking, well I guess I'd better have a go now. But his ability and methods worked brilliantly for Canterbury and extremely effectively for NSW in 1985. Turvey had a great impact on the first two matches and I still regard him as one of the most dangerous opponents I ever faced ... and that's not even taking into account his outstanding cover defence.

To win the Origin series for the first time in 1985 was great, to win 3-0 in 1986 was even better. When we went back to Lang Park in 1987 and won the first match of the series again, I thought we would bring up the hat-trick. We'd won seven out of eight since the third game of 1984. But in the second match at the SCG we went down in the mud, 12-6; Barry Gomersall caned us 10-4 in the penalties and at one stage we went 53 minutes without getting one at all. But that night the better side won, although Sterlo was man of the match with a great performance.

It seemed that one loss sparked the sort of panic from the NSW selectors that they too often displayed before 1985. We had a couple of late changes because of injury before that second game but selectors made no less than 10 changes to the side, either positional switches or changes of personnel, for the third — and I was back in the centres which I wasn't particularly pleased about. My record against Wally Lewis when I had played five-eighth against him was eight wins and four losses, but I was banished to the centres with Andrew Ettingshausen, with second-game centres Brian Johnston and Michael O'Connor switched to the wings. We went down 10-8 in probably the closest and most exciting Origin match of all the games I played. It was my last match for NSW. There were so many near misses in a scoreless second half and when Brian Johnston and myself combined to put Cliff Lyons away at one stage I was sure he'd score — but Gary Belcher ran him down. As it was, a penalty kick landed by Dale Shearer, from yet another controversial penalty awarded by Gomersall (for Michael O'Connor being offside chasing a Cliff Lyons chip kick), won Queensland the match and the series.

I don't think Barry Gomersall was ever up to Origin standard, and I think the Queensland hierarchy knew that. Why he was plucked out of country football to control Origin games and even Test matches I'll never know. He was so unpredictable at times, it was ridiculous.

One regret I have about ending my State of Origin career when I did (other than not being picked to go to Los Angeles for the fourth match of 1987) was that I never played a big match at the Sydney Football Stadium. I finished representative football in 1987, the last year of the SCG as "league headquarters". If my plans to play one more season of rep football in 1988 hadn't been ruined by a knee injury I would have played, perhaps, the first Origin match at the Sydney Football Stadium and the first Test match there, against the Poms in 1988. They would have been two more worthy "firsts" to add to my list.

I played club football at the stadium — the first time in a Monday Night Football match in 1988. The biggest crowd I played before at league's new home was about 20,000 at the World Sevens in 1992. Playing before a half-full (or less) football stadium is not the same as running out to a wildly NSW-biased, jam-packed Origin crowd, and I'm disappointed I missed the opportunity. Then again, not one of my Parramatta team-mates in 1993 had played a big match at the Sydney Cricket Ground. You can't have everything in a career!

The game is now in a completely new era. The SCG was a great place to play when there was a big crowd on hand. There was a big space between players and the fans but the place had so much character to it. People say I played my best football there, and I'm proud of my record of 14 tries in 19 finals at the SCG (I scored a "duck" in four games in 1984!). Everytime you got to the SCG you knew it was for a big match — whether it was finals football, Origin or Test matches. They were big occasions and all of us get pumped up for those. I loved the feel of the place and I really can't fairly compare it to the SFS — because Parramatta have never made a semi-final since it was built, and I had departed from rep football by the time it was built. I like the place — but I never got to taste it at its best ... on a warm, clear day or night, with the grandstands full.

15 Order of the (Golden) Boot

One day in the early stages of the 1986 Kangaroo tour Harry Edgar of *Open Rugby* magazine came up to me and told me I had won the Golden Boot. "Oh yeah?" I thought. "Great ... what's that?" Over the next couple of years as the award gained more exposure and prestige, I began to realise to have won it was perhaps the greatest honour of my career.

People look at other sports and say things like: yeah, Viv Richards is the best batsman in the world, Dennis Lillee is the best bowler; or Boris Becker is the best tennis player or Carl Lewis the best runner. When I think of them my thought is: "Gee, they *were* good, the very best." In 1986 I was voted the best rugby league player in the world.

It was one of only three individual awards I ever won, outside of club awards. In 1985 I won the Lance Todd Trophy for the best player in the Challenge Cup final and in '86 I won my only Dally M award, rated representative player of the year. In winning the Golden Boot I joined pretty exalted company. It's an international award that only seven people have won: Wally Lewis in 1985, me, Peter Sterling and Hugh McGahan (shared) in 1987, Garry Jack in 1988, Ellery Hanley in 1989 and Mal Meninga in 1990. It's a shame the award didn't continue after that — because it was a wonderful concept. I hope Adidas (who discontinued sponsorship) or someone else picks it up again.

I was as proud as punch when Harry Edgar broke the news to me that cold day in England. It was the day of our traditional photo call at Headingley, Leeds. He explained that the award was voted on by journalists in all the league-playing countries, and that there would be a presentation at the Dragonara Hotel in a couple of weeks. I had to keep the news to myself until then.

Later that week, I had to go back to Headingley to get some photos taken with the trophy, which is in fact a gold (painted I think) boot, to fit in with the magazine's deadlines. Therein lies a funny story.

I wasn't allowed to tell anyone before the presentation took place, so I didn't. Not even Julie. The day I was handed the award I rang her — and she couldn't believe I hadn't told her. But everytime I had rung her there had been someone in my room and I wasn't going to break the confidence. The day of the presentation it had been announced that Peter Sterling, Wally Lewis, Garry Jack and myself had been nominated from Australia, along with Ellery Hanley and Garry Schofield from England, plus a Kiwi — Hugh McGahan I think. We got into our blazers and went downstairs and the other players were in the hallway on the sixth floor, wishing us well — saying good luck. I said nothing — although I knew something the others didn't know. The Great Britain coach, Maurice Bamford, wouldn't let his players go; I suppose he didn't want them mixing with the opposition. After dinner came the big announcement. I had to feign surprise, and then make a speech. I was suitably humble and shocked — even though I'd known for some time. I wondered whether this was the way it was at the Academy Awards — if the winners were forewarned with the knowledge that they had won.

When *Open Rugby* came out, there was the shot of me on the day at Headingley plus others from the presentation. The trouble was I had arrived in England sporting a moustache but had shaved it off after the first week. So there I was, moustachioed, holding up the boot and there I was again, without moustache, holding it up at the presentation. Garry Jack was the first to pick up on it. "You knew, didn't you?" he said. Then I told him the story, and he was dirty.

A couple of years later Jimmy Jack was in the same boat, although the Boot was awarded this time in Sydney when the Great Britain side was out here.

It was a nice irony that the old rivals, Wally and me, were the first two winners. I was chosen as five-eighth in the World XIII that was announced as part of the award — and Wally was relegated to second spot. That didn't happen too often.

In the long-running Dally M awards, run by the *Daily Mirror* (now *Telegraph-Mirror*) newspaper, I never even came close to winning the award for five-eighth — let alone the Dally M gold, or second or third place. I must admit it puzzled me. I was picked as five-eighth for NSW, so in the selectors' eyes I was the best five-eighth in the state, but in the Dally Ms it was always Terry Lamb or Cliff Lyons who finished ahead of me. Both of them won gold Dally Ms. Then it was pointed out to me that each position award went on a points tally kept over the season; the other blokes simply polled more than me. It remained an ambition right up to my last season to win a Dally M for best five-eighth but I never even got a fair crack at it, thanks to my shoulder injury.

Canterbury's (formerly Wests') Terry Lamb wasn't far behind Wally Lewis as the best five-eighth I played against. He was a tough competitor and a good one and when I played against him in club football, I always prepared for the game as if it was an Origin or Test match. That was how highly I rated him. If I was just a bit "off" my game, I knew he could get the better of me. I'd have to concede that the reason "Baa Baa" won far more awards than me was that he was more consistent week-in week-out. Terry is the ultimate competitor. There he was in '93 playing such a dominant role for Canterbury and the fact was that he came into first grade within a few weeks of me in 1980. He was still going as strong as ever. Lamb has unbelievable upper body strength for such a little bloke and has always been very aggressive in his play.

Lamb won a Dally M and a Rothmans Medal, had played more than 270 first grade games when this book was going to press (and was talking about playing another season) and played in three premiership-winning sides, despite missing the 1985 grand final. When you talk about the five-eighths of the modern era, he's right up there near the top. He never wore the number six jersey in a Test match, though, so when people talk about me standing in Wally Lewis's shadow to a degree, perhaps you've got to say the same thing about Terry Lamb in relation to the pair of us. Terry perhaps did me a favour back in 1982 when he knocked back a spot on the Kangaroo tour, because he was getting married. If he hadn't made that decision, who knows if I would have made my debut then. In different circumstances it could have been Terry Lamb embroiled in the controversy over beating the tour vice-captain (Lewis) to his Test spot.

In the prestigious Rothmans Medal, I never polled anywhere near the top. In fact, in my 13 seasons (I disregard 1988 when I only played in two matches) I didn't once finish in the top 20. The referees pick the Rothmans Medal winner and I always thought this was ridiculous. How can a ref go out and do his job — concentrate on every knock-on, every ruck and every pass, and then come in and also pick the best player. It shouldn't be the job of the referee. It's no surprise that halfbacks have done so well in that award — they'd be by far the most noticeable players to a referee. You could argue that the refs would be far less likely to remember the players who did a lot of unnoticed work somewhere further out on the paddock.

The winning of the Golden Boot confirmed 1986 as by far my best season. I felt my form was consistently good all season for Parramatta; we won the Panasonic Cup, the minor premiership and the grand final. I played in the NSW side that won the State of Origin series 3-0, taking my only man-of-the-match award in the third game. And I scored five tries in our convincing three-Test series win against New Zealand. I regard the first, scored in the SCG Test, as my best at Test level.

I picked up a double in our 22-8 win at Carlaw Park, both through backing up. I was just a few centimetres away from scoring three, and in fact everyone back home at Parramatta Stadium was cheering my "hat-trick", including my parents. Dale Shearer and I led the race for a grubber kick into the in-goal and we both dived at it in the wet simultaneously. There was confusion among the commentators about who scored the try — although I knew "Rowdy" had got there first. The ground announcer wasn't sure and might even have announced me as the scorer. This information then filtered back to Australia.

The fact that I had to run so far, and do so much work for my second Test try at the SCG, made it very special for me. I got the ball from Wayne Pearce in our own half and had to step one New Zealand player to get into the clear. I beat their fullback Gary Kemble with an "in and away" (that was the closest thing I had to a side-step) and then faced the threat of big Mark Graham coming across in cover. I pinned my ears back and just got to the line — 60 metres downfield from where I had taken the pass. We won that Test 29-12 and then went to Lang Park (my first Test match there), where I picked up two more tries in our 32-12 victory.

Frankly, though, I felt my contribution on the Kangaroo tour a few months later was disappointing. It wasn't that I played badly — but I only scored one try in five Tests on tour, in the second Test against the Poms at Elland Road. It seemed the play didn't run my way too much, what with other players in the side dominating, and I had trouble getting myself into tryscoring situations, in contrast to 1982. My try at Elland Road came when I tagged onto a backline move. Wally Lewis actually commented when he congratulated me: "It's about time you scored."

I thought the Poms would be a lot tougher than they turned out to be on the 1986 tour. We'd heard a lot about how much they had improved and I'd seen for myself there were plenty of good footballers scattered through England when I was there with Wigan in 1984-85. When we ran out for the first Test at Old Trafford, in Manchester, we were greeted by a record British Test crowd of over 50,000, and the atmosphere was fantastic. A couple of the British players took the Union Jack out and waved it around to the fans on both sides of the field, to build the atmosphere — and perhaps to intimidate us. But the Poms were disappointing once the game started, and we won 38-16, scoring seven tries. At that stage Ellery Hanley was their superstar but they put him in the centres, where he seemed to be lost. Once he came in on me in defence and left a huge gap for Gene Miles. I passed to Gene and he strolled over.

This was our second meeting with Hanley. He had been in Australia in 1984 and he hadn't shown much to suggest what a great player he would turn out to be. But it was obvious that he was played out of position, as a winger in Australia in 1984 and then in the centres for the first Test in 1986. He didn't appear in the last two Tests; apparently he carried an injury into the Old Trafford Test but so highly was he thought of that the selectors gambled with him. I think his performance showed that he was below par that day.

My main memories of that afternoon are of the lousy weather. It poured with rain — and then the sun unexpectedly broke through in the second half. In the brief period of sunshine the British scored two tries, as if it had all been rehearsed. But the sun disappeared again (and stayed disappeared for a week) and we got right on top. I recall hanging back in defence in their quarter and leaving a gap for Joe Lydon who scored one of the most memorable of Test tries, when he beat Garry Jack with a swerve and pace in an 80-metre run. I was the bloke who let him get clear.

We won the second Test at Elland Road Leeds by 34-4 and, just as in 1982, the Pommy selectors waited until the series was dead before making massive changes. I'd already played against former Wigan team-mates Henderson Gill and Ian Potter in the first two Tests and then I lined up against my old centre partner David Stephenson at Wigan in the third.

Before the tour we talked as a group about forgetting the undefeated effort of the 1982 side, and of not adding any extra pressure on ourselves by trying to emulate that record. We decided to take the tour a match at a time. But I know that for the guys who had been there in 1982 — Gene Miles, Mal Meninga, Wally Lewis, Peter Sterling and myself — that the longer the tour went on, the closer we edged towards an unbeaten run, that the more important it became to us. Winning the Tests was, of course, always the priority. But we had some very good, very competitive, footballers who starred in the club matches. Ben Elias, Terry Lamb, Des Hasler, Greg Alexander and Gary Belcher played some outstanding football in the midweek games.

Well we made it, finishing the campaign undefeated for a second time, thanks to a much-improved second half in the final Test at Wigan (and knowing that only diabolical refereeing could cost us a match in France). It was a time for some reflection and I thought about how lucky I had been that my only two Kangaroo tours were history-making ones, and that I had played in all Tests on both tours.

I always think it's unfair (and basically impossible) to compare sides from different years. Arguably, though, the fact Mal Meninga was the sensation of the 1982 tour but couldn't make the 1986 side was one pointer to the '86 Roos having been the stronger of those two touring sides. There is no doubt that the opposition at Test and club level was a lot stronger in '86. I don't want to declare one was any better than the other; their records speak for themselves. Additionally, just because the 1990 tourists lost the first Test at Wembley against an English side that had progressed dramatically in fitness, professionalism and skill since 1986, doesn't suggest to me that they were in any way below the standard of the previous two. It's an argument no one can win, and I'll leave it at that.

Viewed from a personal angle the tours of 1982 and '86 were very different. On the first I was single and had only had a couple of full seasons in first grade. I made my Test debut that tour — and the whole experience was new to me. My greatest memory remains scoring a try at Boothferry Park in my first Test. The 1986 tour was my third time in England. I was older, married, in the centres and after playing only two Tests in three seasons (one as reserve), I was established in the Test team. The big thing I'll remember about the 1986 tour was the adulation of the English crowds. They started to flock to our matches towards the end of 1982 and you knew by the enthusiasm of the applause that they were appreciative of our play, as much as they were there to watch their home sides. This was the attitude of the fans right from the start in 1986. It didn't matter where we were playing, they came from miles and miles around. They expected us to play like champions and I think for much of the time we managed it. The cheering and chanting and the general excitement at English grounds was great.

France apart, I enjoyed the '86 campaign a great deal — and I was very proud to have an unexpected Golden Boot to pack in my luggage for the long trip home.

16 Saying No to the Green & Gold

It's an emotive argument; plenty of football's old-timers frown on anyone who decides they no longer want to represent their country. "You should never turn you back on a Test jersey," they argue. Well, I made the decision to stop playing for Australia when I was 27, but I have only one regret — that I didn't go out of representative football the way I had planned. It was a similar scenario to the one I was confronted with in 1993 as I headed into my last year of football.

Goal-setting has always been part of my life. I was 21, only recently a member of the Australian side, when I said to Kerry Boustead near the end of the 1982 Kangaroo tour that I wouldn't go on another tour. He laughed at me and told me that of course I would. Bowie was proved right. But on the tour of '82 I felt I had achieved my dream of playing for Australia. I wanted to move on and the next target was to play for Australia in Australia. I achieved that in 1984. By 1986, after playing what I consider my best Test series — against New Zealand — I had played against every Test-playing nation and in every Test-playing country.

I changed my mind about Kangaroo touring and decided to go to England and France again in 1986. It was an opportunity I felt I should take at the end of the first season in which I'd become firmly established in the Australian side, alongside Gene Miles in the centres. I knew for sure I wouldn't be back for a third 'Roo tour in 1990. I would have been 29, winding down to an extent — and probably rated too old to be considered. But something that happened the night before the third Test in Britain in November 1986 convinced me that my representative days would be numbered. I'll tell about that shortly, but first ...

By the time I'd got home from that tour I had made a decision that I wanted to finish my international career with a series win against the Poms in Australia in 1988. Then I would hang up my rep boots and face the bigger responsibilities in my life — my family and a career outside of football.

At this point I have a confession to make about my Test career that I know will startle a lot of people, and cause some controversy. My confession is that I faked an injury; well "fake" isn't quite the word — *exaggerated* an injury — to miss a Test match in 1984! To this day I don't totally understand why I did it.

I mentioned that my goal after the 1982 Kangaroo tour was to play for my country at home, and especially at the Sydney Cricket Ground in front of my family and friends and all the Aussie supporters. But, with that in view, I pretty much bombed out in 1983. Just as Wally Lewis had become a casualty to Brett Kenny in '82, I became a casualty to Wally Lewis. It was something that I got used to from that season onwards. When 1984 came around, I was determined to regain my Australian jersey for the series against the Poms, though I knew by then my only chance was in the centres.

By that stage Gene Miles and Mal Meninga were the Queensland centres; Mal had cemented his spot as an Australian centre alongside Steve Rogers in 1982, and he and Miles filled the centre positions for the Test in Brisbane against New Zealand the previous year when Rogers was injured. I knew I was up against it, particularly with Queensland dominating the State of Origin series. But Rogers had finished as a representative player, which meant that, after the domination of the Rogers-Cronin partnership for so many years, the position was at least fairly open in '84.

Despite Queensland winning the first Origin match at Lang Park 29-12, I got the call — making the first Test team alongside Gene Miles. Mal Meninga was overlooked. My club form had been good and I went OK in the losing NSW side where I was picked in the centres alongside Steve Ella, with Alan Thompson favoured at five-eighth. The NSW selectors just couldn't make up their minds that year and we had different five-eighths for each match — Thompson in the first, Terry Lamb in the second and me in the third. No wonder Wally Lewis picked up the man-of-the-match awards in the first two games.

We won the first Test at the SCG 25-8 against a Great Britain side that was much, much tougher than the teams they threw at us during the 1982 tour. They were in the match for a long time but just couldn't go the distance at that intensity over 80 minutes. Aiding our cause was the fact that their coach Frank Myler made some peculiar selections, including Ellery Hanley on the wing. Hanley played five-eighth for Bradford Northern and was regarded by many as the Poms' gun player. GB's centres were Garry Schofield, the team's other rising star (with Hanley), and Keith Mumby who'd been around for a while. Schofield was quick and inexperienced; Mumby was slow but a seasoned campaigner. When I walked out onto the SCG that day I looked up at the Hill and thought: "I've finally made it; I'm playing a Test at home."

A week and a half later we played the second Origin match at the Sydney Cricket ground in the pouring rain. It's the match that will go down as the first in Sydney that the public really threw their support behind. There were just over 29,000 at the game despite the weather and they were vocal and tremendously enthusiastic in their support. It wasn't quite Lang Park yet, but finally it looked like the Sydney people had accepted the Origin concept. The match was remembered for a few other things: a wild brawl in the first minute, when the NSW forwards set upon my mate Gene Miles as he ran the ball back from the kick-off, an incredible try by Greg Dowling as he scooped up a Wally Lewis kick which had rebounded off the crossbar, and for the fact that it was Ray Price's last match for NSW.

I suffered a corked thigh late in the game and had to be replaced, by Steve Ella. Our trainer Alf Richards came on and asked me how it was and I told him no good, so I went off to spend some time with an ice pack. The second Test at Lang Park was being played a week later and the side was to be chosen that night. Chairman of selectors Ernie Hammerton came into the dressing room after the match and asked me how I was and I told him I didn't think I would be right, that the leg was pretty sore. Deep down I just wasn't keen on going to Lang Park for the Test and I thought the injury gave me an "out." I really can't pin down what was going on in my mind then. I just had it in my head that I'd be happy not to go up to Brisbane for a week for the Test. Maybe it was because I'd achieved my goal of playing a Test at the SCG. A night match at Lang Park seemed somehow not so important.

When I think about it now I am still amazed at what I did. I wanted to be an international and I guess I knew that was risking my spot in the side if I didn't play in Brisbane. The fact is that my leg *could* have been okay for the game with all the right treatment. I'm not particularly proud to admit that rather strange event in my career. But it happened and I won't hide it.

They still picked me in the Australian squad, as a reserve, with Mal Meninga getting my spot in the centres. The prospect of going to Brisbane was even less inviting if I was going to sit on the bench for the game. The next day I drove down to the SCG for the medical, and bunged on a noticeable limp as I went into the room. I was examined by the ARL doctor Bill Monaghan, and I grimaced as he touched my leg. Doc Monaghan ruled me out and Steve Mortimer was called in as the new reserve. I could have gone to Brisbane; I could have played. In fact, I chose to exaggerate an injury enough to get me out of it. The old-timers won't like this story.

Australia won another reasonably tough Test 18-6 and when the side was chosen that night for the third Test a week and a half later, I was named as a reserve, with Steve Mortimer taking Mark Murray's spot at halfback. I'd relinquished — basically voluntarily — my Test spot to Meninga, but at least I was still in the Test squad and so registered my second Test in Australia — the only one for which I sat on the bench. Just short of two years after Peter Sterling and I had ousted Lewis and Mortimer from the Australian side, they were reunited in the halves for their only Test match together against the Poms (they played together in one Test against the Kiwis in 1983).

We beat the Poms 20-7 and I was out there at the end to chair off Ray Price on the day of his last Test for Australia. Pricey had given amazing service for Parramatta, NSW and his country. At 31 he was still the ultimate competitor in this, his final Test. I'm sure the Poms were glad to see the last of him.

It was almost two years before I played for Australia again, after passing up another opportunity the next season (1985), when I was granted permission to be excused from the tour of New Zealand.

People looking back on the career of Brett Kenny may well get the wrong impression — that he wanted to pick and choose when he played for Australia. I understand that view, but I reject it. I loved playing for Australia. It is rugby league's ultimate honour and my career would never have been fulfilled if I hadn't had that chance. And I would have been very disappointed had I not been picked for Australia again in 1986 — the only year in which I played in every available Test — three against New Zealand, three against Great Britain and two against France.

It wasn't so much that the shine wore off playing Test football for me, it was just that other things became increasingly important. I played rugby league because I enjoyed it and succeeded at it; success comes at some price. Because a football career is so brief compared to the vocations of most of us, there comes a time when a long-term job and family commitments take priority. They were the reasons I eventually turned my back on playing for Australia. Representative football by that stage meant days and weeks away from my job and my family. Because of those earlier sacrifices I'd gone from job to job, a father with no trade behind him, my earning capacity as a footballer nearing its end and facing a fairly frightening prospect of having no security once I finally hung up my boots. It didn't worry me so much when I was younger — but it sure started to worry me later on.

Now, back to that night before the final Test at Central Park in 1986. I roomed with Mal Meninga on that tour. Mal was (and is) a great bloke, fairly quiet like me, dedicated to his family but a bloke who knew how to have a good time. We used to have some friendly wrestles in the room; someone was always coming in and dive-bombing your bed, keen for a rumble. One day Mal picked me up on one side of the room and tossed me right across onto my bed on the other – – just like you'd pick up your kit bag and hurl it. That's when I realised what amazing strength he had. I don't think he realised himself how strong he was. I certainly never relished trying to tackle him. Both our wives were pregnant when we left for the tour; Mal's wife Debbie was due while we were away and Mal knew he wouldn't be there for the birth. Julie had just found out she was expecting the following March so it wasn't quite as difficult for us.

Mal couldn't make the side for the first two Tests ahead of Gene Miles and myself, but we had some injury problems for the third, and Don Furner chose Mal in the second row. Although he was happy to be back in the Test side, he was pretty anxious the few days before the game because he knew Debbie would have the baby any day. On the night before the Test I'd just dropped off to sleep when the phone rang. Mal was downstairs in the hotel. It was his mother-in-law and I had a pretty fair idea of what it was about so I rushed downstairs and rounded him up. The big bloke was over the moon with the news — he had become the father of a baby girl. But at the same you could see the sadness in him that he was so far away. Mal obviously wanted to celebrate, but all the players who weren't involved in the Test match were out. Those who were playing were either downstairs talking or were already in bed. So we rang room service and ordered two bottles of champagne. As the other blokes straggled back home, they'd poke their heads into the room, with its door flung open, and ask what was going on. When Mal told them the news they'd be in there — and we'd order another bottle of champers. Before long, half the touring team was in there, swilling champagne as we wet the baby's head.

Wally Lewis passed on the news to coach Don Furner and asked him to join us, but Don said that while he was delighted, we had a Test match to play the next day and should get to bed. We did eventually, about midnight. It was the only time in my Test career that I had a drink the night before a Test. It might have shown the next day when we struggled in the first half against the Poms, but a lively speech from Wally at halftime hit the spot and got us going and we left England for France undefeated.

After seeing what Mal went through during that time, there was no way I could contemplate being so far away when one of my kids was born. I decided right then that I would definitely not be going on any more tours, to England, New Zealand or anywhere. France were scheduled to tour Australia in 1987 and Great Britain were to tour in 1988. I thought if I was playing well enough to be selected, it would be perfect to play the French Tests, then make the series against the Poms my last. That way I would have started with a Test against the British in England and finished against them in Australia. Nice balance. But just as with my careful plans for retiring from Parramatta five years later, things went a bit awry.

Firstly, France didn't come to Australia in '87, basically because they couldn't afford to — an indication of how far the game had declined in France. A one-off Test against New Zealand was hurriedly organised for immediately after the State of Origin series. The Origin series was really tough physically; NSW won the first match but lost the next two, the decider by only two points, to relinquish the Origin trophy after two years of dominance. I was struggling with form but was picked, as much on reputation as good play I reckon, for NSW and Australia.

The Kiwi Test was played on a Tuesday night, just six days after the final Origin match, and the feeling in the Australian camp was pretty flat. I don't know if it was because it was just a one-off Test or if the Origin series had taken the stuffing out of us. Bit of both probably. Anyhow, the mood certainly wasn't the best.

New Zealand had a new coach in Tony Gordon and six new players, including 19-year-old Kevin Iro who was being boomed as the greatest whiz kid of all time. Iro was lining up with the tough campaigner Dean Bell in the centres, against Gene Miles and myself. Mark Horo, later to become a Parramatta team-mate, was also making his Test debut — and his first Test proved to be my last.

The Kiwis got stuck into us from the start, with Adrian Shelford and Sam Stewart playing above themselves. Unable to lift ourselves to sufficient heights against a very committed team, we went down 13-6. It was my first loss in an Australian jersey — but that didn't worry me so much as an agonising injury I suffered. Sometime in the second half I hurt my neck in a tackle and I couldn't move it without being hit with a shooting pain. I thought it might just be a muscle spasm but I was advised to put a neck brace on, which meant back to the hotel for an early night. The next morning after an uncomfortable night I was not keen on the thought of going to the airport in a neck brace. So I took it off, gingerly, and sat in front of the mirror and tried to comb my hair. The pain was unbearable with even just the slightest movement. I gritted my teeth and put the brace back on.

In Sydney a visit to a specialist and a CAT scan cleared me of any serious damage and I was hoping to be right to play in a couple of weeks.

What I was most upset about was not being able to go to Los Angeles for the extra State of Origin match put on that year. All my life I had wanted to go to LA to see Disneyland, Universal Studios, Beverly Hills and all the other tourist attractions. I thought I would have been fit to play but the selectors didn't even ring me to see if I was okay. They just didn't pick me full stop — and I was really dirty about that treatment. It wouldn't have been so bad if they had at least contacted me and said they had some doubt over my fitness, then had picked me and ruled me out at the medical. That would have been acceptable. But to not even have been given the chance was really disappointing.

I still haven't been to America, but I will one day when my children are old enough to enjoy Disneyland with me. I actually played against Illawarra the weekend of the LA match, which proved I would have been fit. A working holiday in Los Angeles wouldn't have been a bad way to go out, considering the chance to finish against the Poms was taken away from me the next year.

So that was it. I didn't know it — but my representative days had finished. I still had hopes of playing for NSW and Australia in 1988, but someone, somewhere apparently had other ideas ...

Season 1987 was a mid-range year for Parramatta. We won 12 games and lost 12, missing the semi-finals by only three points. But it sure wasn't up to the standards we were used to and became the first year since 1980, and only the second season since 1974, that Parramatta hadn't made the finals. It was a disappointing season for me personally and for the club as a whole in that we were absolutely devastated by injuries. The nucleus of the backline, Paul Taylor, Neil Hunt, Eric Grothe, Steve Ella, plus prop Geoff Bugden hardly played, and Paul Mares, our most exciting forward, was limited to just one match because of a serious knee injury.

I was glad when the season finished and I don't really want to remember too much about it. It was one of *those* seasons that players go through. I'll always regard 1986 as my best season and 1987 my worst (I don't count 1988). I was never fully fit and my form was pretty lousy.

The one shining memory of 1987 is that I became a father when Joshua was born on March 4. Perhaps the restless nights getting used to a baby in the house for the first time might have contributed just that little bit to my poor form as well. But I'm certainly not complaining about that.

Freshened from a summer off, I was keen to prove in 1988 that I wasn't a "has-been." I wanted to help the Eels turn it all around, and to go out of Test football a winner.

We started the season with a good win over Newcastle and headed to Parramatta Stadium for the first time, to face Balmain. I then felt that the likes of Steve Ella, Peter Sterling, Eric Grothe and myself were starting to get used to the fact we'd become the senior players. We now had to set the example after always having had older blokes around for our first few seasons — and particularly Pricey and the Crow until 1986. I was very positive. This was going to be a great season, the start of a new era. Instead it proved to be the *end* of an era — for me at least — and the start of a nightmare. And it happened so innocently.

In the match against Balmain we were making progress up the left hand side of the field, towards what is now called the Peter Sterling Hill. Young Danny

Crnkovich got away down the touchline, and I trailed him. When trapped, Danny tried to lob a pass over a Balmain player to me. I stretched up to catch it and caught a glimpse of Russel Gartner coming in to tackle me. My weight went fully onto my right leg as I propped to step ... and it just collapsed on me. Even before I was tackled. There was some later conjecture that Gartner had hit me high and that the impact had caused the injury. But the reason Russel hit me high was that my leg had already given way and I was on the way down. He was completely innocent. Garry Jack came in and completed the tackle, finished up all over me and with the ball which had sprung loose. Perhaps a try had gone begging, but that was the least of my worries.

I was in serious pain, and as our trainer Alf Richards headed onto the field, I knew I was gone. I was taken straight off and by the time I got to the tunnel I could walk on my own without assistance. I thought: "Great, it's not as bad as I thought." Our doctor, Peter Manollaras, checked me out and said he thought it was probably just cartilage damage because I could walk on it. That night people were coming up to me in the club, and I was telling them I'd only be out for a couple of weeks, that it was only cartilage damage.

The next day — on my 27th birthday — I found it was much, much worse. Arthroscopic examination disclosed that I'd torn the anterior cruciate ligament. I was devastated. I was told I had two options, to have surgery and miss the season or to have intense physio, build up the muscles around the knee cap and take a gamble on the knee standing up. I could last the season or I could bite the dust first match. When 1993 came around with my shoulder problem, that scenario sounded a bit familiar.

I had two weeks to decide, but I needed only two minutes. I decided not to have surgery and began physio the same day and continued every day that week. It was announced in the paper I mightn't be out for the season as was expected; if there was any chance I could play with it, I was prepared to take the risk.

Parramatta were playing Manly at the Stadium on the following Sunday and I was getting ready to leave when I leant down to pick Josh up and put him in the car. He was only just over 12 months old then. I bent down, picked him up and the leg just gave way, completely buckled. I almost dropped him. I thought if I couldn't even pick up a baby, there was no way I was going to be able to play football. I decided right then I'd have the operation. It meant goodbye 1988, goodbye to playing my last Test against the Poms, goodbye to helping Parramatta back into the semi-finals ... and goodbye to employment for a few months as well.

When I look back now I see that injury as the changing point of my career and my life. I'd never suffered any injury in my eight previous seasons in first grade that had sidelined me more than a couple of weeks. Now I was an invalid.

What made it worse was that I had to sit and watch Parramatta get flogged 64-12 by Manly on that Sunday. Can you believe we led 12-6 midway through the first half? The side lost the next five matches in a row from that day and a semi-final spot looked increasingly unlikely from then on. I told John Monie before the match that I'd decided to have the operation; I thought I'd be wasting my time trying to play on the knee. He was disappointed, as was I.

I ran into Ray Price who asked me what was happening with the injury, and I told him. Pricey was calling the game for 2UE and he rushed me up for an interview to break the news exclusively for his radio station. Winning was everything to Pricey, even when it came to ratings.

With my 1988 season restricted to one and a half games, it would have been perhaps feasible to cling to a hope that I could come back and play for Australia in 1989. But I'd made my decision and I wasn't going to change it. For me there was no farewell like the one Pricey had at the SCG in 1984 — just my first loss at Lang Park in 1987, plus a pain in the neck and now a wrecked knee.

The knee injury meant that I became unemployed again. My working life had been an unsettled one after the steady period in which I worked at the Parramatta Leagues Club cellar, from 1981, until I went to Wigan in late 1984. Even then, any time I had to have time off for representative football I had to take it without pay. That disclosure may surprise a lot of people who would presume that because I was employed in a leagues club, I'd still be paid if away on league commitments. I was worried about leaving that job to go to Wigan but everyone kept telling me a player of my profile would have no problems getting a job when I got home, and I believed them. Well, they were wrong. It was a great struggle. Every time I was interviewed I slipped in that I was chasing a job. But it took time. Finally I became a car salesman with Phil McCarroll Ford at Camden after they had commissioned me for a promotion. I was pleased to get the chance and stayed there until the 1986 Kangaroo tour when I left on my own accord. I was working from 8 am to 6pm, driving from Greystanes to Camden five days a week which made it a long day, especially when I had to go straight to training. They were great employers, but in the end I couldn't handle the combination of the hours and the travel.

When I returned from the '86 tour, I tried once again to mention I was looking for work — whenever I was interviewed — and someone from Carbonrib heard it and offered me a job as a sales representative. But with all the injuries and rep responsibilities I had in 1987, I needed plenty of time off, and they told me they couldn't afford to keep me on. Later I worked as a labourer with a landscaping firm and then selling advertising space on the Winfield Cup scoreboards that you see in the clubs. With no representative commitments to complicate things I got a good job with Appletise, and was hoping that job would prove to be the answer. But they changed bosses after 12 months or so and, while they were happy to use me for any promotions, they were pretty tough on the question of time off for football. I couldn't even get away from work early on Friday nights when we were playing — and often had to tear home from the office at Silverwater to home at Kings Langley, have a quick shower and, without having eaten, head to Parramatta Stadium for a match.

Once I got there just 50 minutes before kick-off in a real flap — and played accordingly. Finally, I'd had enough. The last straw came when they wouldn't allow me holidays the following October to take a trip to Cairns which I had won as clubman of the year. The boss's abrupt attitude was: "Sell it or give it away." I gave them away instead.

It was a tough task — trying to combine a secure job with football. I never managed it too well in those earlier years. And I certainly couldn't afford *not* to work. It wasn't until my last couple of years as a footballer that I was in what anyone would consider the good-earn bracket — and by that stage I knew it wasn't going to last very long. I mention all this to present the other side of the story on the "no one should ever turn their back on the chance to play for Australia" cry. I wouldn't argue that playing for your country is the greatest honour a sportsman can achieve. Some may be prepared to sacrifice everything for that, and that's their choice. My own view was that I wanted to set up some sort of future, and look after my family — and if it meant representative football was the thing that had to go, so be it. I'd achieved all I wanted to as an Australian player. But I certainly hadn't achieved much in the workforce and I knew which "profession" of the two was going to pay the bills once I reached 30 or so.

I wrote to Ken Arthurson in February 1989 to explain that I felt I had given good service to Australia, but that the holding of a steady job and my family commitments (Julie was expecting Nikolah by this stage) had become my priority and I would appreciate if I could be stood down from future representative matches. I received a nice letter back thanking me for my contribution and wishing me the best for the future. With that exchange of letters a chapter of my life closed. Jack Gibson was coaching NSW then and had rung me asking me to reconsider; he wanted me in the NSW side that season, but my mind was made up.

So began the second phase of my career; in reality it began with the knee injury at the start of 1988. There were no more semi-finals, let alone premierships, no more State of Origin or Test matches. I was a senior club man now, slower than in my formative years, but still able to do a job for Parramatta. Brett Kenny the footballer of 1989 was a far different creature from the 1980-86 model. I still felt I had something to contribute but was quite aware even then that there were plenty of critics publicly expressing doubts that I would ever be the same again.

I'd signed a new three-year contract midway through 1987, for the 1988, '89 and '90 seasons, and I remember the papers calling it a "lifetime contract." They apparently presumed that the completion of the contract would signal the end of my career. To be honest I was probably thinking along the same lines. As it turned out I did come back better than some people expected and in 1990 I was actually approached via an intermediary to see if I'd make myself available for the final State of Origin match. Coach Tim Sheens had asked a reporter to bounce it off me to see if I'd make myself available. I gave it some serious thought, but I decided that I'd made up my mind and I didn't believe in any Dame Nellie Melbas. If I had gone to Lang Park and not played well I would have been bagged for the rest of my life. If we had lost, an easy excuse would been that the selectors had picked an "ageing" Brett Kenny. The funny thing was that for those first few years after I'd retired from the rep stuff, I always wanted to be regarded as still playing well enough to play representative football if I had chosen to. But when the chance arose, I stuck with my decision.

There was another indication that I had come back strongly when Wally Lewis called me in 1990 to say that the Brisbane Broncos were keen to talk to me. I told him I'd be interested in talking to them but didn't want to do anything until near the end of the season. I gave that some thought. Julie's sister, Lynne, lived on the Gold Coast and living in Queensland held some appeal for us. I knew Wally Lewis and Gene Miles and Greg Dowling well, so it wouldn't have been as if I would be going to a club which didn't have some friendly faces. The thing sort of got away from me — and to tell you the truth I didn't even get back to them, which wasn't too flash. Parramatta came up with a very good offer during 1990 to secure me for another two years and wanted an answer virtually there and then. I was happy with the money and didn't want to look as though I was stalling, waiting for someone else to trump Parramatta, so I re-signed for two more years.

In the latter years of my career I happily devoted myself in total to Parramatta. There were no rep duties, no diversions or distractions — just the club that had given me my chance. For five active seasons and one inactive one while I was injured, I was a club player and nothing else. The disappointment was that during that time my club did not once make the semi-finals, and twice almost won the wooden spoon with me as captain. There were times when I no longer enjoyed wearing the blue and gold.

Failure was hard to live with when you consider that for my previous six seasons in first grade we made five grand finals, and a final, that I had played 17 Tests, 17 State of Origin matches and made two Kangaroo tours.

To re-shape an old cliche — mine was a career played in two halves.

17 Reeling Eels

Paramatta's steady decline from superclub to near-wooden spooners in 1992 (only two competition points taken from Gold Coast on technical grounds stopped us "winning" the spoon) was the result of poor buying policy, a lack of foresight and the fact that too many players were paid too much for too little achievement. Maybe that sounds harsh, and a few of my team-mates mightn't be pleased to read such an opinion, but the club's record backs me up — and I know plenty of people agree with me.

I got into hot water when I spoke out during an interview with the *Sydney Morning Herald's* John Macdonald in August 1989. I was called before the Parramatta board of directors and fined $1000. It was my first run-in with officialdom and I was firmly reminded that, while I was playing, it was not my role to publicly criticise management. I've had to wait until retirement to spell out my feelings, and I don't plan to hold back.

The club can't merely point to the retirement of Ray Price and Mick Cronin in 1986, the last time we won the premiership — or even made the finals — as the start of the decline. I'm sure a lack of thought for the future, tracing from well before that, contributed to the Eels' decline.

A classic example of a player we should have had is Gene Miles. I became good mates with Geno on the 1982 Kangaroo tour and virtually from that time onwards, and particularly through 1984, I tried to get Parramatta interested in him. Geno was super-keen to come to Sydney. He had a job with Rothmans and knew he could get a transfer. All the club had to do was find him somewhere to live, pay a contract fee which wouldn't have been outrageous plus, I think, a transfer fee to the Queensland Rugby League, a system that was still in place then. Geno was already showing the signs at that stage that he was going to be one of the world's best centres, an awesome proposition for anyone he faced.

I spoke several times with Denis Fitzgerald about Miles and passed on Geno's number. Fitzy would say he'd call him, but he never once followed up. If he wasn't interested, he should have told me and I could have told Geno. I was just trying to help both parties by being the middle man. Instead it was a case of: "Oh, I've been busy, I'll give him a call soon." Even then (1984) Mick Cronin was a season-to-season proposition and I wasn't the only one at the club who thought he might finish at least a couple of seasons before he did. It got to the embarrass-ing stage where I'd call Gene to see what Fitzy had said, and he'd say that he hadn't heard from him. I know that Gene Miles would have come to Parramatta for next to nothing. He wanted to play for Parramatta.

The attitude at the club seemed to be that we had a brilliant backline and while Crow was there we didn't need another centre. We had Sterling, Kenny, Ella, Cronin, Grothe, Hunt, Taylor. But that's my point. Mick Cronin wasn't *always* going to be there. The club's problem over all these years has been to wait until the last minute before filling the holes. In most cases that was too late.

When I was approached by Manly in 1984, it was because they had decided they wanted a five-eighth replacement for Alan Thompson. It was the mirror image of the situation with Mick Cronin. Thommo had been there for a long time, was still playing good football but wasn't going to be around much longer. Manly wanted to replace him *before* he'd retired, not after. Their attitude was to start with the best (in their eyes) and if they failed to get him, then to go for the next best. They told me if I decided to stay with Parramatta, they'd go for Wally Lewis. In the end they signed Cliff Lyons. Manly's attitude was that to win a premiership you had to have two first grade sides, and obviously quite a few of those players would be in reserves. At Parramatta we finished up with virtually the opposite — two good reserve grade sides.

When Mick Cronin departed, Denis Fitzgerald suddenly became interested in Gene Miles. Even then we were into 1987, though it was obvious in early 1986 that the Crow would finish that season after suffering his serious eye injury.

Now it was too late to snare Gene Miles. By 1987 he was rated the world's best centre, could command bucket-loads of money and had a heap of clubs chasing him. Manly and Easts were after him and were prepared to offer him a lot more than Parramatta were. Manly had the backing of Kerry Packer and the famous story is told of how Packer flew Gene Miles and Wally Lewis down to his office for talks with him and Bob Fulton in 1986. Three or four years earlier Parramatta could have got Geno a whole lot cheaper. He was keen to come, but Parramatta hesitated and did nothing.

Even when we won premierships in 1981-82-83-86, Parramatta weren't active on the player market. We brought Geoff Bugden from Newtown after he'd won the Rothmans Medal and Chris Phelan from Brisbane. There were no other "major" signings until Mike Eden came from Easts in 1985. We were just fortunate that we had a freakish group of locals come through. And we had seasoned internationals such as Ron Hilditch, Bob O'Reilly, Ray Price and Mick Cronin plus the experienced Steve Edge to create the perfect balance.

By about 1985 it was obvious the club should have been looking to replace our top players. But the attitude was: don't worry, another freakish group of players from the local juniors will suddenly appear and all will be okay. Within a few years it was obvious the freakish new group weren't quite so "freakish" as had been hoped.

I accept there are other sides to the argument. Because so many of us became internationals, the club had to increase a lot of contract fees in the mid-80s. Frankly, not too many of us were on the sort of money that internationals at most other clubs were getting until late in our careers. But we enjoyed playing together and we stuck solid despite larger offers from elsewhere in many cases.

The reality of an horrific injury crisis in 1987, the first season after our last premiership, was another factor. But Parramatta never seemed to be interested in any "insurance" if players were injured, or were nearing retirement. It always seemed an attitude of: wait until it happens, then we'll look at it. In my books, that was not good management. By the time the need came, it was too late to act. No one wanted to play for Parramatta anymore — the attraction of going to a successful club no longer applied.

Too many players who'd had more than enough chance to prove themselves in first grade were kept on — and paid good money. I never asked players what money they were on, but the rumour was strong and reliable that Parramatta had plenty of reserve-graders on $50,000 a season in the late 80s and early 90s. While other clubs had done away with incentive payments, we were over-burdened with them. It meant that because of injury, or because of the team's poor performances, a lot of players were playing first grade and getting rich incentive money to do so. But these players weren't bringing success to the club. They were only getting the chance because of other people's inadequacies or bad luck — not because their form was so good it demanded that they be in first grade. Basically, money was being wasted in large amounts.

When Gold Coast, Brisbane and Newcastle came into the Winfield Cup in 1988, player payments sky-rocketed. Because we were always strong in reserve grade and had some young players with "potential", other clubs came knocking on their doors. Fitzy promptly upped his offers to keep them. The trouble was, as Peter Sterling once wrote in an article, we were paying for potential not achievement. I can name a long list of players who never reached their potential. With some of them it was because they got to the comfort zone where they were getting paid well, and playing first grade, despite not reaching the level that should have been demanded of them. In their defence, a lot of players were also thrown into first grade because of injuries to established players, or simply because we had no one better. Probably plenty of them didn't get the benefit of undergoing a good apprenticeship in the lower grades. Also they didn't have the benefit of having a lot of experienced players around them to guide them, as I had had when I first came into first grade. Ultimately, Parramatta was littered with players of "potential" who could perform in first grade well enough for two or three weeks, but lacked consistency past that. They spent seasons yo-yoing between firsts and seconds and in the end lacked confidence. That Parramatta broke the salary cap in 1991 was unbelievable and proof surely that there were too many players getting too much money for too little achievement. I feel those who hadn't proved successful first-graders should have got a lot less, as I and players of my time did, and the club should have offered more for established, proven topliners.

When it came to spending and buying policy, Fitzy kept announcing publicly that he wouldn't meet the outrageous figures that some players and managers were after. The player market blew out at two levels: money for the topline in-demand players almost doubled over a couple of seasons, while the borderline first-reserve grader was demanding heaps more as well because he was the type of player Gold Coast and to a lesser degree Newcastle needed.

In football as in life you generally get what you pay for — and it seemed we got a lot of the latter instead of a few of the former. Parramatta were buying players who were little better, if any better at all, than the players we had. The policy was a shambles.

Back in 1987 the club did the right thing by buying Bob Lindner to replace Ray Price. Lindner was the Test lock and I thought it was great that we had gone right to the top to replace Pricey. Unfortunately Bob Lindner didn't regularly show the form for us that he did in representative games. But he certainly played some good games and copped a bit of unfair criticism. I watched almost all the 1988 season from the sidelines and I thought Bob was among our best players in several matches. But he'd set himself a standard for Queensland and Australia and many people thought he didn't match that at club level. The same thing happened to me and Sterlo too, and you have to cop it. Not unreasonably, more is expected of you when you're an established international.

The other criticism was that Lindner didn't play enough football. Statistics show he played 13 (out of 24 rounds) in 1987 and 14 (out of 22 rounds) in 1988. But the club was not at fault, they bought the right player.

Mick Cronin's departure meant we needed a centre and a goalkicker. So what did we do? Brought a Rugby Union player in Jeff Perl because he was a goalkicker — although many people had doubts he would ever be a first grade player. He came on as a replacement in firsts *once* all season. We bought an Australian Schoolboy in Michael Erickson who was 18 and really should have been given the chance to settle in with the lower grades. He ended up playing 15 matches in firsts in 1987 and I still maintain the reason he struggled a little in later seasons was because he was rushed into first grade too early. If the club bought him as an instant replacement for Mick Cronin, that was a far-fetched concept. As a long-term replacement for Cronin and Steve Ella, it would have been fair enough. Michael was an exceptional player, but should have had 12 months in the lower grades.

The other goalkicker Parramatta bought was Rod Slater, a prop from the country who, once again, had "potential." Injuries conspired against him and he played just eight first grade games for the club over three years.

It turned out that John Muggleton became the side's regular goalkicker after Steve Ella got injured. That's what ruined 1987 — injury. Look at the sorry story — Steve Ella two games, Neil Hunt four, Geoff Bugden six, Eric Grothe eight, Stan Jurd nine, Paul Taylor 11, Brett Kenny 14 — and you can see how the 1986 grand final winning side was ripped apart. But right there was the message. Players were getting older and taking more time to recover from injury, players were nearing the end. Of *course* there were going to be injuries.

I thought I'd play centre in 1987 and young Brian Jackson would be brought up as five-eighth. Many people saw him as a real prospect for the future, but Brian ended up as another player who failed to live up to expectations.

In 1988 we obviously needed strengthening in the front row. Terry Leabeater had been around for a long time and wasn't showing anything like his form of 1986 and Geoff Bugden, the other "Bookend", had had persistent injury problems for a few seasons. We got Mark Clinton, who was a real good toiler but, compared to the standards of most clubs, was no more than being in the category of players who you could bring up to firsts to fill in for someone else. The sort of player who would do the job for you, and then head back to reserves. Our other major buys were Craig Izzard, Mark Robinson, Andrew Fitzhenry and David Liddiard from Penrith, who had all played in the reserve grade grand final.

Izzard was a player with ability. To this time he still hasn't shown himself to be a consistent first-grader over an entire season. Robinson again was a winger of "potential" (that word again) in the Eric Grothe mould, but he had injury problems and didn't make it. Andrew Fitzhenry never proved himself consistent enough to command a regular first grade spot, and David Liddiard — well, he was a good case in point about the whole Paramatta buying policy. Could someone please explain why Parramatta would let David Liddiard go then two seasons later buy him back from Penrith — for more money! It's like a company having a blue collar worker and letting him go across the road because he wasn't worth what they offered to pay him, then a couple of years later bringing him back as general manager because the other mob saw something in him.

We did the same thing with Brett Garnon in 1988. He was a whiz kid who was going to be a star but didn't reach his potential and went to Cronulla. Ultimately we brought him back (from the south coast by this stage) — as (another) goalkicking centre replacement for Mick Cronin? We signed Gary Vernon from Brisbane as well — another in the category of "good toiler" who played more reserve grade than firsts.

The other major change in 1987 was that, without Mick Cronin and Ray Price, Sterlo and I and a few others had been suddenly been elevated to status of senior players. It had always been a case of me being between Mick Cronin and Peter Sterling, with them calling the play. Sterlo would direct things around the rucks and when Crow called for the ball, he got it. Now, I had to take on more responsibility without Mick Cronin, Steve Ella, Paul Taylor, Neil Hunt or Eric Grothe outside. I think it took a lot of us a season to get used to taking on Pricey and the Crow's leadership responsibilities. I thought that in 1988 we would come to grips with that, but then I missed almost the whole season and we were thrown out again. Looking back, we never had the grand finals backline together after 1986. We got closest in 1988 when I was the only one missing for a long period.

In '88 we finished 11th, I played just two games because of my knee injury but a lot of the other established players played a fair bit of football — Bugden 17, Ella 17, Grothe 13, Mark Laurie 11, Sterling 13, Paul Taylor 21. None of the recruits played more than 10 first grade games.

From that time on, it was a different Parramatta. The scenario was the same — we bought players who wouldn't have been automatic choices at many clubs, plus we had our own "potential" stars who for one reason or another didn't come up to expectations.

Category one — Jeff Perl, Craig Izzard, Mark Robinson, David Liddiard, Andrew Fitzhenry, Gary Vernon, Rod Slater, Andrew Langford, Ian Gately,

Mark Bugden, Peter Johnston, Jeremy Ticehurst, Brett Atkins, Peter Martin, Mark Horo, John Fearnley, Phil Tiernan, Pat O'Doherty.

Category Two — Danny Crnkovich, Tony Cosatto, David Rowles, Brian Jackson, Brett Scott, Glen Liddiard, Scott Mahon, David Penna, David Woods, Matt and Phil Adamson, David Black, Jason Bell.

I'm not trying to be unkind, and in some cases injury intervened to spoil promising careers, but the point I'm making is that over a six-year period Bob Lindner was the *only* highly established player Parramatta bought, while gambling on what most people would consider borderline first-graders — or buying, or retaining, players of "potential." Of all the youngsters whom it was hoped would go on to be representative players or even internationals, not one of them did.

It might be a hard analysis, but when you look at the end of the 80s, the results seem to support the view of many of our critics — that we had a lot of players in that good reserve grader-but just a first-grader bracket. In firsts we finished 7th in 1987, 11th in 1988, 8th in 1989; in reserves we finished 2nd on the ladder (3rd after losing the final) in 1987, 2nd (4th) in 1988 and 1st (2nd) in 1989. President's Cup enjoyed similar success — 3rd in 1987, 1st in 1988 and 1st (3rd) in 1989. The $64 question is: why were we strong in the lower grades but not in firsts? From that 1988 President's Cup winning side only David Woods, Greg Drake (although injured), and Scott Mahon were established first-graders at Parramatta in 1993.

By 1989 there were only Peter Sterling, Paul Taylor, Peter Wynn, Mark Laurie and myself left as regular first-graders from those great years up to 1986. Others were still there but Eric Grothe, Steve Ella and Geoff Bugden had major injury problems, while John Muggleton, Steve Sharp and Michael Moseley were more often in reserves. By the start of 1990 Paul Taylor had been dumped, Eric and Steve had succumbed to injury and Geoff Bugden was on a three-year contract — but didn't play in 1990 because of injury — Again I must question the sense in signing "Buggo" for three years when he'd already had trouble staying on the field because of injury.

Coach John Monie left at the end of 1989 and that was the time when there should have been a major clean-out. Jack Gibson did exactly that it in 1981 when he joined the club. I saw Jack around the dressing rooms a bit in 1980; whether he was eyeing off the job I don't know, but by the time he started in 1981 he'd got rid of all the players he felt hadn't come up to scratch or were unlikely to. He rebuilt and plenty of young players got their chance alongside established senior players in a successful first grade side. The fact that we weren't successful in the late 80s made it more difficult to blood players, and that was a problem. Very likely it was a big factor in some blokes not kicking on. By 1990, you could tell who was going to improve and who wasn't — we had plenty of middle-of-the-road players who had been there a long time.

Familiarity was certainly a problem. John Monie had been at the club nine years, six as first grade coach. Too many people were too used to him and each other. I'll always remember John addressing players before a match late in the season and telling us there were a few whose contracts were up and that they hadn't performed too well and if they didn't finish on a good note, they mightn't be wanted by the club the next year. It didn't matter to him, he said, he was off to Wigan soon and didn't have to worry about it. To me, it was a sign that he'd had enough. I think at that stage John was offside with a few players and had also lost some respect for some of them. It was time to go. I don't want to take anything away from John Monie. He was a fine coach who achieved the rare feat of coaching a side that won the Panasonic Cup, premiership and minor premiership in the same season. His record since, with Wigan, has proved his ability. But I'm sure he'll admit that by the end of 1989 he'd been at Parramatta too long. Things had soured.

I supposed the club dreams of finding its new Ellas and Sterlings. There was a parade of hopefuls, from the bush and the juniors — players such as Delroy, Crnkovich, Cosatto, Jackson, Woods, Bell, Mahon. They were fine in the top grade for two or three weeks but a lot of them just couldn't handle the pressure of first grade on a sustained basis. Five-eighth Brett Scott was another example of this syndrome.

The far better option would have been to give them more experience in the lower grades, buy some established first-graders and bring the young talent up progressively for 15 or 20 minutes in firsts, or for a match here and there. Too many didn't get that luxury of time — because there was no one else. That was Jack Gibson's way — under-23s players would go and have a shower, then sit on the bench for firsts and get the occasional run. The fact of us not winning games made it more difficult still.

Lee Oudenryn is a classic example of a player who should have had time to settle in the lower grades. When he hit the first grade scene in 1992 he'd only had three seasons of rugby league behind him. But Mick Cronin had little choice but to play him. The club had waited and waited on other young players — and they had not come up to scratch.

The club showed enormous patience as it "waited" for these young potential stars to bloom (most never did). Mick Delroy was an interesting case in that Easts came in with a big offer, a ridiculously large offer according to the rumours, and Parramatta let him go. They didn't think he'd come up to expectations and warranted the money he was asking to stay. It was a tough decision, but probably the right one. But Delroy was something of an exception. There were a stack of others who had offers from other clubs and Parramatta ended up paying ridiculous money to keep them. In the process the club busted the salary cap despite coming near to last!

It wasn't until the end of 1992 that the club made a conscious decision to let a lot of players go. They copped some flak for it but they finally bit the bullet. I'm not saying I agree with all the choices of who they didn't want to keep but I applaud the club for finally taking a stance. There was a lot of discontent among some players at that stage and something had to change. With experienced campaigners like Michael Speechley and Paul Dunn joining the club, players such as Scott Mahon and David Woods started to show their true ability in '93. Additionally, a new crop of fresh players came through from the juniors. Time will tell whether they make the grade. In '93 Mark Horo was having his best season and Dallas Weston became a top first-grader. The clean-out should have come earlier.

Of the players let go over those few years, I was most disappointed of all with the departure of Andrew Leeds at the end of 1991. He was the only player I reckoned we definitely should have kept. I thought he was playing well; he was signed as the Australian Test rugby union fullback in 1989 and he played pretty consistent, solid football for three seasons. He was a talented player. Apparently, it came down to money, although I understand he didn't sign for a fortune with Penrith. He had a good season at Penrith and then went to Wests where his form was outstanding.

There was a fair bit of criticism when the hard-tackling front-rower Peter Johnston was allowed to go to Souths, but I won't blame the club for that. He spoke with Peter Sterling a good deal during the negotiations and he was happy with the money and happy with what the club had to offer, but apparently he just couldn't make up his mind and finally made the decision to go to Souths. When Johnston first came over from rugby union he wouldn't have played first grade at many clubs. He was a good defensive player and the fans used to talk of his big hits; they didn't always notice the tackles he missed. He improved, particularly in his last season for us in 1991, but I don't regard him the wonderful player and huge loss that some people made out.

More of an issue was the players we *didn't* sign. When Mick Cronin joined as coach in 1990, I was hopeful still that we could breathe some new life into Parramatta. We came within a point of making the semi-finals and that season a lot of the players I've spoken about had their best years — Mark Barnes, Brian Jackson, Danny Crnkovich, Greg Drake, Andrew Langford, Glen Liddiard. Sterlo had a terrific year, winning the Rothmans Medal. Matt Goodwin also performed well; he was a good first grade player and added a toughness to the pack.

I was delighted to play under Crow. I admired the bloke so much and I always thought he'd be a great coach. He was a major reason I re-signed towards the end of 1989; I knew he would bring a fresh approach. By the end of that first season under Crow, the club finally decided to go after some big names. In 1987 they'd come close to signing Greg Dowling, who wasn't happy with the initial offer from the Broncos, but at the last minute he decided to stay in Brisbane. At the end of 1990 Parramatta spoke with Mario Fenech. Peter Sterling, who had lunch with Fenech and Denis Fitzgerald, maintains that Fenech would have come to Parramatta if Fitzy upped his offer by a fairly modest (comparatively) $10,000. Mark Geyer was another forward we chased but he stayed with Penrith; apparently Paul Sironen was also approached. At the end of 1991, with Canberra's money problems public, the club went in for Laurie Daley, Brad Clyde and Glenn Lazarus as well as Newcastle's Mark Sargent — but all four stayed with their clubs. A year later the club made a genuine approach to Clyde again, as well as Andrew Ettingshausen. Once again they stayed with their clubs.

The move into the big arena of chasing the topliners was a long time coming. Parramatta now were not as attractive to these players as we were in 1987 and '88. And it seemed we always left our approaches until too late in the year. Most clubs are now on the phone by April or May. I just don't think the club had the right attitude towards player acquisition or retention. There was never any urgency in our approaches. I know through my experiences with Manly and Balmain that both clubs certainly made me feel more wanted than Parramatta ever did.

Fitzy always declared he wasn't concerned about what our supporters were saying about him not doing the right thing with players. He felt he was doing his job, he had faith in the local juniors and would not pay the ridiculous amounts for outside players. But it seemed he was only too happy when we had players approached by other clubs to up their contracts and give them what they wanted. I think he was concerned that the supporters were going to be dirty on them if he let these players go. A lot of them were placed on huge incentives. Apparently in 1991, the club paid close to $500,000 — almost a third of our salary cap, on incentives.

I suppose some people might dismiss my criticism. Many probably believed that Peter Sterling and I were getting most of the Parramatta salary cap between us, and that we were both overpaid. Sterlo and I had a lot of seasons at the club and weren't getting fortunes for much of that time. At the end neither of us would complain about what we were being paid — but we'd be happy to line up our achievements for the club with anyone else's.

Good luck to our players, they'll take what the club is prepared to pay them, and so they should. Younger players often came up to me and asked for advice, or talked about their contracts, and I used to have a shot at them. I'd tell them of the days when I was playing for $1000 a year in under-23s and $5000 a season as a first-grader. They'd come back and say that would be worth $15,000-$20,000 now. They'd be trying to justify why they were on so much money and why they should be retained on that money. But I told them straight, when they sat down to re-negotiate, they'd have to say what they had done, why they were worth a certain amount. Their only argument was that "I've played x amount of first grade games for Parramatta." And I told them if I was Fitzy I'd say: "Hold on, look at the results; we're near the bottom of the table, you haven't done enough." They really didn't have much pull. Yet the club was still re-signing them for good money.

The fact that we just missed the semi-finals in 1990 raised hopes for a good year in '91. But with Sterlo's shoulder injury reducing his year to just one match and other players not being able to maintain their form, we hit rock bottom in 1991. I inherited the captaincy and for the next two seasons was in charge of the worst-performed Parramatta sides for almost 20 years. We didn't win a trial or Challenge Cup match in '91, and then lost our first seven matches — our season was gone before most sides were even warming up. We'd come to over-rely on Peter Sterling. Sterlo controlled just about every play and no one did it better than he did. All of a sudden he wasn't there and we had to start doing things differently. It's no total excuse for us having such a bad '91 season. You shouldn't decline that much because of the loss of one player — but what a player! His exit certainly contributed.

I believe that by then the attitude of many players at Parramatta wasn't good enough; they weren't always geared 100 percent towards the game of rugby league. Some were happy to go out of a night and have a good time — which is not a bad thing to do — but they didn't have the ability to do that *and* play at a high standard week after week. The system at Parramatta allowed them to get away with it. Confidence obviously crashed too. We seemed okay at training but once we got out on the paddock, things didn't happen.

Inevitably my captaincy came under fire from some people. I had the tendency to blow up, and I'll admit there were days when I just didn't enjoy playing. They were the least enjoyable years of my career. But what kept me going was the certain belief that I didn't want to go out on such a low note. I always clung to the hope that we'd start the climb back, and I believed that we could.

18 The Rebellion of '92

Ron Massey was Jack Gibson's right-hand man when we won three premierships at Parramatta in 1981-82-83. He was the perfect sidekick for Gibbo, a coaching co-ordinator who dotted the i's and crossed the t's for the super coach. "Mass" had been with Jack for many years, went to Cronulla with him — and then took over as the Sharks' chief executive for a couple of years. He was a very knowledgeable and capable man, and when Parramatta decided to bring him back to assist Mick Cronin in 1992 I thought it was one of the smartest moves the club had made. A few months later I found myself chairing a meeting of 40 players after a Tuesday training session, most of whom were bitter at Ron Massey. We had a rebellion on our hands.

I'll outline the background. It was my opinion that discipline had gradually dropped off at Parramatta since Jack finished in 1983. John Monie was a top coach and Peter Louis was successful with the reserves. But John was pre-occupied with firsts and without a co-ordinator such as Ron Massey, it seemed that little by little the discipline, the standard of rules and regulations and the desire of the players to meet them, dropped in the lower grades. That atmosphere filtered through in the next few years as the lower grade players became first-graders. When Mick Cronin came along in 1990 he, too, had more than enough on his hands with the first-graders at training. Meanwhile, Denis Fitzgerald seemed to be loading himself with more and more responsibilities. He became leagues club chairman and an alderman on Parramatta City Council. Reserve grade coach Bob O'Reilly was certainly no disciplinarian. As I have mentioned before, a lot of players were in the comfort zone — getting paid pretty well for mediocrity as far as results went.

I regard Mick Cronin as a good coach. He knows the game well and keeps things simple, which was Jack Gibson's great asset. A lot of people believe Mick is too nice a guy, too soft, to be a good coach. I disagree. Mick quickly showed he could be tough when he had to be, but was never going to be the shouting type. He had a young side and he had trouble at times just putting on a simple tap move at training. He'd simplify things as much as possible, but the blokes sometimes would stuff them up anyway. They'd be in the wrong position, or just couldn't understand what we were doing. So Mick would have to simplify it again. Come Sunday, our execution of things we finally got right at training would more than likely go astray. The coach must have been pulling his hair out.

Now and then blokes would come up to me and say how hard and strict training was at times and that they knew that in the 80s we used to play cricket and volleyball and other games on some Tuesdays, providing some variety and fun. The difference, I told them, was that we were winning in those times so we could *afford* to have some fun. I remember when we used to skylark in the backs while the forwards were going through a move and then we'd get called over and be able to go through the move like we'd been paying attention all the time. When players joked around in a similar way with Mick Cronin as coach it was different. He pulled me aside one day and told me that it might have been okay back in the old days when we were young, and winning. We were so used to each other we could snap back to attention and do it right, but these blokes weren't going so well and couldn't switch on and off like that. He asked me to take more responsibility and to lead the way — and he had a point. In later years I certainly had to play a different role.

Generally the attitude and the discipline was way below what it had been in the first half of the 1980s.

By this stage the reserve grade wasn't performing as well as it once consistently did. Up until 1989, we were constantly in the finals of the lower grades but, while the President's Cup side finished fourth in 1990 and top of the ladder in 1991, the reserves missed the semi-finals both years. In fact, they finished 12th in 1991 — their worst result for many years. Mick Cronin had a situation in which the firsts were near the bottom of the table and performing poorly, but there was little pressure from players in reserve grade. Something had to be done to lift the standards right through the club and I was confident Ron Massey's return in the summer of 1991 would be a step in the right direction. While Crow could coach the first grade, he didn't have the time to be worrying about what blokes were doing elsewhere. Ron Massey was brought back for that reason.

But Ron didn't go down well with a lot of players. He's a very straight-down-the-middle sort of bloke and he could be pretty abrupt with the way he spoke to them. After relatively easy-going years the players weren't used to being told so directly what was required of them. And, as is always the case when a team is losing, problems get magnified. A lot of pressure was put on a lot of players. Some handled it, some didn't. Halfback Jason Bell, for example, handled it well. But I thought a player such as Glen Liddiard, who had a tonne of talent but never much discipline, couldn't come to grips with it. He asked for a release before the season even started and went to Penrith.

Discipline and enthusiasm certainly improved at the start of the year. Mass had sorted a few blokes out. We won our first match of the season against Souths, 26-20. But we lost our next five, and problems started. A lot of the dissent came from reserve-graders who thought they should have been given a go in firsts. Some of them became very disillusioned because they just didn't know where they were headed. We weren't winning games in firsts but there were very few changes to the side and whenever replacements were made, it was only the fresh reserves on the interchange bench who got a run. A lot of players wanted to know why, and I was getting used to being the father confessor, juggling all their comments and complaints.

I went to Mick Cronin about it. A few of the other blokes spoke to him about it as well. He said: "Put yourself in the place of the players in first grade. You're losing, it's towards the end of the game — would you like to be replaced?" He also felt that in a losing game, with fresh reserves on the bench and no one injured, it would have been unfair to make necessary changes. I could see his point of view but I could see the also the players' view too. It must have been very hard sitting on the bench and thinking that the opportunity was coming because the side wasn't going well — and then not getting a look in. It got to the stage where some reserve grade players didn't even bother sitting on the bench. Jason Bell was one who got into a bit of strife. He told the coach he wasn't right to sit on the bench, because he was injured. In fact, he was quite okay. He'd had enough of sitting on the bench and not getting a run.

There were players who believed Ron Massey was having too much input into team selections. That belief, coupled with Ron's sometimes blunt manner brought it all to a head. There was a blow-up at halftime in the reserve grade game the day we played Illawarra. Several players had a go at Massey about something he said in the dressing room, critical comments he made about their performance.

A few weeks earlier, in Canberra, the President's Cup had to play on the Saturday night while the other grades played on Sunday. We all stayed at the same motel and the President's Cup players were told they couldn't go out drinking on Saturday after the game, because the other players had to play next day and they weren't to be distracted. It was explained (by Massey) that if they wanted to go out and have a drink they could pay the freight at another motel and stay the night there. He told them that while ever they were with the Parramatta club, they had to do as they were told.

It was subsequently discovered that a few players did go out drinking and Massey was upset about it. It all came to a head the following weekend, after a few things were said during the week at training. A lot of the players were at Jason Bell's 21st birthday party and a few approached me and said they'd had a talk amongst themselves and a lot of them weren't happy about the way things were going. I suggested we have a meeting of all players and get everything out into the open. I knew there was nothing worse than them stewing over it and keeping it to themselves. So we decided to get the captains of all three teams to speak to their players and call a mass meeting. I wanted to get it all sorted out as quickly as possible. The under-21s were in the top five and the reserves weren't far away; it was important to clear the decks and concentrate on football.

The meeting took place the following Tuesday — just the players, no-one else. We got together in the Ray Price lounge at the Parramatta Stadium — an ironic twist, considering Pricey was the most outspoken person on players' rights I've known. It was the only time in my 14 seasons with the club that such a get-together took place. The funny thing was that the coaches walked past and realised a meeting was taking place. They thought it must have been to organise our end-of-season trip, and walked on, not suspecting a thing.

As club captain, I was voted to chair the meeting. We made sure all the points raised were written down and decided that we would take them directly to the board of directors. Everyone had the chance to have a say. The question of the night in Canberra was brought up, and a few President's Cup players asked who had the right to tell them they couldn't go to the disco after playing a match. They were young blokes, a little immature as far as facing the commitments of grade football were concerned. I told them that in the context of a professional football club they had to face certain responsibilities and make certain sacrifices. I think a lot of them had trouble facing the fact they had to start thinking and acting for themselves — and that they couldn't just keep sailing along with the crowd.

They then raised the subject of the way Ron Massey addressed them. If you didn't know Massey well you could get the wrong impression about him. Things didn't always come across the way he meant them to. With him, it was easy to take things the wrong way. Several players also said they were told Massey virtually had the full say in who was selected and who was replaced on the field. The reserve-graders again claimed they weren't getting a go and felt Massey was also standing in their way of playing first grade. There were other complaints as the meeting rolled on.

The New Zealand halfback Stu Galbraith, who'd only been at the club a few weeks at this stage, spoke up and made a good point: would all these problems be so great if we were winning? Would we even be having this meeting if we were winning? And whose fault was it that we weren't winning? It was a telling point.

I didn't particularly agree or disagree with things that were said but we wrote everything down, with the plan that I would approach Denis Fitzgerald at training on Thursday and request a meeting with the board. In the meantime, the whole thing leaked out to the press — the full story of the meeting. A lot of us were filthy about that. We thought we had done the right thing. We'd met and now were about to approach the club's management in the interest of getting everything sorted out as amicably as possible through the right channels. Fitzy said a reporter had telephoned him the next afternoon inquiring about a players' meeting concerning Ron Massey. Fitzy called the players together and was addressing us when Ron Massey actually walked out of the tunnel. Fitzy had to ask him to go back inside. From what I hear, a lower grade player was responsible for leaking the news. The story was on the back page of the Telegraph Mirror and headed discussions on radio all that weekend.

The ridiculous thing was that Jason Bell was portrayed as the bad boy, as the one who instigated everything. He honestly had nothing to do with it and wasn't even at the meeting! Bell was a 17-year-old halfback star in the President's Cup side that won the premiership in 1988 and everyone had him tabbed as the heir apparent to Sterlo. He was put up to firsts the next season but played a lot of centre, because Sterlo was still there. Jason just wasn't the thinking-style half-back Sterlo was and was never going to fill a similar role. He was great with the ball in his hands, he could beat a man and was a tough defender. But a lot of times he wouldn't run. Maybe he felt he had to fill the organiser's role; he'd been switched around between positions a fair bit, and if there was some uncertainty in his play, well, it was understandable.

Jason wasn't doing the job Crow wanted, so the club signed Stu Galbraith from New Zealand and "Belly" was dropped straight to reserves the week Galbraith arrived. I thought he had picked up his discipline and had knuckled down, but it was true he didn't get on well with Ron Massey. Bell went to Mick Cronin and discussed his situation and apparently had something of an argument with Massey. At least he brought his problems out in the open and spoke for himself. By the time of the meeting, Bell had decided he was leaving the club and he saw no benefit in going along and stirring up any trouble. Yet his name was the one most mentioned as the troublemaker — because all the talk had started at his 21st birthday party.

A players' delegation ended up getting a meeting with representatives of the board in president Alan Overton and Fitzy, plus Mick Cronin. We got together in one of the sponsors' boxes the following Tuesday night and all the issues were thrown up. Crow gave us his side of the story, the players gave their side and Overton and Fitzy gave their views as far as the board was concerned. They made it clear that Ron Massey had been re-appointed for 1993 — which is what I told the players at the meeting — and that the club wouldn't be getting rid of him, no matter what the players said. It suited me; I was happy for him to be there. It was agreed that Mass may have been a bit too abrupt in the way he said things, and while it didn't bother some (including me), it bothered some others.

Mick Cronin explained his selection policy, and told us that Ron Massey wasn't picking sides as had been claimed. He spoke well and we all left the meeting happy enough. Alan Overton then addressed a gathering of all players downstairs and told them that everything had been sorted out. We got on with training.

The only thing I worried about — and I spoke about this privately with the Crow — was that at team meetings, when performances and team matters in general were discussed — Ron Massey seemed to take charge at the expense of Mick. But Mick explained that Massey had done exactly that in 1981 with Jack Gibson and had been doing it that way for many years. The coaching caper was relatively new for Mick and he thought: "Well he's good at it, let him do it." I told him that was fair enough, but I felt the players wanted to hear more from him, and he agreed. Personally, I didn't have another problem with the Mick Cronin-Ron Massey partnership. I thought the whole thing was a bit of a storm in a teacup, although I would admit I found Ron Massey was more easy-going in the early 80s than he was in 1992. Then again the atmosphere is always different at a winning club compared to a losing one.

Massey softened his stance for a while after that. The change was noticeable. I felt a little bit sorry for him in that, while all this drama was going on over a whole week, he didn't seem to be consulted by anyone at the club. He called Mark Laurie and myself into the office later that week. He addressed "Pebbles" first and asked him about the situation (Laurie wasn't very happy with things and hadn't been getting on too well with Massey). Then he called me in and asked me why I hadn't let him know we were having the meeting and why he hadn't been given the right to reply to the criticism. He had a fair argument. I explained to him that it was something the players brought up, not me, and that

Queensland rival (and 1986 Kangaroo centre partner) Gene Miles stops Kenny in his tracks.

Above: "The team I didn't want to join". The 1985 NSW side that won the Origin trophy for the first time. Back row: (from left) Kenny, Cleal, Roach, Tunks, Wynn, Jarvis, Grothe. Middle: Alf Richards, Chris Mortimer, Jack, O'Connor, Ella, Larry Britten. Front: David Barnhill (manager), Ferguson, Steve Mortimer, Terry Fearnley, Pearce, Elias, Peter Moore (manager).

Left: Relief! Kenny, pictured here moments after fulltime with Wayne Pearce, scored the match-sealing try to wrap up the 1985 Origin series.

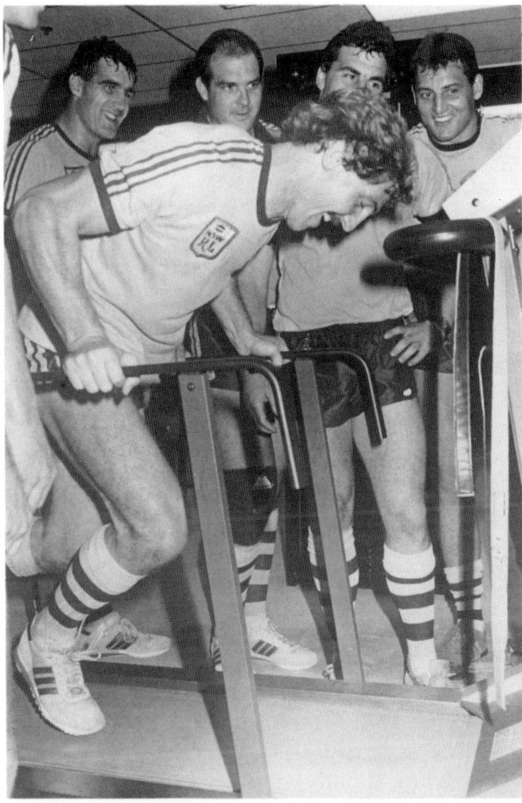

Left: Dedicated trainer? The Blues ham it up at Kerry Packer's Sydney gym, the Hyde Park Club, in 1986.

Below: Missed me! English Tiger Garry Schofield hits the turf in a Parramatta-Balmain club match in 1985. Kenny describes Schofield as the best English opponent he faced.

Above left: The perfect ending, Ray Price and Mick Cronin, savouring their victory lap after the 1986 grand final. Above right: Champagne flows! It's 1986, the last time the Eels had any reason to celebrate. Brett blames lack of foresight for the Eels' decline.

Below: The Bookends and Little John. Terry Leabeater and Geoff Bugden about to hoist high their winning coach of '86, John Monie.

Right: One of the last shots in his healthy days. From 1988, a serious knee injury forced a change of style.

Below: The Guru, Eric Grothe. Too much wasted talent, but gee he played good guitar and piano.

Bottom left: Coach Monie — up there with the best of his time.

Bottom right: Ray Price, the greatest ever competitor.

Above left: Ellery Hanley — Kenny rarely saw the best of him, as he played out of position in Australia in 1984 and was unfit in England in 1986.

Above right: Mal Meninga, Kenny's roomie on the '86 Kangaroo tour. "Mal's experience of being so far away when his wife had their first child convinced me I would never tour again."

Left: The perfect backline trio, Lewis, Kenny and Miles, even though "Bert" hankered for the Aussie No.6 jumper.

Golden Boot winner Kenny, minus moustache, in 1986.

Left: Second time a Kangaroo in 1986, but only one more Test followed despite all the best laid plans.

Below: Bert and Geno, the perfect combination — on and off the field.

Bottom: Back at Central Park, Wigan, as a Kangaroo in 1986. "I didn't know how they would receive me," remembers Kenny.

Above: Aussie on Aussie. Brett beats a despairing Mark McGaw in the Australia-Leeds clash of 1986.

Right: On the way to his only try of the 1986 Ashes series, at Old Trafford. "About time," said Wally Lewis.

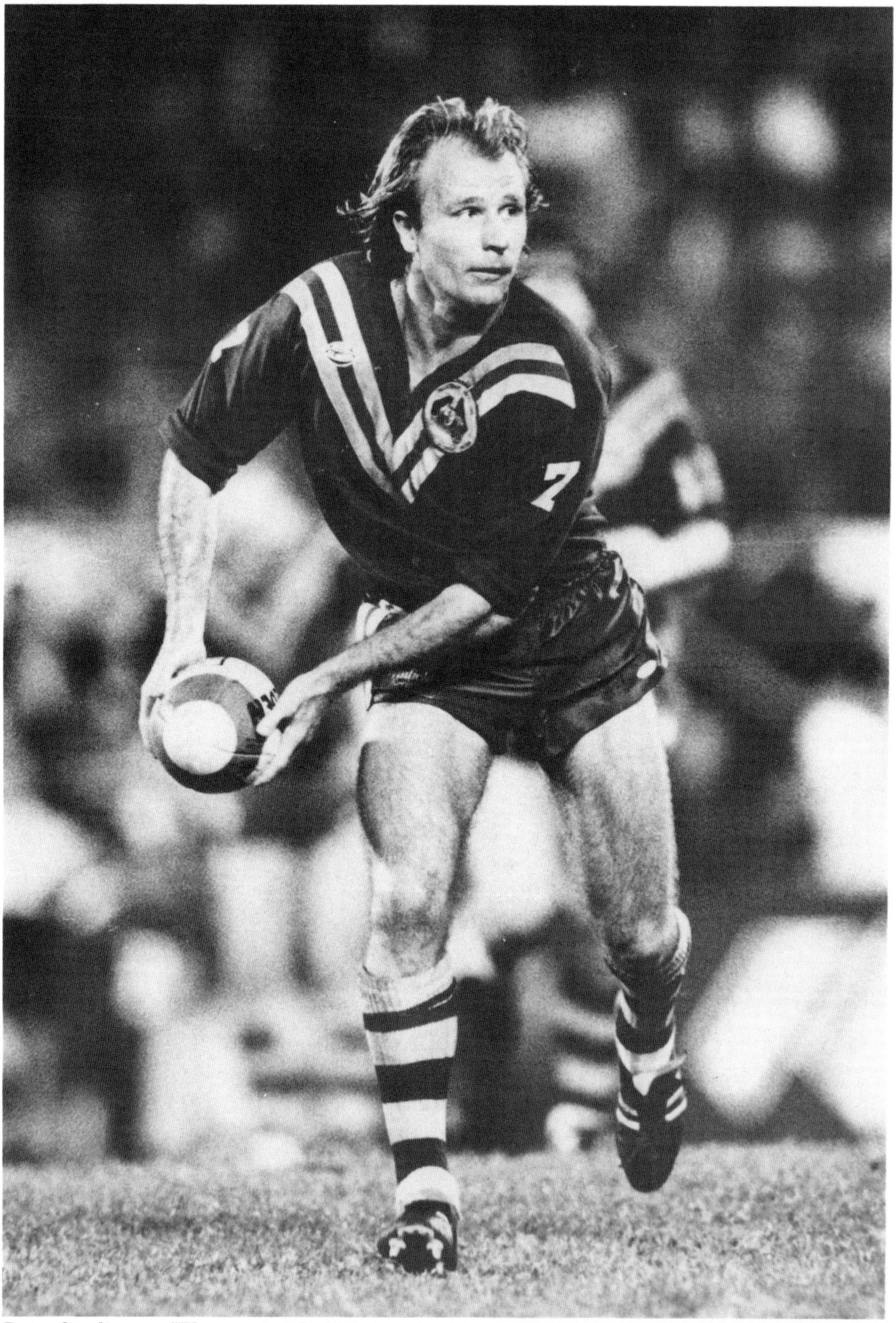

Peter Sterling — "The greatest half I played with or against. I just wish I had his lifestyle."

The Emperor of Lang Park, King of Origin. Did Brett Kenny live in Wally's shadow? "No."

Above: Out of reach of Norths' Mario Fenech. Inset: Kenny lines up the only goal-shot of his first grade career, at the WACA in 1992. The shot missed, "but gee I showed some style!"

Above: The one black mark! Getting the marching orders from Greg McCallum in 1989.

Smiling survivors, Brett Kenny and Terry Lamb. Lamb won many player awards but, with Lewis and Kenny in front of him, was unlucky to never wear the green and gold No.6.

The night of the comeback. "Old man" Kenny tackled by Souths' "young gun" Craig Field, May 14, 1993.

Right: Balmain coach Alan Jones, the man who almost stole Brett Kenny from Parramatta. "He made me realise I could have done a lot more with my life."

Below: Long-time Parramatta chief executive Denis Fitzgerald.

Right: Mick Cronin, the first-grade coach at Parramatta from 1990. If only he had the players to show what he can do ...

Below: The league world thought it was the end. In agony at Newcastle 1993 ... because of bruising to the "good" shoulder.

Saluting the kids. Waving to Nikolah and Joshua as play resumes on comeback night, against Souths in 1993, at Parramatta Stadium.

Fitzy knew about it afterwards. Why hadn't Fitzy let him know? When I realised we wouldn't get the opportunity to speak to the entire board, I wanted Ron Massey at the meeting. Mick Cronin was there, so Mass may as well have been too.

Assessing Massey's role at Parramatta, I'd say he was there to assist the coaches wherever possible — with an emphasis on first grade. He had to make sure the players were doing what was required, they were on time for training and functions, and had all the information they needed. His was a manager's role as much as anything else. I don't think his role was to govern team tactics or selections but he would offer suggestions — and that was fair enough. He'd been around a long time and had a good knowledge of the game. That was perhaps the crux of the whole thing; no one knew exactly what he was supposed to do or exactly what he did. To the players, Massey's role lacked definition.

I was assured that the suspicion that he was dictating team selections was ill-founded. The complaints on that score came from players in the under-21s. I was told Mick Cronin and Ron Massey would call each other to discuss team selections and performances and then would sit down with the other two coaches (Bob O'Reilly and Gary Pethybridge) and discuss things further in the selection meetings. But the coaches always had the final say on their teams.

For example, when it came to making changes on the field, the under-21s coach Pethybridge might want to make a change during a game and Massey might say, don't forget this bloke, or if you take him off you haven't got this bloke. He would make suggestions but again the final decision lay with the coach.

Ultimately Gary Pethybridge left for Penrith and quite a few of the under-21s followed him there. Plenty of the players who had been stirring the pot at Parramatta ended up leaving. For a time there was certainly a lot of discontent in the place. The decision was made to stick with Ron Massey and Mick Cronin, and the club weeded out the players they didn't feel would do them service. My own view is that a lot of players who left would not have gone much further if they'd stayed at Parramatta. Plenty of them were approaching 21 and if players are still in President's Cup at that age these days, often they don't have a first grade future. The player I was most sorry to see us lose was the strong young forward Phil Adamson. I thought he had a good future. He was the type of bloke who, whenever someone was egging him on, he would keep going. But he loved to have a good time and was caught up with the wrong blokes too often. Throughout a session other blokes would want to muck around and he would go along with them. If they weren't mucking around, he was fine. With a lot of those other players gone, I thought he would have blossomed at Parramatta in 1993.

I would have liked to see Jason Bell stay too, but it was his decision to leave. He just wanted to get out and start afresh somewhere else. More than anyone else, Jason Bell reminded me of what I was like when I first came into grade football — in the way he was both on the field and off it. I remember when I made a mistake I'd be guilty and drop my head a little and probably make two or three more mistakes after that. Jason was the same way. It wasn't until I got older that, after a mistake, I'd just get up, forget about it and get on with something else. That was very much due to the coaching of Jack Gibson. Belly was also like me at training, always keen to muck around and have fun.

It's fair to ponder why some of these young Parramatta players hailed as future stars simply didn't kick on. Was it the fault of the players or the coaches? In Phil Adamson's case, Mick Cronin saw his biggest problem as his defensive workload. It wasn't good enough. I know Crow spoke to him many times about improving that area and told him that if he did he'd be in first grade. Phil didn't do it; he was too lazy. With other players the reasons varied. I suppose the whole system of talent identification, retention and development, from management down to coaching, has to take some responsibility for the fact that so many good youngsters didn't succeed. But frankly the question of "success" is mainly up to the player; it's how much he wants success that dictates whether he will be just a good grade player, a good first grade player, or something even more. I feel, in some cases, players were happy with playing reserve grade or President's Cup. They earned good money and didn't have a great desire to go any higher. And they didn't.

It is up to the administration and coaching staff at any club to weed out these players. At Parramatta that took long enough to happen. That's where the 1992 and '93 seasons will be judged as a crucial time at the club. If Ron Massey's re-emergence did one thing, it brought everything to a head at Parramatta. We had a clean-out of players and the club decided to start afresh. Players had to handle tougher disciplinary demands. The benefit was starting to show in 1993 when the club had a much better start to the season than in the previous two years. I must admit I was worried before the 1993 season that so many players had left, and the club hadn't bought many to replace them. But players began to take their chances, and we got away to a great start.

Morale had improved 100 percent and players such as Cameron Blair and Mark Horo started the season as well as they ever had. Paul Dunn, and Michael Speechley to a lesser degree, proved to be large influences in the new-look Parramatta, 1993. Speechley shows his experience on the field but doesn't talk much off it, whereas Paul Dunn's experience and knowledge rubbed off tremendously on other players in both areas. He was always talking to the players. The talk was always positive and Dunn quickly became a big influence at Parramatta in 1993, a real leader for the younger players.

Well before I was injured in the Sevens I had decided to give up the captaincy. It was my last season and I felt someone else might get more out of the players than me. It was more logical for someone who was going to be there long-term to take over — and I could be there to help in their first year. I was proud to be Parramatta captain, although I never aspired to it, nor to captain my country or anything quite so lofty. When Peter Sterling was injured in 1991, I was the next senior player on the ladder, and it was only natural I took over. For the most part, I enjoyed it, just as I enjoyed being the senior player in the club and being able to impart my knowledge and experience to the younger blokes. I had to come to terms with the fact that all of a sudden there was no Sterlo, or Eric Grothe or Steve Ella around, just myself and "Pebbles" Laurie, who was a pretty quiet bloke. Having so many youngsters around probably kept me on my toes and kept me young too. They used to stir me about my age and I'd have a shot back, telling them to come and see me when they were 32 — to come and see me and tell me what *they* were doing then. As a 31 or 32-year-old father of three, I was playing with the likes of Michael Buettner, in his first year out of school and with not a care in the world.

My relationship with the administration changed too. I'd learned from a few things I'd done in my earlier years; I have told of being fined for having my say about player recruitment. I had talks with club president Alan Overton and I was starting to see things through different eyes. I worked as well as I could with Denis Fitzgerald, although I wasn't in full agreement as to the way he ran things.

I suppose I'd be rated an "emotional-type" captain. I wasn't the Ray Price type who would do things and say "follow me" and hopefully the others would follow his example. I wasn't the Steve Edge type who would always keep calm and know exactly what to say. I guess I let emotions take over a little bit. At the time of my captaincy we were losing games and making silly mistakes all the time. I knew the team was a lot better than it was showing — and I would rip into players behind the goal line. Anyone who was at the games could see me flying off the handle behind the goal line and blokes would be walking back after missing tackles and I would be screaming at them.

I admit that after the 1992 game at the Gold Coast, when we butchered the match with schoolboy errors and went down 26-6, that I actually apologised to the team for going off my brain at them. I came in after the match and knocked a big tank of water over in a fit of rage. David Penna told me later he was getting changed at the time and all he could hear was this big smash and the sound of water splashing. Luckily, I do cool down pretty quickly. I still felt the need to apologise later but several players came up to me individually and said they didn't mind, they needed something like that to ram home how badly they'd played.

I had my critics as a captain, and people have told me they've heard comments from within the club that I wasn't a good captain and that was one of the reasons we didn't play well in 1991 and '92. That's their opinion and they're entitled to it. But the opinions of such people was not the reason I gave the captaincy away. I tried to be positive during play but after we'd conceded a try, I'd rip in. The frustration used to build up inside me and then spill over. It surprised Parramatta people because when Mick Cronin and Ray Price or Steve Edge were there, I'd say little behind the line. Pricey would certainly rip in and then Crow would end with some quiet, positive comments. When Sterlo was captain I was a bit like Pricey, I'd point something out and yell a bit, but Sterlo would be the settling voice and pick his words carefully. When I was captain we had a fairly young side, but I knew they should have been producing more.

I realise what some people said when the side had a good start without me in 1993 — it was because I wasn't there screaming at them. There was a theory that they were better off without me. It's been reported back to me plenty of times that certain people were saying in 1992 that I was too old and too slow and should have given the game away. One of the blokes I worked with told me that when I was out with a shoulder injury in '93 he was discussing with a customer how well Parramatta were going. "You know why," the bloke said, "because Brett Kenny is not playing. He's getting too old, he's too slow. Slows the rest of them down too much."

There weren't too many complaints in 1991 when Sterlo got busted and I was shifted to lock. I didn't miss a match, won the clubman of the year award and some people were even tipping me to win the Rothmans Medal. I was happy with my form. But by 1992 when I moved back to five-eighth, there were people who were out for me. I was never going to be the same player I was in the mid-80s, I was older and slower — the knee injury played its part there — but I thought I had improved other facets of my game and believed I was still contributing positively to the team. I knew I could still play the game at that level and believed I was still setting myself a high standard, and trying to set the standard for the rest of the team.

I never wanted to finish my career with people saying: "He's too old, he should have given the game away earlier." You can say you don't listen to critics, but no one likes to hear things like that. In football you have to do it for yourself, not for them. John Monie, in a message sent from England for my testimonial, said that he felt I could finish my career the way I started it. It's never nice to hear people say that you're "losing it." But Ray Price and Mick Cronin faced similar criticism and in my books they finished right at the top. I knew I wanted to do the same – – and that's why I was keen to get away at the end of 1992 and decide whether I had the desire, the ability and the fitness to go through another season. Even after the shoulder injury knocked me for six, I still knew in my heart I could get back. I still dreamed of a last day at the football, of doing a final victory lap around Parramatta Stadium — saying goodbye to the fans and with them thinking: "He gave us great service ... right to the end."

19

Regrets ... I Have a Few

The work required for this book has provided a process of revealing self-analysis for me. I have played football because I've enjoyed it — it has been my life. Most of the things I have in life have directly or indirectly come from rugby league. I find it a fairly daunting prospect to contemplate life without football.

I have no trade, and that probably is my greatest regret. It virtually means that when football is gone, I am starting over. I've had a dozen jobs, and these days I drive a truck for a fruit juice company. I won't say that's embarrassing, but when I look at what some other footballers of my era have done with the profile they've gained from their careers, I feel a little inadequate. It's a regret I have, and something that I hope I may be able to rectify. I'd dearly like to join the media. After 14 seasons in first grade, perhaps people would like to know my thoughts on rugby league through a newspaper column or through television or radio. I was short on the confidence to push myself in earlier years and I guess that hasn't helped me. I know early on I wasn't regarded as being much of a speaker in public, but I have grown in confidence over the past few years and feel quite comfortable with the task now.

But retirement is a difficult time for a sportsman, bringing about a complete change in the life he has been accustomed to. I'm certainly looking forward to having more time with Julie and my three great kids Joshua, Nikolah and Mitchell. I've stuck by the creed of paying cash for everything I can since I first left school, so I have few debts and a lovely house at Glenhaven. I certainly wouldn't be crying poor, because league has been kind to me financially in my last few seasons.

But I haven't earned any sort of fortune. There's a large tax component to contend with, plus the fact that you only get two pay packets a year — in June and October. I believe that needs changing — that clubs should look at paying their players monthly or even weekly in some cases. I know that a few clubs already do. People who have seen me pull up in my truck during the summer have asked me: "Is this your off-season job; you don't HAVE to work during the season do you?" I sure do, and always have — or tried to.

To work in rugby league, on the administration side, would be great. Not coaching, I have no ambition whatsoever to do that — past kids' level anyway. For a time I actually thought I might have a future in league, off the field, when I briefly worked for Parramatta as a development officer. That is a chapter with a bad ending in my working life. The opportunity I had was taken from me in bitter circumstances.

I'd had enough of working at Appletise when they wouldn't give me time off to take a trip to Cairns, my prize for winning the clubman of the year award in 1991. When I resigned, I explained the reasons to Denis Fitzgerald and asked if there was any chance of some part-time work at the club to tide me over until after Christmas. After that I'd look for something else. He came up with the plan that I could work in the office as a development officer. Development manager Mark Donkin had had trouble getting players to go out to schools with him and help with the workload, so it was certainly an opportunity.

I was aware it mightn't last, but things were going really well. Mark showed me the ropes thoroughly and it really opened my eyes to what goes on behind the scenes at a professional football club, There was so much more involved in it than going around schools and teaching kids how to kick and pass. Mark put a lot of time into me and I was starting to get fairly independent in what I was doing.

We had a staff meeting in early January and were told that Matt Adamson, one of our lower grade players, was going to start as development officer at the end of the month. Matt had just re-signed and the job was an extra lure as part of the deal. Most of the staff thought he would be an extra and there would be three of us in the development office. Mark and I talked about how we would all work together. Maybe I was naive, but I had no hint whatsoever from Denis Fitzgerald that I would be finishing up. I even asked officer manager Kevin Wise and he seemed to think I'd be kept on.

The day arrived when Matt Adamson was scheduled to start, a Monday. Denis came to see me after the Sevens and asked if could he have a word with me at work the next day. The next morning Fitzy called me in and said I had to finish up. "Matt's starting, we can't have two of you; you're going to have to go," he said. I asked when, and he said that day.

Why the hell couldn't Fitzy have told me a month earlier what would be happening? At least then I could have looked for a job, had some notice of what was in the wind. I'm not complaining about being put off *per se*; I knew from the start the position most likely would be temporary, although I'll admit I did get my hopes up that it would last. But the impersonal, inconsiderate way I was called into the office and told "see you later" was one of the most disgraceful things that has happened to me in football. In my view it was poor management and poor human relations. The Parramatta administration obviously knew for a whole month that I was going to be given the bullet, yet waited until the last day before telling me. If I'd been told a few weeks earlier that I was finishing, it would not have been an issue. But nothing was explained, not a word was said; I had begun to presume that I would be kept on because I was going well at it.

Mark Donkin couldn't believe it either. All the time and effort he put into training me was down the drain. The experience of that job, though, for all the disappointment at the end of it, really convinced me I wanted to work in rugby league. It's the thing in life that I know best and what I enjoy most. The ironic thing was that Matt Adamson asked for a release from his two-year contract after just one season and cleared out to another club — Penrith. At least I'd given 12 years loyalty to the club, rejecting pressures to leave Parramatta at different times. They had to employ someone else — and Michael Buettner now has the job.

The episode played on my mind when my contract was up at the end of 1992, but the fact was I wanted to finish my career with Parramatta, and I felt I owed it to the coaches and players. I certainly didn't feel I owed anything to Denis Fitzgerald.

Someone in my family was so irate about it they called the press and there was a great ruckus, and frantic phone calls to try to stop the story breaking. I had Fitzy and club president Alan Overton trying to get me to retract my comments when the story did appear. I didn't go looking for a story to be printed, but I was filthy and I certainly wasn't going to hide my feelings when asked. Fitzy was quoted in the story as saying: "When Brett resigned from his sales rep job I said we would employ him as a development officer on a casual basis. At the time I stressed the position was casual because of our commitment to Matt Adamson. When Adamson was injured late last year and could not start, we kept Brett on and he has done a great job. Yesterday we had no alternative but to stand Brett down because there is no other job in the club at this stage. It saddened me that Brett was put off but I had given my word to Matt Adamson. This is Brett's testimonial year and apart from ensuring he gets full support from the club to make it a success we will do our best to find him a job. There are already a number of possibilities, anyone of which could bear fruit this week."

Luckily Steve Edge, my ex-team-mate and Parramatta's marketing manager, helped out in my quest for a job. Edgey made a few calls and within a couple of weeks I had the choice of two jobs and elected to take the one with Berrivale after talking to Ken Ives, who is a keen footy fan. When I accepted the position he told me it wouldn't be available for a month or so, as he had to go through head office in Adelaide and get a few things sorted out. I thought it didn't sound too definite, that maybe they were going to fob me off. But it finally came around and in '93 there I was working for Berrivale, delivering fresh orange juice to supermarkets and grocery stores in a two-tonne truck. They're a big company and hopefully I can advance there.

People seem to hold a misconception that top footballers don't have to work. These days a lot of them don't. It's easier for the new generation because they can be 21 and earning between $100,000 and $150,000 a season — and if they're good enough, get it for the next 10 years. I only reached the $100,000 mark for the last three years of my career. For the first half of my career I didn't earn what anyone would regard as good money. Most people my age were earning close to what I was, or more, with their regular jobs.

There are a lot more "fulltime professionals" in the game today, although everyone at Parramatta has a job. Peter Sterling was the only exception, but he always had some sort of media income. With players having to go into camp for such long periods leading up to representative matches these days, I'd imagine it's becoming even harder to hold down a good job, although it seems the sales rep field has proved that using a footballer's profile can be beneficial. Many players these days combine a good career with their football.

I doubt that fulltime professionalism right across the board will ever come. The likelihood is that it will always be restricted to just the elite. I don't think Australia has the population and financial resources to support fulltime professional sport as America and Britain can. I question why the NSWRL and ARL can't supplement the contracts of top players, as the Queensland Rugby League did with their internationals in the early 80s. Players make a lot of money for the League, especially in the State of Origin series, which is a $1 million gate every time they play a match.

I suppose my work-football experience is more like the older guard, akin to the players in the era before me who would work as garbos or in a leagues club cellar (as I did for a few years) or driving trucks. Blue collar men. A lot more players seem to fit in tertiary studies and build towards more solid careers in the 90s.

My greatest regret is that I didn't do more with my schooling and that I never completed a trade. If I could have my time over again that is one thing I would definitely do. I started as a carpenter and studied at Tech fulltime but couldn't get a job. Not that long after I was playing grade football, and then suddenly first grade — so my ambitions were focussed on the football field. I used to dream of making lots of money, having a nice car and using my name if I was successful. I guess I haven't chased that dream as well as I should have. I've never endorsed one product, never done any media work other than a few promotions for 2WS. Never even done a Lowes ad! The only time I've appeared in an advertising campaign was in the full-page colour advertisements for Winfield to promote the State of Origin — the ones featuring Wally Lewis and myself arm-wrestling.

No doubt one of my problems has been that I don't chase things. You ask me for an opinion, I'll give it to you. You ask me to do something, I'll do it. Don't ask and I'll probably overlook it. It applies to around the house too ... just ask Julie! Perhaps readers of this book will realise that footballers do have strong opinions, but we don't necessarily try to ram them down people's throats. In my case, I've probably got an image that I don't care about things. I care alright, but I don't necessarily voice my opinion at the time. It may take me a while to come up with a solution or a particular point of view — while others will be more immediate and boisterous about it. I'll sit back and think, and wait and my solution might come later. That's just me. Maybe I've taken a lot of things for granted too. People probably look at me and think: with all you have done in the game and with the high profile league now enjoys, how the hell is it that you are going to end up driving a truck? It's a fact of life with me, but I am encouraged about what has happened for a lot of players in the last few years. There seem to be more opportunities after playing days are over. Maybe it will turn out to be the case with me, too.

I'd like to think I've been pretty good with my money. We're in our third house and we owned the previous two when we sold them. The money I received from my stint with Wigan virtually paid off our first house at Greystanes. We paid off the mortgage on our current home with my testimonial money.

Strangely enough, the shoulder injury of '93 helped prepare me for life after football. There was no training, no playing for a while — and that's something

I'm going to have to get used to. I am at the end of a career — and at the crossroads of my life. I don't dwell on it too much; I believe in fate to a degree. I'm a Pisces, a bit of a dreamer. I'll just take it as it comes from here.

Coaching at the top level is not a consideration for me. I've always played to game to enjoy it, and I don't think coaching first grade is an enjoyable thing. The stress, the pressure and the demands are unbelievable. After 14 years of going through the pressures of being a first grade player, I want a break. My family has been through it too, they deserve a break. I'd love to coach kids, though, to teach them the game and not to worry about whether they win or lose. I'm talking about 10-year-olds or younger. By the time they get to their mid-teens winning becomes all-important, some parents become over-ambitious for their kids and the enjoyment factor can be lost. I'll never forget coaching Guildford's under-10s the year I started in first grade; I'd love to do it again.

I believe I am very fortunate in that I have just *enjoyed* being a footballer. I've loved playing and I have been fortunate I have derived a lot of success and financial reward from it. To think I've played so many seasons of first grade, played for my country, gone on two undefeated Kangaroo tours, played at Wembley and won the Lance Todd Trophy, won four grand finals, won State of Origin series, the Golden Boot award. It's hard to believe how many "firsts" I've been fortunate enough to enjoy — first Parramatta premiership, first unbeaten Kangaroo tour, first Australian to win the best player award at Wembley, member of the first NSW side to win the State of Origin, and member of the first side from either state to win the series 3-0. Rugby league has been extremely good to me. I guess I've always known that, but these last few months of my career have really brought it home to me.

Regrets? None really, except the injury in '93. My last season was very special to me. To have had to go through it with the burden of a shoulder problem that needed surgery, but without the luxury of having that time, was extremely disappointing. But there's no use me crying about it, just overcoming it. That's just football ... and life.

How would I like to be remembered? Well, I hope people will remember me for the good things I did. I suppose some will think that I didn't get excited, didn't look interested at times, that I had good periods and not so good periods. I think there's probably a perception of me — ah, Brett Kenny — he just took things as they came.

The assurance I can give is that I wouldn't have been playing, and kept playing, if I hadn't enjoyed it and sustained my interest in the game. Yep, I can assure you I got nervous, I got keyed-up — but I've always been one to keep things inside. Perhaps people will remember me as someone who played the game the way it should be played. I hope I brought pleasure to the fans of the game, and especially to the Parramatta people. That's important to me. It's a great thing for a human being to be able to do — to bring pleasure to other people through something he himself loved doing.

20 Life According to Bert

Over my years in the game I've rarely come out publicly with strong views on rugby league. I always stuck to the belief that my role was to play the game and that I'd leave others to dissect it. If my opinion was sought, though, I wouldn't shy away from saying what I thought, especially in my later years. My comments on Parramatta's buying policy had got me into trouble, and I spoke out a few times about my rivalry with Wally Lewis. Probably the only other time I hit the headlines for something I said rather than what I did was in 1985 when I declared I was tired and didn't care if I played for Australia again.

None of that means I haven't held firm opinions. People are always coming up to me asking about aspects of the game. So in this chapter, for what they are worth, I offer my views on subjects which I feel strongly about. I have also tackled the most common questions I've been asked over the years — about people, places, events and issues.

People

IN-GOAL ADJUDICATORS: I feel they often get paid for just sitting in the sun. Too many times they are not in the right position when they have to make a decision. How many times have you seen a replay of a try and the in-goal man hasn't been close enough? In such cases it's left to the ref to make the decision himself. The in-goal guys should be positionally excellent, and they should get as close to the action as they possibly can without hampering play.

I also believe they should be able to rule on touch line decisions close to the goal line, and to assist the touch judge and referee in touch-in-goal decisions. A good example was a situation in an Origin match in 1993 when the ball was kicked downfield and clearly bounced over the top of the corner post, yet the touch judge 30 or 40 metres downfield ruled it went into touch. The in-goal adjudicator was actually much closer but was not entitled to have an opinion. In tough try decisions in the corner, the referee, touch judge and in-goal adjudicator should all consult. Sometimes this happens.

REFEREES: I know it will surprise (even amaze) a lot of Parramatta supporters, but the best referee I played under was Greg Hartley! There, I've said it. Hartley got on well with players, never chastised them, always called them by their names. Generally he gave players a lot of respect — and in return he got it back. A lot of refs today don't do that; they tend to treat you as a stern schoolmaster would his pupils. If you treat people in such a condescending way, chances are you'll get treated the same way in return.

JACK GIBSON: Jack was the best coach I had. I learned a lot about the game, about the disciplines of the game in particular, from him. He simplified things, he knew what was required to win but he never over-coached; he felt players needed a certain freedom to express themselves on the field.

JOHN MONIE: I was very fortunate to go from Jack Gibson to John Monie as my coach at Parramatta. His record confirms that he is obviously a very good coach, a very good tactical coach, particularly when it comes to set moves and out-manoeuvring the opposition. From what I have been told, a lot of the first grade tap plays came from John — in the period in which Monie was reserve grade coach under Jack. That alone shows how well respected he was when it came to tactical plays.

FRANK STANTON: I didn't think at the time that Frank Stanton was the type of bloke I'd like to ask around for dinner, nor, perhaps, that he was such a good coach. But after the 1982 Kangaroo tour I realised what he was about, and what he had tried to achieve on that tour through a tough disciplinary approach. He was a lot better, and much more effective, than I first thought. He was the bloke who stuck his neck out and gave me my first break in Test football. I'm very thankful for that.

JOHN PEARD: I have a lot of respect for my first coach at first grade level. He was the man who gave me my start and put me on the road to the career I've been fortunate to enjoy. Peardy took a big risk by putting such an inexperienced 19-year-old in his side at Parramatta, and he continually helped boost my confidence throughout the season. I hope that what I have been able to achieve since has given John Peard at least a small sense of pride.

MICK CRONIN: As a great player he had a big influence on my development, and that of a lot of Parramatta players. As a coach we haven't yet seen the best of him, because of the quality of the teams he's had at Parramatta. I think he displayed with NSW Country in 1992 what he was capable of. Some people tended to downplay Crow's achievement with that Country side. The fact was, Country won for the first time since he played in the winning side of 1975. It was a coaching feat that Warren Ryan couldn't achieve.

People say that Mick Cronin is too nice to be a coach, and the bloke certainly is a gentleman. But how would outsiders know if he's too "nice" to coach, whatever that means? He has great knowledge of the game and generates a lot of respect from players. He is also extremely honest. I just wish he had more experienced teams at Parramatta to give him the chance to show his true worth as a coach.

MEDIA: The media play a big part in rugby league and I've had no great problems with them over the years, although we have been instructed at Parramatta not to speak to, or at least to be very wary of, certain members of the press gang. The *Telegraph-Mirror's* Ray Chesterton, in fact, is banned from the Parramatta dressing-room. Apart from isolated incidents, I've always got on well with media men and women. My one major problem over a lot of years came when I was misquoted about the Wigan-St Helens match of 1985. I subsequently emerged from that whole business not looking too good. Reporters have often rung me up, written their story and then called back to check that I am happy with what I was quoted as saying. I've always appreciated that. It's a field that interests me, and I'd like to join the media in some capacity now that I have retired.

My firm advice to new players in first grade is to think carefully about what they say to the media. A lot of times, if things aren't put quite right, it can come out looking very wrong indeed when you see it in print. A throwaway line can suddenly look a whole lot more dramatic than you thought. The game gets such coverage now that it would be the smart thing for clubs to invite people involved in the media to training at the start of the season and have a session with the players. Advice on how to handle the TV cameras, radio microphones and reporters in general would be extremely helpful.

ERIC GROTHE: The Guru ranks as one of the greatest wingers Australia has produced. Apart from being a sensational footballer, he was very talented in other areas as well, particularly musically. Eric could play guitar, piano and drums. I'll always remember when we were in camp with the NSW side in Sydney and a few of us had gone to see a movie in the city. We were walking back to our hotel, looking for a cab, when we passed one of Geoffrey Edelsten's luxurious 24-hour medical centres. There was no one in it except for a receptionist — and this big piano. Eric's walked in, sat down at the piano and started to play the theme from *Chariots of Fire*. The receptionist was startled, and so were some of the players.

I don't think Eric ever realised what football talent he had, especially in the area of pure pace. I'd rank him as probably the quickest player I've been associated with; we'd be doing sprint training and Steve Ella, Neil Hunt and myself would be flat-out against each other and Eric would be there beside us, cruising, looking across with a smile on his face. If we were asked to do two 200-metre sprints, he'd always do the first one flat-out and then come up with an excuse (usually his crook knees) and get out of the second. Yet in a game he could run 90 metres to score a try; they'd kick off to him and if he made a break he'd run another 90 metres. He only ever put in extra effort if it was really necessary.

He also pulled off some of the best try-saving tackles I've ever seen, coming from impossible positions to stop certain tries. In our first game at Parramatta Stadium, he launched himself at St George five-eighth Steve Robinson right on the line and intentionally punched the ball from his hands just as Robinson was about to throw his body over for the try. The ball went over the dead-ball line. It was intentional alright. In the 90s it would have been a penalty try, because you could no longer intentionally strip a player of possession.

STEVE ELLA: Whenever Steve Ella is mentioned, I think about his incredible courage and determination. His brilliant career was plagued by bad knee and shoulder injuries. He was fabulously fast on his feet. I'll never forget a grand final against Manly when he stepped Paul Vautin and left him grasping at air. His ability to change direction at top pace was pretty close to unbelievable.

Injury finally took its toll and he retired at 28. If it hadn't been for the injuries, Zip would still be playing today and by now would be regarded as one of the best the game has ever produced.

NEIL HUNT: Hunty was a fine player who didn't receive the recognition he deserved. Neil, or "Guilty" as Jack Gibson christened him (because every time there was a problem he tended to look like the guilty party), got a lot of respect and admiration from me, not just as a footballer. He was never on a great amount of money compared to the higher-profile players, but he was able to look after himself and his family by being smart with his money. He has the lifestyle others on better money couldn't have because he was always very sensible. We still keep in touch and will always be good mates.

PAUL TAYLOR: Tas was a great character and a great defender who once completed 52 tackles for Parramatta in a single match. He enjoyed having a good time as much as he enjoyed his football. It could never be said that he was one of the great trainers. One day that sticks in my mind was when we had our regular 10km time trial at Mt Pritchard on a Sunday morning. Tas had been out for the night; in fact, I think he got home just in time to get his training gear and head to Mt Pritchard. He looked dreadful and you could smell the grog on him a mile away. He headed straight out in front and beat everyone home!

RAY PRICE: One the great players and great competitors of rugby league. At Parramatta Pricey also had a reputation for being extra tight with his money. I'm not sure that was entirely right; he looked after his money very well, and never said no if there was something worthwhile he could buy for his family. Pricey was a dedicated players' man. He used to get into a lot of strife with the management at Parramatta because he was so willing to stick up for himself and the other players. Pricey had a big influence on me staying at Parramatta when I received a good offer from Manly in 1984. He sat me down and had a good talk to me and virtually convinced me to stay because it would be better for me.

PETER STERLING: He was the greatest halfback I played with or against at any level. On a personal level it was well known that he was an avid gambler, his diet wasn't the best and that he was articulate and confident. The thing about Sterlo is that people always want to be around him. He started up a horse racing contest at Parramatta, involving 26 players, and each player drew a letter of the alphabet each week. For every winner that started with his letter (in Sydney and Melbourne each Saturday), he got a point. The first to get 15 points took the pool and we started again. It proved very popular and even in Sterlo's last year when he suffered the shoulder injury that stopped his career, he still had to come down once a week and run the contest. Blokes are still wanting to get it going again, but no one has Sterlo's organisational ability. He was also the king of trivia, organising nights to raise money for the end-of-season trips.

Sterlo was always excellent with the media, and it was no surprise at all that he joined the fourth estate fulltime after his playing days ended. He was immediately successful. Holding down jobs was never a strong point with Sterlo — and he had a few opportunities over the years — but he has worked hard with Channel 9 and deserves his success.

WALLY LEWIS: He's the best five-eighth I have seen and I can't argue with those who claim that he was the greatest player the game has produced. I found him a very honest sort of bloke, very much a family man who also did a lot for charities and organisations. That's something that not too many people know about. People believe what they read in the paper about Wally — that he can be surly and selfish — but off the field he has always seemed very kind-hearted, and popular with the other players.

LAURIE DALEY: Many people rate him the new superstar of the game and have tagged him the world's best player. I wouldn't go that far yet. He is an excellent player, but I would agree with Rex Mossop, who caused a bit of a stir when he said Daley couldn't be regarded as a "great" yet. Rex pointed to those times in a game when his coach or team-mates might be looking for him to turn a match around, but he didn't step forward. He can be very quiet in games, or dynamite. He reminds me a lot of myself early in my career, especially when I was in the centres. Then, like Laurie today, I wouldn't get involved too much early in a game. I would wait for the action to come to me as he does. Laurie will at times do only as much as he feels he has to. But he has all the skills in attack, kicking and defence and is physically very strong for a five-eighth. I didn't play against him much, because he was injured a few times when we played Canberra, but when I did I had to be on my guard because he is a player quite capable of wrecking the reputations of any opponent.

DENIS FITZGERALD: There is a popularly-held view that Denis is a very good administrator — and he may well be as far as the NSWRL are concerned or in the perception of the Sydney media. He has certainly always had the interests of the club in mind inwhat he has done. He was responsible for turning Parramatta's administration around in the late 1970s and early 80s. But I believe that at times he has not been in touch with his players, and not as efficient and professional as he should have been. He has done extremely well as chairman of Parramatta Leagues Club. The club is a far better place than it was in the early 80s when I worked there. With its different lounges and bars, entertainment and facilities for members, the place has improved dramatically. Much of that improvement is due to the input of Denis Fitzgerald. But the time given to the leagues club, and to his duties as an alderman on Parramatta Council, has been to the detriment of his responsibilities with the football club. In my view, it happened too often that he didn't have the time to address certain things. At those times he wouldn't delegate other people to do the job. There are some dealings I had with Fitzy, documented in this book already, which threw doubt over the view held of him as a top-notch administrator. Often with him it came down to poor human relations.

It is now halfway through 1993 as I write this, and certain aspects of my final contract with Parramatta still haven't been sorted out — even though I signed the contract last December. They should have been sorted out before the start of the season. Not all are Denis Fitzgerald's fault, yet he was the man handling the negotiations. At Parramatta, he is the man who has to get things done.

It is my opinion that in the past few seasons he has had too much control at

Parramatta. In his position as general manager employed by the board of directors, he is totally answerable to that board. Instead it has seemed at times that he held total power, and was answerable to no one.

I would never suggest that Denis did not have the club at heart in all he has done. It's just that he has a tendency to see things his way only; the checks and balances that are a required part of any successful administration at any club have seemed to be missing at Parramatta. If there is blame for the lack of success at the club after the golden years of the early '80s, I believe it must be assigned to the board of directors (significantly, there were some personnel changes in 1993) for not having kept a tighter reign on Fitzy. Some members of the board have even stated in the press that they should have had more input — and claim that that will happen from now on. We'll see.

FANS: I suppose supporters are the same all over the world, you get good and bad. At Wigan I was a hero after Wembley and they didn't want me to go home. A few days later I was the villain because I didn't turn in a blinder. At Parramatta the fans were very supportive when we were winning. In less successful times they were quick to claim that I was getting too much money, was too slow and should have retired. I know a lot of Parramatta fans used to reckon I was a hopeless captain as well, only when we lost, of course. Everyone has an opinion in rugby league and when you're not winning, everyone has a theory why. The majority of fans have been good to me over the years, though, and Parramatta fans are among the best and most loyal. I just hope they remember me for any pleasure I gave them on the football field.

Places

CUMBERLAND OVAL: Compared to Parramatta Stadium, Cumberland Oval was a terrible ground as far as facilities went. But it was home for the first two seasons of my career and I'm sure it intimidated opponents. They had to enter the ground on the opposite side to the stand and take the long walk in front of the hill, copping flak from our supporters, I would have hated to be an opposition player walking in to Cumberland. The dressing room facilities were awful; we had three tiny rooms (one for firsts, one for the lower grades, one for getting rubbed down). Things improved marginally when Jack Gibson had one wall knocked down to make the main room bigger. When we went out for our warm-ups before a match we had to walk along a corridor, through a wire door, and push through the mob at the canteen. Cumberland's grandstand was tiny and old, but I don't think anyone who went there would forget the stamping of the feet on the timber floor, the stand vibrating as the fans screamed: "Parra (stamp, stamp, stamp), Parra!"

PARRAMATTA STADIUM: The new ground gets my vote as the best in rugby league, but I'd love to see it improved even more by being fully enclosed, with stands all around. That's the way it was planned — like an American superdome — but funding couldn't be found. It's akin to the Sydney Football Stadium in one way in that it is so comfortable, for players and spectators, that you don't get such a strong home-ground advantage — except through the weight of numbers in the crowd. Players just enjoy playing there, and feel very comfortable with such good facilities. How different from Cumberland where the surface was hard and facilities outdated, or (the old) North Sydney Oval when it was like a rock, or Caltex which was sandy and always windy, or Gold Coast because it was so far away and just being there made you feel like you were on holiday.

SYDNEY CRICKET GROUND: It was a wonderful place to play, because you knew whenever you were there it was a big game. It had so much character, so much open space and great atmosphere when it was full. But the dressing rooms were old and lousy (I've had plenty of cold showers there) and needed updating 20 years ago.

SYDNEY FOOTBALL STADIUM: As with Parramatta Stadium, the facilities for players are top-class and the crowd is close. Despite getting a lot of wear, the playing surface is fine. For the fans it looks great, but as has been widely reported it's not as functional as it should be, particularly when it rains. I can't compare it to the SCG or other grounds as far as atmosphere goes, because it's never been even half full when I've played there and that's a disappointment.

CENTRAL PARK (WIGAN): The thing that hits you first about English grounds is how old they are, so different from the reasonably modern grounds in Australia with their cement stands and grassed hills. Many of the grounds have old wooden stands and terraces; Central Park at Wigan is one of the best of them, comparable to Headingley, Leeds. I haven't seen the ground since a new stand was added at the clubhouse end, but it sounds first-class. I'll always remember the contrast between English and Aussie grounds in the dressing rooms too; at Central Park there were just three or four showers and two big baths! I took the shower. Atmosphere-wise, it was a great place. It could fit about 30,000 and the crowd always seemed bigger than it was because the people were so close to you and made so much noise.

CARLAW PARK (AUCKLAND): I only played there once, but for an international ground the playing surface was a disgrace. It was sandy and boggy and could hardly take any water before being flooded. The stands on both sides were more like those at an English ground; old and very close.

LANG PARK (BRISBANE): I never minded playing there. It was a place that provided great atmosphere, dominated by its massive grandstand. You'd feel the tension and excitement as soon as you walked in. The crowd is much closer to the players than most Sydney grounds. The dressing rooms were old fashioned, though (when I was going there, anyway), and could have done with some brightening up. The big argument now is whether State of Origin games should be taken away from Lang Park and sited at the larger and more modern ANZ Stadium (QEII). I'm a traditionalist, yet if the facilities are 10 times better, you have to ignore tradition and move with the times.

WEMBLEY (LONDON): This is the greatest football ground of my experience. I watched FA Cup soccer finals there as a kid (on television) and was astounded at the size of the place and how immaculate it looked, with its strip-cut grass. I'll never forget the thrill of playing there in 1985. The place has a certain air to it

— it's unique, almost magical. The dressing rooms are immaculate, tiled and sparkling clean — and so huge. And that long tunnel which leads from the dressing room to the pitch. The closer you got to sunlight (if there happened to be any), the louder the crowd noise. It's a phenomenal place, providing a memory I will treasure all my life.

Onfield/Off-field

SWEARING: I understand that if kids hear first-graders swearing, it could become a problem in junior league. But the fact is that "language" is a part of life in modern society, like it or not. Rugby league is a frantic game played by grown men and in the heat of the moment they can lose their control and swear. I feel a lot of referees take too much notice of it. I'm no angel in the language department on-field. Swearing is caused by frustration and anger with yourself or team-mates; it's a heat of the moment thing which should be ignored. But it's not. There was a good example of the sort of things that go on in my comeback match against Souths in 1993. One of our players had the ball taken illegally from him, but referee Tony Kelly ruled a knock-on. We were behind at the time and not playing well. I got frustrated and started swearing about the decision. The ref called me over and told me to apologise or he'd send me to the sin bin for 10 minutes. I knew we couldn't afford to have a player off the field, so I apologised. But I thought to myself: "What's the game coming to when men can't swear on the football field?" If I swear in front of a woman, I most certainly apologise. That's not acceptable behaviour. But we're talking rugby league here — one of the hardest games in the world. If a player swears, he should be told to go back to his position and calm down. If he continues, *then* the ref has every right to call him over and ask him to apologise.

FOOTBALL BOOTS: Firstly, an admission. I have never cleaned a pair of boots in my life. I keep wearing them until they fall apart. When it's been really muddy I'll go to the extremes of giving them a wipe-over with a wet rag. The best I have played in are Puma, which I first used in 1982, although the Kangaroos were actually sponsored by Adidas. I now wear Asics, which are very comfortable too; they made me a blue and gold pair of some suede-type material which are very light. They look pretty fancy. I'd like to see the boot manufacturers consult players more and get their opinions on what would be an ideal boot for rugby league. Personally, I'd like to see the studs repositioned around the boot — not so much on the ball of the feet. When they're there they always seem to give me trouble.

A FOOTBALLER'S LIFE: People tend to think that it must be great to be an international rugby league player who has done just about everything in the game. It *has* been good, and being a footballer has got me a lot of things in life I could never have otherwise dreamed of having. But on the other side, it's not as rosy as some people imagine. Moneywise, I've only hit the higher brackets in the last few years, and you have to consider we are heavily taxed on income which we can only earn over a decade or a little more. Career people can expect good earnings for 20 or 30 years once they reach a top level. You see a lot of figures in newspapers about what players supposedly get; often you can halve the published figure to get the real amount and then halve it again before you get to what the players actually get after tax. Getting two cheques a year means you have to spread your money out, which can be difficult for someone with a wife, three children and a mortgage. Footballers have bills just like "normal" people. But I'm not complaining. The game has been good to me.

One personal complaint concerns the World Sevens, not my favourite tournament, and now installed as a regular feature of the league year. We get paid very little for going down to the Sydney Football Stadium for three straight days. Furthermore, we had to pay to park our cars in the public car-park before crossing the road to put on the entertainment people came to see. You can presume that the promoters are making lots of dollars from the players' efforts. We are informed that it's an Australian rugby league-sanctioned tournament, and as such part of our commitments for the season. A free car-park ticket would be nice, though!

PREPARATION: A lot of hard work goes into being a footballer, significantly more these days than 10 years ago. After four or five months of pre-season training (using Parramatta as an example), teams train three times a week during the season plus two weight sessions. On Tuesdays at Parramatta we do a lot of physical work and a small amount of ballwork, while Thursday and Friday or Saturday morning sessions are almost entirely ballwork. On top of training there are matches, and club promotions; it adds up to a fair bit of time away from home for someone with a family. I've had times when I've been getting ready to go out and the kids say "daddy's going to football" — even if I'm not. They are so used to it. I fully accept that to be successful you've got to put in the work. The fans see no more than the finished product on a Sunday. The hard work needed to become a successful player, and to build a successful team, happens away from the crowds.

BEING WELL-KNOWN: Footballers these days are high-profile figures and being recognised in the street or a restaurant is a regular event. It goes with the territory — and it rarely bothers me. When I'm out with family or friends it can be a little bit difficult. Probably the only time it can get overbearing is when you're at a restaurant, halfway through your main meal and kids come up and ask you for your autograph. Sometimes I just wish they could at least wait until I've finished eating. People with me often say "don't you think that's rude" — but I normally say the kids can't be blamed, the parents are just over there.

DRUGS: The use of drugs in sport is a very contentious issue. I stand firmly against their use as performance-enhancers. Tests cast serious doubt about whether they provide any "help" anyway. I'll admit, though, there was a time earlier in my career, in 1984 or 1985, when I seriously considered taking steroids for a few months during the off-season to build myself up. I talked to a bodybuilder and he told me even if I was taking steroids I'd have to do an enormous amount of heavy weight training to gain any substantial weight. I would still have to do the hard work — but could ruin my body in the meantime. I figured I could probably get the same result by drinking a lot of milk with protein powder and doing the same heavy work. And that's what I did, adding some beef in the upper body. I didn't stick with it long enough. Taking steroids, or any drugs, may give you a short-term advantage, but in the long term can only do damage to your body. For a cheap gain for a few seasons of your career, you may have to pay the price of looking back one day when you're battling major health problems. The price to be paid is simply not worth it.

I am in agreement with the NSWRL's drug testing policy. My only objection is I wish there was a way to test players before games or at some other time and not after matches. Being required to give a urine sample after a game, often isn't easy — considering the players have just pushed their bodies to the limit for 80 minutes and have no excess fluid left. I have known players to be held back for three or four hours after a match, sinking can after can of soft drink or beer or water, trying to pass some urine. I've been tested twice and both times had my family waiting for me for a couple of hours.

GOALKICKING: You may be surprised to know it, but I kicked a few goals in my younger days. One day when Guildford were playing at Seven Hills, we were running away with the game and it was my "turn" to kick goals — and I landed a conversion from right on touch. I had only one chance in grade football, against Canterbury at the WACA in 1992, a kick not far in from the right touchline. I took it back too far, well past the quarter line, and missed. But I watched it over and over on the video and I thought the style I showed was pretty damn near perfect! I could have had a great career as a goalkicker if it hadn't been for that Cronin.

BEING SENT OFF: At first I was really disappointed that I would finish my career with a "record" — being sent off just once, against Balmain in 1989. Now it's water under the bridge — and at least I know what goes on down in Phillip St on Monday nights.

I was marched for a high tackle on Balmain fullback Michael Moss and copped a one-week suspension — one lousy week. Looking back now, the circumstances were extraordinary. All week we rehearsed countering a set move from the scrum the Tigers had put on the previous week, in which Moss came through and received an inside ball. I had it sussed out to perfection except for one small thing ... Moss didn't get the ball. The five-eighth dummied to him. I followed through, and collected Moss high without the ball. He did an Academy Award dive, and all the Balmain players screamed: "Send him off! Send him off!". Greg McCallum accommodated them, dismissing me on a touch judge's report — the touch judge who had been on the far side of the field.

Video at the hearing showed that it wasn't intentional and I actually spun around and ended up facing my own tryline after contact. That, plus my good record, saw me cop just the week off — but it was enough to tarnish my clean slate.

INJURIES: If you aspire to play first grade football, you've got be able to play "hurt". During a season you carry niggling injuries much of the time, most of them unknown to the watching public. It's a fact of life for a footballer. I've played with any number of niggling injuries — corked thighs or arms, calf muscle strains, sore shoulders. The game is so competitive now too that if you miss a match or two you are giving another player an opportunity — and you could find yourself out of the side for a few weeks, or even the rest of the season.

TESTIMONIALS: They were originally designed to honour and aid (financially) players who had given a club loyal service, and who had not made a fortune along the way. In this era in which players earn really good money, I sense a building resentment to them. I was certainly honoured to have been awarded a testimonial year and I feel that if they are organised by people outside of the club representing supporters who want to show their appreciation for what you have given them as a footballer, then that's fine. Clubs these days use them as a lever to get long-service players to re-sign as they approach their 10th season. It's now a "tactical" move in the game — and you couldn't expect a player to walk away from such a lure. It boils down to good business I suppose, although a fair way from the original spirit of testimonial years.

Kenny's Formguide

TOUGHEST OPPONENT: Wally Lewis. A great player who could change a game whenever he felt the need and was always so difficult to stop.

TOUGHEST INTERNATIONAL OPPONENT: Dean Bell (New Zealand). I faced him in a few Tests and he was a hard, tough player — very competitive and strong. He rarely had a bad game.

BEST BRITISH PLAYER: Garry Schofield. I first came across him while I was at Wigan in 1985 and he was about 19, making a name at Hull. I faced him in quite a few Tests and found him to be a great opportunist, a top competitor and good defender. He had a fine all-round game. I marked him in my last game against the Poms, when the Eels played the touring 1992 side at Parramatta Stadium. That was an important match for me; I'd never lost to an English side while playing for Australia and I didn't want to start then. I told my team-mates that before the game — that it was my last chance to play against Great Britain and that for them it might be their first and last chance. I'm glad to say we made the most of it and that I had a good game against Schofield, who was by then their captain and number one player.

MOST UNDER-RATED PLAYER OF MY TIME: Steve Sharp. "Sharpy" never got the wraps he should have. He was an unfashionable player in that he didn't make a lot of breaks and do the glamourous things. But he was very effective for Parramatta and made life a lot easier for players around him. His team-mates knew his value. I still believe he was largely responsible for turning the 1981 grand final our way when he came on as a replacement.

BEST YOUNG PROSPECTS IN 1993: Brad Fittler, Michael Buettner, Jacin Sinclair. Fittler may have already played for Australia, but he should just keep getting better and better and become the cornerstone of Australian sides for a long time ahead. He's better suited at five-eighth and might even end up at lock, because he'll get bigger and he'll slow down a bit in later years (I can speak with authority on that). He has Laurie Daley to contend with for the five-eighth spot — a similar situation to what I went through with Wally Lewis. In their case both Fittler and Daley can play centre (or even lock). Both have to be in every Australian side picked.

From what I have seen of Jacin Sinclair, he has every skill needed of a top-class centre and seems to be coming to grips with his short fuse. He is tall and strong, a good defender and can slip a ball with one hand in a tackle. I've seen him put on a couple of great around-the-corner passes. And he has a kicking game too.

Michael Buettner shows maturity beyond his years and I see him as Parramatta's next regular representative player. He has a very good head on him — he never gets flustered on the field. The way he handled goalkicking duties when he was just 18 was remarkable. And he has a lot of natural talent; he can defend well, has good positional sense and can do things with the ball. I think he'll just keep improving in the next couple of seasons.

MOST MEMORABLE TACKLE: A tackle made on me by Wayne Pearce in a Parramatta-Balmain match. I was running across field, slowing fractionally to pick up Steve Ella who was veering back inside. But he was a little too far away, so I had to straighten and go myself. As I did, I ran straight into Wayne Pearce's shoulder. He hit me right in the mid-section then drove me backwards into the ground, and as I hit the turf his shoulder seemed to go further and further into my stomach. I was winded badly but I was taught never to let an opponent know he has hurt you. So I got up, played the ball, and all the time kept my eyes on Pearce. When he moved away to rejoin the play, I collapsed in a heap on the ground and waited for the trainer to come out and help me get my breath back.

MOST INTENSE PLAYER BEFORE A GAME: Steve Mortimer, during the 1985 State of Origin series. He never stopped geeing people up, talking to himself and others — all the way from the hotel, on the bus trip and into the dressing room before the game. He worked himself up so much it was unbelievable.

DREAM TEAM: Below is my perfect Australian team, selected from my 14 years' experience with and against them:

Garry Jack, Eric Grothe, Mick Cronin, Gene Miles, Kerry Boustead, Wally Lewis (c), Peter Sterling, Steve Roach, Royce Simmons, Craig Young, Wayne Pearce, Steve Folkes, Ray Price. Reserves: Mal Meninga, Steve Rogers, Les Boyd, Terry Lamb.

The most difficult positions to decide were the two centres. I played with some of the best of all time but had to squeeze Mal Meninga and Steve Rogers onto the bench and leave Steve Ella out. Sludge and Mal could cover several positions and would be super-subs in this dream team.

Garry Jack just beat Gary Belcher; "Jimmy" was the ultimate competitor. Grothe and Boustead picked themselves, although Michael O'Connor went close to selection. With Wally and Sterlo no explanation is needed, and the same with Pricey. I had to find room for Wayne Pearce in the second row, and once again there was a blanket finish for the other spot. I settled on Steve Folkes, a tough competitor who would balance the pack perfectly with runners like Price and Pearce. Young and Roach were good defenders as well as top ball-players, just the men to give you the upper hand up front. There may be some surprise that I've picked Royce Simmons at hooker in front of Max Krilich or Ben Elias but Roycey was a tough, consistent performer, a little quicker than Max. He was a faultless defender and a good man to have on your side. Les Boyd would just miss out on the starting line-up but has to be in the squad; he could cover second row or prop and would be an impact player when he came on. Terry Lamb is Mr Versatility and, as did Steve Ella, probably suffered because of that when rep sides were announced. He was always the perfect man to have as a reserve.

Insights

FAVOURITE MOVIES: Basic Instinct, Silence of the Lambs.

FAVOURITE TV SHOWS: Happy Days and Home Improvement.

PERFECT HOLIDAY: A trip to the United States, starting in Los Angeles and a tour of Disneyland and Universal Studios, then a week or two looking around other parts of the States.

PERFECT DAY OUT: A game of golf in the morning, then home to pick up the family and take them to Taronga Zoo. In the evening Julie and I would go out for a nice dinner by ourselves then get home and see the kids tucked into bed.

WHAT I LEAST ENJOYED ABOUT BEING A FOOTBALLER: The way people expected me to be. It was as if I had to fit a certain mould, a certain image that people had created for me. I always had to smile, could never be upset or dirty on the world. I've been told a thousand times that it's just part of being a "celebrity" — but I still wonder why can't people accept me for the way I am. I know that early in my career I was seen as being "dumb" because I wasn't so comfortable in speaking in public, and lacked a classic radio announcer's voice. It used to really worry me what people thought of me and I'd always dress and act like I thought "they" wanted me to. As I started playing regularly for Australia I started to feel I had nothing to prove. In later years, people had this perception of me that I didn't have to work, that I must be very comfortable, and it was almost degrading for me to drive a truck. But the fact is I am me — not some Ken doll you buy in the shop and dress up the way you want him.

WHAT I MOST LIKED ABOUT BEING A FOOTBALLER: The competitiveness and the mateship. I just liked playing, competing against good players. Early in my career when I was fitter and faster I loved running the ball, then later as I got slower, I concentrated on becoming a better tackler and I enjoyed that competitiveness. I enjoyed making good hits, having a good tackle count, showing younger players I could still compete with them. Through football I've been able to meet, and keep, some great friends — from Queensland and England as well as Sydney. They are friendships I would never have made if it wasn't for league.

HERO-WORSHIPPING: Top sportsman have their idols, too. I'll always remember the night I finally met my childhood idols John Sattler and Bob McCarthy, I was tickled pink. I met Rod Marsh when I was over in Perth and Geoff Lawson as well. After the 1982 grand final I thought it was great when I was introduced to my namesake Grant Kenny; I'd expected him to be bigger than he was. One year I was watching a grand final with Andrew Ettingshausen in the Ladies' stand at the SCG — it might have been 1987 — when Prime Minister Bob Hawke yelled out from a few rows back "Hey, Bert, how are you?" On the

Kangaroo tour of 1982 we went backstage with AC-DC after a concert in France.

I have a couple of daydreams. One is to have Jimmy Barnes and John Farnham come to one of our games and then come over the club for dinner, a few drinks and a talk. They both seem to be good, unassuming blokes. That would be fantastic. The other is to play a round of golf with Greg Norman, no pressure, no coaching or anything (although if he wanted to give me a few tips I sure would listen!).

WHO WOULD I LIKE MOST TO HAVE HOME FOR DINNER? I was asked this recently as part of a local newspaper profile and I answered ..."Elvis Presley. If he was dead, I'd want his ghost to tell me what happened and why; after all the mystery about his death I'd like to know the real story. If he was alive and had been in hiding all these years, I'd keep his secret and let him go back to his peace."

WHY DO I ALWAYS WALK ONTO THE FIELD LAST? I used to run out like everyone else, but at times I was buggered before kick-off and would have to get my second wind. The thing was, I thought you HAD to run out when you were in grade. Then I saw Canterbury walk out slowly for the 1984 grand final and thought: "Hey, maybe you don't have to run out at all." From the next season I started walking out. Mick Cronin was still at the end of the line for the next two seasons; he always went out last. But once Crow retired, I joined the end of the queue and it has been a sort of superstition ever since, except the two years when I was captain; I'd walk from the front and everyone would rush past me.

IF ONLY I COULD TURN BACK THE CLOCK: If I could have one moment again it would be my only kick at goal in first grade — at the WACA against Canterbury. I wouldn't have taken the ball back so far! Off the field, I would have concentrated more on my school work and on getting a trade behind me instead of sacrificing everything for football.

THE DAY I WAS "SHOT": I've left this to last because it's something I have kept quiet about all these years. A few years ago I was walking past a pub in Parramatta when a big brawl broke out. Someone produced a pistol and fired a shot. The bullet ricocheted off a wall and hit me in the back. I thought at the time that someone had knocked me when they all rushed past. It didn't really hurt that much but when I got home I discovered a big wound in my back, with the bullet lodged inside. I didn't want people thinking I hung around rough pubs, so I never told anyone. The bullet was so precariously placed that doctors decided to keep it there until late in 1992 when it moved slightly and they decided to cut it out. I went to training one night with a dressing on it and the son of our trainer, Peter Cohen, noticed it and asked what had happened. I told him the story but asked him to keep it quiet. I've still got an ugly scar on my back. Peter's son also asked me about the scar on my neck and shoulder, so I had to explain to him about the shark attack as well. Now he thinks I'm another Indiana Jones! Believe me about the bullet? Young Master Cohen did and I haven't had the courage to tell him it was just a mole I had to get cut out. When he's old enough, he can learn the real story by reading this book. I never did mind a practical joke.

21 Anatomy of a Comeback

D-Day for Brett Kenny was approaching fast: May 14, 1993 — the night I returned to the playing field for the run to the line in my final season. It was the beginning of the end; the last gamble of my career. I had dodged surgery and it had been three months since I hurt my shoulder in the World Sevens. The time had come to put it to the test. I thought of 1986 and the casino below the Dragonara Hotel, Leeds, and the night when I walked in, put five pounds on a number and walked out with 175 pounds ($400). I hoped that sort of luck was going to be with me for these three months in 1993.

I had been busy during my convalescence, working on this book — recalling the glories and the disappointments, recording information for a story for which I didn't know the ending.

The last few days before my comeback match against Souths were anxious ones. I kept this diary of the week, to give you an insight into the routine and thoughts of a footballer facing such a moment — the (last) return from major injury. I kept a tape recorder with me all week. I hope drivers who spotted me thought I had a new-model compact mobile phone because I must have looked strange talking to myself as I drove my truck from delivery to delivery, or my car to and from training and the match.

This is what I recorded:

MONDAY: It's 6.30 am on Monday morning and I'm heading off for work for another week. It's not just another week for me. In four days' time I'll be playing first grade rugby league for the first time in a long time. It's my first premiership game for this year and my first since August 1992. I've got reservations about the game, just how my shoulder is going to stand up. I won't know that until sometime Friday night, so for the time being I've just got to worry about getting off to work and doing my job. But I know it's going to be a long few days. It'll be hard to concentrate on anything other than the thought of making a tackle on Friday night, or getting hit by a South Sydney player.

A few deliveries out of the way now. It's getting on to midday and I'm pulling into the car-park of Parramatta Stadium to do my first weights session of the week. I'll spend about an hour or so in there, then grab a bite to eat and get back to work. I've been doing weights and hitting the tackling bags for over a month and the shoulder has felt good. I feel confident the shoulder will stand-up but there is always that nagging doubt. I remember what Dr Johnston said: "It might last the season, it might last five minutes."

Four o'clock and I find myself back at the stadium again. I've just done a photo shoot for the local paper with Michael Buettner, my centre partner on Friday night. The headline is going to read The Master and the Pupil. While the photo was being taken, memories came flooding back of 13 years ago when I was standing in the same place as Michael Buettner and the fellow alongside me was the Master, Michael Cronin. I'm getting a bit nervous about playing now — but excited as well. It's all hitting home. I've become so used to being at training but not playing — running out for a football match is going to feel quite strange.

TUESDAY: It's 4.40pm and I'm back at Parramatta Stadium for training. I had a good relaxing afternoon and evening with Julie and the kids last night and slept well. I feel most comfortable of all being at home. The injury has meant that I've been home more these past few months than I had been during a football season for a long time.

Today has been a good day workwise. I got a lot done (I make about 13 deliveries a day) and the busy routine has helped me keep my mind off football pretty well.

Tonight we'll do mostly ballwork, seeing the match is on Friday night. I'm looking forward to it — to actually touching the ball. It will be the first ball session I've had for a long time and I'm hoping I'll be able to get through it without any mishaps or errors. First I'll go up to the gym and hit the punching bag for a while, then go down the dressing room and go through my normal routine. Nothing different.

Well, it's 8 o'clock and I survived it. It was a pretty tough session for us, but I enjoyed it immensely. It was so good to be back running around with the team again. I felt a bit tired, I must admit. It was straight to the shower afterwards and it'll be straight home; I don't think I'll be up too late tonight.

As it turns out, I won't be playing in the centres after all. Mick Cronin was walking out of the coaches' room just as I arrived and said: "Speech is out, you're at five-eighth." Michael Speechley's knee is still giving him trouble but David Woods, who also has a shoulder injury, will come back early and play in the centres. So I'm back in my favourite number six jersey. I know it means I'll be a bit more involved and certainly have to make more tackles but if the shoulder is going to get a test, it may as well get a real good one.

WEDNESDAY: Late morning. I'm back at the stadium for my second weights session of the week. Sometimes it feels like I live here. I've had a hectic morning with work, plus quite a few calls from the media. Channel 7 and Channel 10 have rung up wanting interviews this afternoon. I've had a phone call from 2KY also, asking for an interview with them early this evening. It seems like a broken-down old bloke making a comeback is of interest to someone. One thing about the calls from the media is that if it hadn't sunk in by now that I'm coming back, it sure has now!

All this attention has helped me focus on the game. I'm starting to think a lot more about it. I've been pretty relaxed until now, but each time I think about playing I get that little bit more nervous, and anxious ... but excited too. I'm really looking forward to the training session tomorrow night, our last session before the match. For now, it's into the weights which have become even more important to me because I need as much strength in the upper body as possible to cope with the shoulder problem. Then I'd better get some work done for Berrivale before all the interviews. After all, they're paying the bills — and to be honest, sitting in this truck gives me some solace. There's just me, my thoughts ... and the pager.

It's 3.30pm Wednesday and I'm on my way home. I've just done an interview with Channel 10 at Berrivale's office at Blacktown, and I'm on my way home now, where a Channel 7 crew are waiting. Just before 5.30 I've got to do another interview with Peter Peters on 2KY. Looks like I'm in the news again!

I've just watched the news and Channel 10 announced I was in my testimonial year. I didn't have the heart to tell them that it was last year, not this year.

THURSDAY: It's five past four and I'm running a little late for training. I had to make a few phone calls from home to speak to various reporters, and get back to Peter Sterling to arrange a time to do another interview tomorrow, to be shown before the Nine coverage on Friday night. There seems to be more and more attention every day from the media as the game gets closer. It's as if everyone in the city is watching, waiting to see if I'm going to survive or not. It's going to be great to get down to training and just be with the boys running around with the football. That brings me back to earth, reminds me that it's not just Brett Kenny running out on Friday night but the Parramatta football team. I've got to play my part in the overall performance and we must win. We've got to beat Souths to keep up our confidence and keep our finals hopes alive.

The time is dragging a bit. All the interviewers ask the predictable questions, to the extent I can tell what they are going to ask before they open their mouths — how's the shoulder feeling? What have I done to get it right? How do I feel about the match? What will happen if I break down?

I'm just going to make it to training in time; we're starting at 4.30 today instead of 5pm. As I drive into the car-park of the Parramatta Leagues Club, I wonder how many times I've driven through here, how many times I've walked through here after a match and gone through to a crowded bar to have a quiet drink, win or lose. On the outside particularly, the club hasn't changed much over the 13 years I've been here. The club and the ground next door really are like a second home. I've never really thought about the familiarity of driving in and out a few times every week or about it stopping in a few months time, but I feel really keen to get out there tonight for my last session before I run out against Souths. I'm not going to have much time to muck about.

That was good. The training went well and we had a nice barbecue afterwards. We usually have it after the Friday or Saturday morning session but, because we're playing on Friday, we had it tonight. Only one problem — I slightly strained my calf muscle on Tuesday and it was pretty sore tonight; I'll have to work on that overnight. Wouldn't that be a scream — Brett Kenny with the bung shoulder drops out because of a calf muscle strain! No, it'll be okay by tomorrow, although it will be sore when I cool down after the match. Can you believe I got another call from another reporter after training? I don't even know the man's name or where he was from. I've never had so much media attention in my life!

I'm into the last 24 hours. It's just after 7.30pm and I'll be running down that tunnel about this time tomorrow night. I'm looking forward to it; I just want to get it over with now. I've got to be positive and to enjoy the moment. Getting nervous is healthy, but I can't let it overtake me. Keeping occupied will be the key.

FRIDAY: 6.20am. THE day. I didn't have a good sleep; when I went to bed I felt like a kid on Christmas eve, I just couldn't wait for morning to arrive. Now I'll just get off to work as normal. Friday's not a real hard day for me at work, so I'll get everything done as soon as possible and get home and relax a little bit before the game tonight. I wonder what it would be like to be one of those "fulltime professionals," the players who don't have or need a job? Having to work has certainly helped this week. Being idle would have been murder.

It's now five to 10, and I'm about to do *another* interview, with 2GB. Then I'm off to do my Channel 9 interview with Sterlo. It feels a bit strange, that. For all those years he was the bloke next to me on the field at Parramatta, the bloke who I felt for at Wembley. Mind you, he doesn't look much like that player anymore; where has the hair gone? Strange too that same shoulder injury ended his career.

The interview went well, nice and relaxed. Sterlo asked what training I'd done since the injury, about the side's performance and anything I saw watching from the stand. I told him I thought the backs could have got the ball more.

Now it's getting close. I have just finished the last delivery for the day and I'm heading into Parramatta to see Graham Shaw, our physiotherapist, to pick up a another brace for my shoulder. Then it's home to do my paperwork for the day's work. I'll relax for a bit and get ready to leave.

Everywhere I've made a delivery today, or seen people from work, they've been wishing me well. It's been like that all week, but more so today. It's nice to know people sincerely want me to go well. I certainly can't escape the fact I'm playing a football match tonight!

It's twenty to five. I'm about to hop into the shower, then I'll help Julie bath the kids and get them ready, have something to eat, pack my bag — the ritual I have done hundreds of times (except when I was at Wigan!) — then to Parramatta Stadium for the sixth time in five days.

It felt strange packing my bag. I checked it, checked and double checked again, I'm pretty confident now I haven't forgotten anything. Anyone would think I'm nervous. Finally, we're off! Julie can drive, I think.

Whooo. We've made it, we're into the car-park. The crowds and the traffic are building up and fortunately we have our own carpark just beside the leagues club. I'll make sure Julie and the kids are comfortable. I'll watch a bit of reserve grade and then head down to the dressing room about 6.30pm.

Into the final hour and I feel good. The waiting is just about over. I'll go through the usual ritual — costume, shorts, jacket, go to the toilet, on the rubbing table, get my back and shoulders rubbed. I'd better get the calf muscle rubbed, it's still sore. I'll then take my time, get my ankles strapped, get my socks and boots on and throw my jumper on. My jumper on? Seems a long while since I've done that. I'll be good and ready to go out the back and warm up when the conditioner calls us.

We're back inside after the warm-up. I'll get some grease on my knees, put the shoulder brace and my shoulder pads on. I had a chat with David Woods as we walked back into the ground. I told him the side had been going well and we were the two blokes coming back from injury into the side; we couldn't let them down. I think Woodsy will go well. He sure adds some thrust out wide; he's got a lot of talent.

I feel a bit tense, but it's a nice mixture of tension and excitement. To be honest, I haven't thought about the shoulder much. I've thought much more about *playing* again after such a long break. I hope my fitness stands up OK. My shoulder will be fine. I've done everything possible; I've got a brace which will stop my arms going in the wrong direction, preventing any undue stress on the shoulder. I just want to get into the game as soon as possible, make a few tackles, throw a few balls — play rugby league.

It's now the final wait. The nervous time until the touch judge comes along and taps on the door and calls "ready".

Well ... here he is. It seemed a long time tonight before we heard that tap, tap, tap. I'm as ready as I can be. I'll take my regular position, last in the line, and follow the boys down the tunnel. I'm a footballer again. In an hour, an hour and a half, I'll know the answer ... (deep breath) ...

Here we go.

Curtain Call

An appreciation by Neil Cadigan

On the night of May 14, 1993, Brett Kenny slow-walked onto Parramatta Stadium, just as he had hundreds of times before. He wasn't the last in the line of Eels, but the other players quickly overtook him as he neared the sideline.

This night there was an edge of anxiety among the crowd of 16,020 which had gathered for the match against Souths, and the cheer for Parramatta reached its crescendo once the fans locked in on Kenny. Seemingly without a care in the world he ambled out for his 251st first grade appearance. In line with the routine of more than a decade, he broke into a slow jog towards the north-east corner; he glanced up momentarily, grabbed his shoulder pads around the collar and walked back towards halfway. He had a career behind him — and 80 minutes, he hoped, ahead.

In the Ken Thornett Stand were Ray Price, Steve Ella, Steve Edge, Mark Laurie, Ron Hilditch, Mick Cronin and Peter Sterling, all of them part of the Brett Kenny career, and now observers of the last stage of his battle to finish in some sort of personal glory. There were comments and nudges about his lairy blue-and-gold custom-made boots, and the thoughts of some went back to the infamous Graeme Langlands white boots episode of the 1975 grand final. With that thought came another emotion — the hope that the bright new boots were not a bad omen.

Souths kicked off to the northern end and the game was running. Every time Brett Kenny made a tackle or ran the ball in those opening minutes, all of us in the crowd tried not to cringe. But as the minutes ticked by and he went a little harder each time into a tackle, you could almost taste the relief in the crowd.

Then came a moment that all Parramatta had feared ... or so it seemed. After slipping a quick pass to centre Michael Buettner, Kenny was crashed to ground by a Souths defender — and didn't get up. Trainer Peter Cohen sprinted on as the crowd held its collective breath. Kenny sat upright, his left arm hanging limp. He knew what those in the stand were thinking, he guessed what the commentators might be speculating. Sterlo, or someone else, would perhaps be saying: "That's it, he's done his shoulder. It's all over."

But the news was good. Kenny had only been winded; the pain was worse than usual. If only he'd had some match fitness, he would have recovered more quickly, he thought. Instead he was down for a minute-and-a-half — and then jogged behind play for another minute before packing into a scrum.

Brett Kenny was OK ... this time. Towards the end of that first half, when he drove his left shoulder into the midriff of rampaging Souths forward Mark Carroll, his confidence grew. That was THE test. He passed, took tackles, started to pack more punch into his own defence. He survived. It was his fitness that had him dragging, looking distressed for much of the match.

But some of the old Kenny magic was on display all the same. He looked to have set up a fair try for Dave Woods early in the second half, but was called back for a shepherd. His rustiness showed. A pass was intercepted by Rabbitoh Darrell Trindall, but Kenny breathed easier when the Parramatta cover ran Trindall down. Twice Kenny was penalised for "holding on" in a tackle; the second time referee Tony Kelly marched him 10 metres for back-chatting. In the final five minutes he threw a pass which flew too high for winger Danny Crnkovich and went to ground. Souths snared possession and scored a couple of rucks later. Behind 7-2 at halftime, Parramatta went down 15-2.

With three minutes to go, coach Cronin called Kenny off. The warrior walked up the tunnel, into the dressing-room ... and kept walking. He circled the dressing-room five times, cursing that he had not been allowed to play out the game, and that the Eels had lost after such a good run of success. He cursed too that he hadn't been able to do the things that had become second-nature over the years.

"I was filthy I came off," he said an hour later. "I guess I was looking for a fairytale beginning — to come out and have a good game and for us to win. It just didn't go that way. I got frustrated. I can't remember ever being taken off before when we were losing and when I wasn't injured."

But the ultimate value of his 251st game, really, was that he survived it unscathed. The stats sheet showed that he made 23 tackles, many with his left shoulder. Along the way he'd thrown some classy passes, found some gaps for team-mates. It was mission accomplished, or the first step anyway. With the match under his belt, his touch would gradually return. He had goals, to break Ray Price's record of 258 first grade games, to see Parramatta much higher up the ladder than the previous year, to play that final game against Balmain at Parramatta Stadium.

It was almost an hour after fulltime before he left the dressing-room. Outside he was greeted by Julie, Nikolah and Joshua, whom he'd caught a glimpse of as play was about to resume in the second half. The Kenny clan was the subject of the wave that was spotted by a million television viewers. Before he reached them after the match he was warmed by a rousing cheer from the 30 children who had waited for their hero to emerge. The old man of league still had his fans.

His dad, Alan, came over and asked the obvious questions: "How did you pull up? How was the shoulder?"

"Fine," came the reply. "I'm just tired and disappointed."

He walked with Julie and friends to his car and drove straight home. There he relaxed with a can of beer, to ponder the evening.

The split premiership rounds at State of Origin time meant it was two weeks before Parramatta played again — against Newcastle at Newcastle. "That won't help my match fitness," he mused.

A fortnight later, Kenny ran out onto Marathon Stadium to the roar of another healthy crowd of 17,530, this time in the number-13 jersey (against Souths he had worn the number-six). Again he went down for treatment early, again the problem was no more than being badly winded. Parramatta were far from impressive in the first half, and trailed 8-2 at the break. Three minutes after halftime, Newcastle won a scrum, and blond-haired half Jason Martin hared away and then straightened up. Moving across field, Kenny took him head-on, the impact zone right on the point of his shoulder. He looked in trouble.

Eventually he rejoined play, but gingerly, and it quickly became obvious he was a casualty. He packed into another scrum with both arms virtually hanging loose. Radio 2UE commentator Ray Hadley was the first to screech out the deathknell. "Kenny's shoulder's gone! " he told his listeners. "That's the end of a great career."

Sterling was there for Channel 9 and he too declared that Kenny was favouring his bad shoulder. He feared for the worst. Kenny finally retired to the bench on the sideline, radio "sideline eyes" and TV cameramen circling, then converging on him like vultures. UE's Greg Prichard, ignoring Kenny, questioned Parramatta doctor, Peter Manollaras. "It's his other shoulder," said the doc. "His left shoulder is as good as new!"

Yet fears that the great Kenny career had ended weren't completely allayed. In the dressing-room later, Dr Manollaras speculated quietly that Kenny may have fractured his collarbone. Metres away, Kenny was telling reporters it was just badly bruised and that he'd be okay. X-rays the next day proved the player, and not the doctor, right this time. In two to three weeks he would be fit to play.

Brett snapped next day that the media pressure was getting to him. His message was: "Get off my shoulder".

"While I appreciate everyone's concern, I just want people to get off my back – – let me play football. The left shoulder is great, it's the least of my troubles. It's the rest of my body that is worrying me — I'm suffering from a disease called ageing."

Aided by another split round, he recovered in time for the next match, a home game against Illawarra — although Dr Manollaras was cool about him playing. Parramatta had surrendered meekly in the second half against Newcastle, going down 28-8. The capitulation against Illawarra was worse still. The Eels were hammered, 34-4. This time Brett was one of the first out of the dressing-room. "I should have bloody retired," he muttered to his dismayed wife. He was shattered by the spineless performance, and his third straight loss since returning. It had been eight matches and 10 months ago that he had last tasted victory — against Wests at Campbelltown on August 2, 1992.

His exasperation reached boiling point the following Saturday, when the Eels were shamed 36-8 by Norths. A trademark intercept, as he snatched the ball from Bears forward Craig Wilson, only centimetres from the Norths player's body, before racing away to score, gave him the only joy of a first half in which Norths scored 26 points. As he approached the goal-line, he smiled at former team-mate Glen Liddiard (the Norths fullback), as if to say "can't you catch an old man?"

On June 27, and ironically against Wests, Brett Kenny remembered what it was like to win. Parramatta led the Magpies 16-0 at halftime, 22-6 at fulltime. He could only laugh when headlines about deep-seated problems at Wests dominated the newspapers. It was at the same time a year earlier that the Eels were embroiled in their own internal troubles. His second try in two weeks brought his tally to 106 tries for Parramatta, putting him behind only Terry Lamb (142) and

Phil Blake (110) on the all-time try-scoring lists — of players still in the game.

The relief was enormous, at the end of a week which had had the critics calling — yet again — for his retirement. He knew what the sceptics were saying behind his back; the remarks had a habit of finding their way, second-hand, to his ears.

"Too old ... past playing first grade ... the side's gone worse since he's come back." One theory was that, like a lame racehorse, he should be put down ... or at least put out peacefully to pasture. His performance against Wests was his best since returning, although the game reached no great heights. Cronin leapt to his mate's defence before a dressing-room throng of reporters: "He came back into a team that was going at its worst, and he went out there not knowing if the shoulder was going to stand up and not knowing if he was going to play again if it didn't."

Week by week the Kenny career was winding down, and with hopeful elements of a good finish. The victory over Wests left Parramatta on 12 competition points — one fewer than their total for the entire 1992 season. With nine rounds remaining, his goal of seeing his beloved Eels start the climb back seemed certain to be achieved. The shoulder had stood up better than he had imagined. The vultures were circling, but a little higher in the sky now; he genuinely believed their was some life left yet in the Kenny body — and that he had at least a couple of five-star performances in his make-up. As long as he remained healthy ...

The fleeting hope that the Eels would make the finals for the first time since 1986 had almost vanished. But the prospect of seven home games in the final 10 rounds meant they were certainly not about to concede. Into the middle of the last winter of his football career, Brett Kenny was on target to make his date with retirement — on August 29 at Parramatta Stadium against Balmain, the club that had almost stolen him away in that last year.

The glory of premierships and Test matches were long-since filed away in mother Marj's scrapbooks — but Parramatta's last man standing, a relic from a magnificent Parramatta era, still had something to offer rugby league. In a Parramatta side of modest ability, he still shone as the man of class. In some ways it was sad to watch the most naturally gifted player I had seen restricted to such moderate achievements with Parramatta in his last playing days. Yet age and decline has in no way diminished his outstanding achievements. Thankfully Brett Kenny played his football in the era of the video — and his fans have collected visual reminders of his stunning capabilities, to last long after he has hung up the blue and gold boots.

To chronicle the last months of his career for this book was an exercise in the observation of humility at work. The one thing that never changed about Brett Kenny, from his debut against Newtown in 1980 to the last pass he threw at Parramatta Stadium in 1993, was that, even though he happened to be one of the greatest footballers of his time, he never placed himself above, or below, anyone else in society. To have the chance to walk around Parramatta Stadium on his final day; to say thanks to Eels' fans for their support and to say goodbye with dignity and pride — these things meant the world to him. His ultimate goal (of many) was to bow out on his own terms. As the last ink was placed on the pages of *The Natural*, fingers were firmly crossed throughout the length and breadth of the district of Parramatta, as he inched closer to that final, modest ambition.